FOUNDATIONS OF PSYCHOPATHOLOGY

John C. Nemiah, M. D.

*Professor of Psychiatry, Harvard Medical School
and Psychiatrist-in-Chief, Beth Israel Hospital*

INTRODUCTION BY KENNETH E. APPEL, M.D.

*Professor of Psychiatry, Chairman of the Department
University of Pennsylvania*

NEW YORK   OXFORD UNIVERSITY PRESS

TO MY FATHER

sed puerum est ausus Romam portare docendum
artes . . .

. . . at hoc nunc
laus illi debetur et a me gratia maior.

© 1961 By Oxford University Press, Inc.

Library of Congress Catalogue Card Number: 61-6299

printing, last digit: 38 37 36 35 34 33

ISBN 978-0-19-501137-1

Printed in the United States of America

My purpose in writing this book is threefold: (1) to present the basic psychological concepts of psychopathology, (2) to illustrate these concepts with the clinical observations they are devised to explain, and (3) to indicate the relevance of the concepts to the practice of medicine. It is intended as an introduction to the discipline of psychopathology for those with little or no knowledge of the subject. It is meant to provide the reader with the idea of the methods and fundamental principles of one approach to the understanding of mental disorders. And it is designed to give the student beginning his work with patients a basis for understanding the emotional components of physical illness.

I make no pretense to completeness of either fact or theory. I have been concerned primarily with observations and ideas derived from psychoanalysis which, arising from the study of clinical phenomena, is the framework of psychological theory most useful for understanding them. I have tried to present basic general concepts and fundamental ways of thinking about psychological facts rather than to describe the specific psychopathology of the wide variety of clinical syndromes. I have, for example, used selected aspects of hysteria, obsessive-compulsive neurosis, and the phobic reaction in order to demonstrate the general principles of symptom-formation, not to elucidate the details of the psychopathological processes specific to these psychiatric disorders. I have, in other words, been more interested in the rules of grammar than in parsing individual sentences. Finally, in a book devoted to psychological theory, I have not attempted to explore the neurochemical and neurophysiological bases of disturbed behavior.

Since this book is intended as an introduction, a large share of the text is devoted to quotations from recorded interviews with patients, to autobiographical descriptions of the experiencing of illnesses and mental processes, and to detailed case histories. The student beginning the study of psychopathology has usually had little or no experience with patients. He has, therefore, little familiarity with the phenomena which the terms and theories of psychopathology denote and explain. The extensive use of verbatim material is designed to allow the reader to see for himself what the terms signify and how the theories are related to the observations. It is included not so much as evidence for the abstract concepts as to demonstrate the nature of the particulars from which the conceptions arise. It is not my purpose to prove the validity of these theories, but to present the basic elements of a useful body of fact and theory concerned with psychopathology.

Like the man who writes it, no book is an island, entire of itself. I could not begin to acknowledge all the bonds that tie my volume to the thoughts and influences of others who have shaped my ideas. I must, however, express my gratitude to those who have played an explicit part in its growth and development. Originally conceived and delivered as lectures to second-year Harvard medical students, it is offered now as a text for those who helped to mold its early years—the students of medicine beginning their study of psychopathology. I am particularly grateful to those of my colleagues and friends who in reviewing the manuscript have been responsible for much of the precision it may have achieved in its growth from the spoken to the written word. Without the warm encouragement of my Chief of Service, Dr. Erich

Lindemann, and without the sort of climate conducive to writing which he has provided, I should not in the first place have attempted the making of this book. In addition to his great kindness in writing the Introduction, Dr. Kenneth Appel has given me numerous valuable suggestions about the content and organization of the material which I have tried to incorporate into the text. To Dr. Stanley Cobb I am deeply grateful not only for his helpful comments on what I have written here, but as well for his teaching and encouragement over the years. I am especially indebted to Drs. Peter Sifneos and George Talland for their meticulous attention to the details of the manuscript and for their corrective influence on many points of fact, phrasing, and theory. The critical eye of the student has been provided by two members of the Harvard Medical School class of 1961, Drs. Douglas Welpton and Axel Hoffer; I have adopted several of their suggestions which will, I hope, increase the usefulness of the volume to the medical undergraduate.

Besides those who have lent critical aid to the manuscript, I must mention several persons whose help has been invaluable in turning this work from fantasy into fact. Mr. Douglas Ross and the staff of the Oxford University Press have been unfailing in their interest and assistance in all the phases of its making. My secretaries, Miss Cherrell Cahoon and Mrs. Carol Richards, have typed and retyped with unruffled cheerfulness, even under the pressure of deadlines. I am grateful to my cousins, Mr. and Mrs. Cornelius Wood, for the retreat of a quiet room on Cuttyhunk Island where much of this was first written. And finally, if it had not been for the constantly understanding behavior of my wife, Muriel, there would have been no book at all.

J.C.N

Belmont, Massachusetts
December 1960

ACKNOWLEDGMENTS

I should like to express my appreciation to the following persons, publishers, and journals for their kindness in allowing me to include in my text material from their clinical files or publications: Dr. Erich Lindemann and the *American Journal of Psychiatry* for the quotation from "Symptomatology and Management of Acute Grief,"; Drs. Ida Macalpine and Richard A. Hunter and William Dawson & Sons, for the quotation from the translation of *Memoirs of My Nervous Illness* by D. P. Schreber; Mr. Morton P. Prince and Macmillan for the quotation from Mr. Prince's father's book, *The Unconscious* by M. Prince, 2nd ed.; Dr. Robert Shaw and the *Harvard Medical Alumni Bulletin* for the quotations from "A Mixture of Madness"; Dr. Peter E. Sifneos for the quotation on pages 148-9 from a recorded clinical interview.

For the excerpts on pages 244, 247, 249, and 252 from J. C. Nemiah, "Emotional Factors and Poor Motivation for Rehabilitation," *Arch. Phys. Med. & Rehab.,* 36:771, 1955, and on pages 41, 43, 45-6 from J. C. Nemiah, "The Psychiatrist and Rehabilitation," *Arch. Phys. & Rehab.,* 38:143, 1957, by permission of the *Archives of Physical Medicine and Rehabilitation;* for the excerpts from *Studies on Hysteria* by J. Breuer and S. Freud, by permission of Basic Books, Inc., for the excerpt from S. W. Mitchell, "Remarks on the Effects of Anhelonium Lewinii (The Mescal Button)," by permission of the *British Medical Journal;* for the excerpts from *Swann's Way* and from *The Sweet Cheat Gone* by Marcel Proust, by permission of Chatto and Windus Ltd. and Random House, Inc., and the Modern Library, Inc.; for the excerpt from *Going Native* by Oliver St. John Gogarty, copyright © 1940 by Oliver St. John Gogarty, by permission of Duell, Sloan and Pearce, Inc.; for the excerpts from *Agent of Death: The Memoirs of an Executioner* by R. B. Elliott, by permission of E. P. Dutton & Co., Inc., and John Long, Ltd.; for the excerpt from *Wisdom, Madness and Folly* by John Custance, by permission of Farrar, Straus and Cudahy, Inc.; for the excerpts from *Selected Writings of Gérard de Nerval*, translated and with an introduction by Geoffrey Wagner, copyright © 1957 by Geoffrey Wagner, by permission of Grove Press, Inc.; for the excerpt from J. C. Nemiah, "Anorexia Nervosa: Fact and Theory," by permission of Paul B. Hoeber, Inc.

For the excerpts from *Selected Papers of Karl Abraham;* from "Studies on Hysteria" by J. Breuer and S. Freud and from "Mourning and Melancholia" by S. Freud, *The Standard Edition of the Complete Psychological Works of Sigmund Freud*, Vols. II and XVI respectively; from *The Notebooks of Malte Laurids Brigge* by Rainer Maria Rilke, translated by John Linton, all by permission of the Hogarth Press Ltd.; for the excerpts on pages 102-3, 106-7, 108, and 110-11 from J. C. Nemiah, "The Lecture: A Reconsideration," *J. M. Educ.*, 35 (2): 183, 1960, by permission of the *Journal of Medical Education;* for the excerpt from *The Candle of Vision* by AE (George William Russell), by permission of Mr. Diarmuid Russell and Macmillan and Co. Ltd.; for the excerpt on page 268 from T. Brown, J. C. Nemiah, J. S. Barr, and H. Barry Jr., "Psychologic Factors in Low-Back Pain," *New Eng. J. Med.*, 251:123, 1954, by permission of the *New England Journal of Medicine*.

J.C.N

INTRODUCTION
BY KENNETH E. APPEL, M.D.
Professor of Psychiatry, Chairman of the Department
University of Pennsylvania

This is in many ways a new kind of book in psychiatry. It does not represent the customary working-over of well-worn concepts for presentation to students; nor is it a new textbook of psychoanalysis. There is nothing treadmillish, schematic, or pat about it, nor is it partisan in approach. Clear, accurate, and scholarly, it sketches pathways and byways of explorations into human nature—its vicissitudes and distortions, its blind alleys and tragedies, its pathos and potentials for creative integration.

Briefly, based on psychoanalytic explorations, it is a running, vivid account of dynamic psychiatry, important for all psychiatrists today. The patterns flow naturally and the concepts come appropriately—concepts which, as the author points out, are inferences, constructs, and models developed in the interest of understanding the complexities of the human mind and behavior. They are introduced practically and usably, not theoretically, dogmatically, or academically. Although the book does not include a discussion of the new biochemical substances and maneuvers so necessary in their appropriate use for combating the great problem of emotional and mental disorders, the author emphasizes the importance of multiple etiology and different levels of understanding and therapy. Whether the discussion is focused on a surgical patient with a laminectomy, a girl dying from anorexia nervosa, a man with a bleeding duodenal ulcer, the homicidal schizophrenic, a woman depressed following the loss of a mate, the patient fearing death from cancer, the auxiliary help of a physiotherapist prescribed postoperatively for psychological reasons, the use of intravenous sodium amytal to reach unconscious motivation, the employment of psychoanalytic investigations, or of free associations and fantasy in the discovery of motivations, the disappearance of a phobia "through unfolding of fantasies and feelings," the use of a propitious dream in helping a woman to accept pregnancy—in all this one finds a skillful integration of both medical and psychological understanding.

This book is not merely one on psychopathology. It is a sympathetic, clear, understandable portrayal of much that is essential in psychiatry, human nature, its fallings by the way and its rehabiltation. As such it might have been entitled "Psychological Medicine." Students, teachers, nurses, physicians, and interested non-professionals will find the text of this volume and its well-done glossary and bibliography stimulating and useful. If, for example, physicians and psychiatrists were to learn the chief "tactics" in interviewing described and demonstrated in its pages, they would find them a valuable aid to the better practice of medicine and the reduction of suffering. Psychotherapy is effectively illustrated by full and telling excerpts from actual interviews. By listening and asking questions, awareness increases and resources develop. Psychotherapy is not something mysterious and esoteric, but an unfolding of fantasies, feelings, motivations, understanding, and capacities. "In order for a person to look upon himself as having value, he must feel that he is loved by other people, that he has strength and capabilities"—that is important in life and psychotherapy. One finds here not just theory, lectures, and recommendations, but practice itself before one's eyes.

From St. Augustine to Proust, from Robert Burton to Weir Mitchell to Freud, the author weaves perspectives from clinical, historical, and literary sources. This is a book that should help to prevent opposition to and misconceptions about the psychological understanding of human nature. It should help to improve the cultural climate of psychiatry— and an improved attitude toward psychiatry, psychiatric problems, and psychiatric patients is much needed for the solution of many of society's critical problems.

December 1960

CONTENTS

logical conflict—His mysterious anxiety—The usefulness of fantasy—The aggressive impulse—His anxiety explained—Its possible source—Defenses and inferences—A psychological model to explain behavior—The Unconscious—Dynamic and psychogentic aspects of psychological conflict.

PART III

Symptom Formation

PART IV

Emotions, Illness and the Therapeutic Relationship

"A great wonder springs up in me, and I am seized by astonishment," wrote St. Augustine as he reflected on the nature of human memory. "And men go forth to marvel at the heights of the mountains, and the vast floods of the sea, the broad courses of the rivers, the encircling oceans and the revolutions of the stars, yet pass themselves by." *

It is a hard task that Augustine would impose upon us. The marvels of the earth and the stars, of the whole physical universe, obtrude themselves almost unbidden upon our senses and our minds; our gaze easily and naturally turns outward to the multitude of things that surround us; but it takes an active effort for most of us to direct our attention upon ourselves—upon the thoughts and fantasies and feelings of our inner mental life. We tire, our interest flags, we do not like what we see—and turn back to the sensations that stream in so willingly from without. True insight comes rarely and spasmodically.

The goal ahead of us in this book is not necessarily self-knowledge, however helpful that may be for understanding the human mind. Our task is to grasp certain basic concepts fundamental to the discipline of psychopathology—not simply as abstract, theoretical ideas, but as conceptions arising from and made living by the observations which they are fashioned to explain. For this reason we shall frequently in our search for facts be turning our attention to what patients

* *Confessions*, Book X.

can tell us, directly or indirectly, of the workings of their minds. It is almost as difficult to look upon the self-revelations of others as it is honestly to observe ourselves; in both situations we find ourselves liable to be maddened, saddened, and frightened by what we see.

It would be far easier if we could avoid the patient as we explore the realm of psychopathology; it would be far simpler if we could limit ourselves to examining the chemistry and physiology of his brain, and to treating mental events as objects alien to our immediate experience, or as mere variables in impersonal statistical formulae. Important as these approaches are for the understanding of human behavior, they cannot alone uncover or explain all the relevant facts. To see into the mind of another, we must repeatedly immerse ourselves in the flood of his associations and feelings; we must be ourselves the instrument that sounds him.

In the fifteen centuries since Augustine wrote we have learned to see deeper into the seas and farther into the heavens. Even the moon has at last lost her modesty and shown us her backside. While we have machines for exploring the physical universe that Augustine never dreamed of, our techniques for penetrating the human mind have changed little, if at all. Patience, time, the ability to look without prejudice, thoroughly and inquiringly at inner experiences, the willingness to take mental events seriously—these are still the tools of our explorations. Nor does our search necessarily bring us to truths unknown till we have come upon them. Every man and every age, working against in-dwelling resistances, must rediscover for itself the same basic psychological facts. It is not so much the insight as the language which describes it that changes.

For the patients who reveal themselves to us in the pages that follow, their efforts have been toilsome, time-consuming, and often painful. They have labored to enlighten us. To understand them we must return the compliment.

Part I

Form, Fantasy, and Interviewing:
Exploring the Design of
Psychological Illness

1

Aspects of the Organism:
The Mind and the Body

"A Gentlewoman of the . . . city [of Basil]," wrote Robert Burton * over three hundred years ago, "saw a fat hog cut up; when the entrails were opened, and a noisome savour offended her nose, she much misliked, and would no longer abide: a Physician in her presence told her, as that hog, so was she, full of filthy excrements, and aggravated the matter by some other loathsome instances, in so much this nice Gentlewoman apprehended it so deeply, that she fell forthwith a vomiting, was so mightily distempered in mind and body, that with all his arts and persuasions, for some months after, he could not restore her to herself again, she could not forget it, or remove the object out of her sight."

As Burton's brief history indicates, it has long been known that the dissonance of the mind is heard on the organs of the body. The plight of the Gentlewoman of Basil demonstrates several essential ingredients of the relation between emotional disturbances and disorders of body function: 1) An emotionally distressing event may precipitate the disorder. 2) The physiological disturbance is often an exaggeration of a common and normal bodily companion of the emotional response; nausea and vomiting, for example, are not infrequently concomitants of the feeling of disgust.

* Burton, Robert, "The Anatomy of Melancholy," London, G. Bell & Sons, Ltd., 1923, Vol. I, pp. 388-389.

3) A prolonged physical response that persists beyond the immediate reaction to the stimulus constitutes an illness that may have grave consequences for the physical and emotional health of the sufferer. 4) The behavior of the physician plays an important part in worsening as well as bettering the patient's symptoms.

These generalizations are as true and important now as they were then for the theory and practice of medicine. It has been variously estimated that over one half of the patients who consult a general practitioner or an internist are suffering primarily from emotional disorders. Not all of them, however, come so conveniently labeled. Some, it is true, turn to the doctor in the priestly role he has tried so hard to shed. They come to him complaining of emotional problems and dissatisfactions. Most patients are not so courteous. They come because they hurt, and leave it up to the physician to find out the reason why. Their ailment appears as a bodily complaint, and the emotional conflict that lies behind it can be readily overlooked by the practitioner who is not conversant with the vagaries of the mind.

The vagaries, however, are there to see for anyone who takes the trouble to look for them. As the Gentlewoman of Basil shows us, the disturbance in function that follows on a distressing event is manifested in both the psychological and physiological systems of the organism. This is an important fact that we must pursue further.

We have been speaking so far as if the emotional disturbances were primary and the bodily disorder secondary. Often the reverse appears to be the case: in patients with visibly damaged brains or with severe toxic or metabolic disturbances, psychological function is grossly deranged as the apparent result of the physical disorder. To speak thus in terms of cause and effect implies the assumption that man is composed of two fundamentally different substances, mind and body, and that the two in some way reciprocally affect one another. It is the fashion in current thought to sidestep this vexed problem of the dualism of mind and matter. The assumption is made that the basic unit which reacts to stimuli is neither the mind nor the body, but the organism. The organism responds to the external forces impinging on it both physiologically and (if the organism has consciousness) psychologically; each of these is only a mode of the whole response of the organism. Neither takes precedence over the other. The child reaches out for the lollipop—that is the reaction of the organism, which on analysis is found to be simultaneously the psychological experience of delighted desire and impulse to grab, and neuro-muscular physiological activity.

As usual, when it comes to practice we find ourselves forced to compromise our principles—we find ourselves thinking and theorizing about the organism in either psychological or physiological concepts. This is the result at least of our present state of ignorance, if not of a basic condition of man's mental faculties. It is, for example, more rewarding for an understanding of the experience of anxiety to examine it in psychological terms than to explore the neurophysiological activity that goes with it; conversely, we learn more about the disorder of respiration in heart failure by studying the pathophysiology of the heart and lungs and the chemistry of oxygenation than by examining the experience of dyspnea that may accompany the physical processes.

We do not, therefore, have to declare ourselves for monism or dualism to see that for a practical understanding of the human being, sometimes it is the language of psychology and sometimes the language of physiology and biochemistry that is more apposite; and when we are lucky, we occasionally catch a glimpse of the complex interrelations between these modes of discourse. It has been the strength of scientific investigation since Burton's time (mostly in the present century) to have amassed a wealth of observed fact and to have created intelligent theory in both the psychological and physiological realms, and at the same time to have discovered some of the relations between them. It is our purpose in this book to focus on the psychological observations and the basic psychological principles that help us to understand and treat the sick human being. Let us begin by examining a patient who will illustrate for us the relations between psychological and physiological functioning and will at the same time introduce us to a fundamental psychological fact—the ubiquity and potency of fantasy.

Mary S., aged sixteen and one-half years, grew disgusted with a close friend who began to put on weight by eating candy. The two girls agreed to go on a reducing diet, although Mary weighed only 114 pounds. A year later she graduated from high school and obtained a job as a stenographer. She began to lead a very busy life, working during the day and going dancing at night with a young man who paid her attention. As her activities increased, her weight loss became more apparent, and soon her menses disappeared. Up to this time her dieting had been a voluntary control of eating, but now her appetite failed. Some months later one of the patient's sisters lured her boy friend from her; Mary began to feel tired, and had to force herself to keep active. The onset of dizzy spells caused her to consult a doctor, who suggested a tonsillectomy. After the operation, she refused to eat, but continued her active pace, including dancing every night. She now weighed 71 pounds. Two months later she had become so dizzy and weak that she could no longer walk, and was finally brought to the hospital weighing 63 pounds. In three days, two and a half years after beginning her diet, Mary S. was dead of bronchopneumonia (57).*

* Numbers in parentheses refer to books and articles listed in the Selected Bibliography.

The immediate cause of Mary's death was, of course, her pulmonary disease, but the stage had been set long before she developed pneumonia. Her illness began when she first started on a course of dieting that eventually turned her into a barely-living skeleton, the easy prey of an intercurrent infection. *Anorexia nervosa* (such is the name given to her condition) is an uncommon disorder, but one that blights the lives of young women, a tenth of whom die of its effects. It has been of interest to clinical investigators because the relations between the psychological and physiological are clear.

The regimen of starvation which these patients impose upon themselves has widespread physical sequelae. Apart from the striking loss of weight, the function of the anterior pituitary is diminished as a result of the inanition. There follows a secondary diminution of function of the target endocrines (especially of the thyroid and gonads, to a lesser degree of the adrenal cortex) with a measurable drop in blood and urinary hormonal levels, and the related clinical manifestations of lowered body metabolism and amenorrhea.

So prominent are the endocrine disturbances that anorexia nervosa has been frequently confused with the state of panhypopituitarism of Simmonds' disease. An important clinical fact, however, that distinguishes anorexia from this latter disorder is the nature of the disturbance in eating that sets the train of bodily changes in motion. When this is carefully examined it becomes apparent that "anorexia" is a misnomer, since many of these patients voluntarily refrain from eating, often in the face of considerable hunger. Indeed when pressure to eat is brought to bear upon them by anxious relatives, they will hide food, flush it down the toilet, or make themselves vomit after a meal—anything to avoid the permanent intake of nourishment. Paradoxically, they will at times indulge in orgies of ravenous overeating.

A young woman of seventeen, for example, in secrecy behind a locked door would wolf down two loaves of bread,
a pound of peanut butter and a quart of beer, all within half
an hour; then, overcome with shame, she would tickle her
throat to induce the vomiting back of the entire meal. In
other patients eating is the focus of odd behavior: one lived
only on pickles and tea; another dined on scraps chosen
from the garbage pail; a third ate only what she could filch
from the discarded trays of her fellow patients in the hospital.

We can begin to understand these bizarre patterns of behavior only when we explore what the patient thinks and
feels about food and eating. When we turn to such psychological experiences, we find a wealth of imagery and feeling
accompanying and motivating the external actions. Many
patients are afraid of eating, and if they do swallow food
are acutely anxious until they can vomit. "I am afraid the
food won't go down because my stomach and intestines are
all shrunk up," said one; another feared that "something
awful will happen" if she took food; a third that she would
choke to death in her sleep if her stomach were full. Some
feel guilty when they eat, and others experience a variety of
bodily sensations which they explain variously and curiously
to themselves. "After I eat," said one young woman, "my
stomach feels bloated as if I were eight months' pregnant,
and I have a sensation as if a baby were rolling around in
there." She was concerned that food and water increased
the size of her breasts, about which she was sensitive. At
times she would feel sexually aroused, but abruptly her desire for sexual intercourse would change to hunger, and she
would rush to the kitchen to gorge herself.

What becomes clear as we listen to our patients talk is
that the biological, nutritional function of food and eating
has become inextricably entangled with a variety of personal
feelings and fantasies that distort and disturb alimentation.

Eating becomes frightening and forbidden because of the meaning with which the patient endows it; from this follows the self-starvation, the bodily changes, and too often, death. The clue to the meaning attached to food and eating lies in the patients' fantasies—the imaginative thoughts through which they view and color their world. Without a knowledge of their fantasies we cannot trace the origin of their devastating sickness.

Fantasy must be the central concern of anyone who wishes to understand the psychopathology of illness. Our task, therefore, in the two chapters that follow is to examine further the nature of fantasy, to discover that it may appear in a variety of forms, and to discuss the methods of interviewing by which we are enabled to elicit it from our patients.

II

FORM AND FANTASY

Joan A., a woman of 56, was trying to describe a profoundly moving experience to her doctor:

> I * felt that it was too much, you know, because there seems to have been a transition—oh, a fraction of a second, you know. That date I'll never forget. I mean, I wouldn't—
>
> *Dr.* What happened then?
>
> *Pt.* Well, I got that—it seems as if there was too much —for goodness' sake go check on your records for that time, you know.
>
> *Dr.* Too much what?
>
> *Pt.* Well, I don't know what this—this—whatever it was, you know, with my head—that—like shock treatment. I don't know. See, I can't—you can't—could you remember for the last two years everything that has transpired? You wouldn't. Well anyway, it seems a fraction of a second—this—something it probably—I mean, I knew I was on my bed. And, I tell you, that was a great second— all this thinking and then this light, you know. And I tried to see it in the sky. I've tried to see it in sunsets or—or anything like that. And—and the peace and the ecstasy of the rapture.... That was April 16th, 4:30 in the afternoon....
>
> *Dr.* How did that come about?

* All indented passages, unless otherwise noted, are excerpts from recorded interviews, autobiographical accounts, or the writings of other observers.

Pt.   Oh, that? Right—right after—well, as I said, not simultaneously—I'd better be accurate. It happened and I —whether you could say it happened simultaneously ... Later on I don't know—I don't know whether I analyzed it that way, but that would be to me your spirit leaving you and, you know, going off ... Well, whatever it was, you know, when I came back, it was just (snaps her fingers) like that, don't you see? I—I—I wish I—you know, it was the most wonderful feeling. And—

Dr.   What did it feel like?

Pt.   Nothing. Because I've been at peace with the world—the world and myself and everything else, you know.

These incoherent stammerings convey the impression that something of major cosmic and personal significance has burst upon her awareness. It is clear that what she has experienced has moved her deeply. But *what* it is she has experienced remains a mystery. Words are inadequate to communicate it. Her vagueness leaves us perplexed and in darkness. Her language refers to an ecstatic state of mind that few, if any of us have known; it recalls for us no comparable sensations or knowledge. We cannot, therefore, share her feelings or know at first hand what she is talking about. She has caught a glimpse of a world from which most of us are excluded.

Presently the patient said more about her enlightenment. God had revealed to her that she was chosen to convert all men to Christianity by reliving the agonies that Jesus Christ had suffered two thousand years before. A great and tremendous power was abroad in the universe—a power currently working for the peace and welfare of mankind, since it was now controlled by the Pope and the President. But there was grave danger that the Communists might seize this force to bring about incredible evil in the world. There were hints that even now the power was not always in friendly hands:

> I thought I was possessed by devils because for the simple reason my mind and my heart and my body are pure as far as it's within my power to be. And they would put ideas of sex in my mind . . . difference between a male and a female, and all that. Of course, they would be fleeting, and all that. But they weren't natural, because they were not my own thoughts. They were put there especially. I wouldn't mind if they were anywhere but in church.

Here, as clinicians we find ourselves on welcome and familiar ground. Her ideas of being a messiah, of being controlled by external agencies, of cosmic forces at work in the universe are well known to us as *delusions*. We have seen them repeatedly occurring in patients with major mental illnesses. Our initial puzzlement recedes; it is with a sense of relief that we say, "Why, of course! This woman has paranoid schizophrenia."

In thus classifying our patient, we have performed one of the important tasks of psychopathology. We have observed and characterized aberrations of mental functioning; we have grouped these aberrant functions into their proper classes; and we have indicated the clinical syndrome to which they belong.

Unfortunately this sort of categorization tends to fog a more complete understanding of the nature of the mental disorder at hand. Once sorted and labeled, the patient is swallowed up in an ocean of schizophrenia. As one of thousands of roughly similar cases, her own peculiar manifestations of the illnesses are lost from sight. Attention is shifted away from an attempt to understand her immediate experience, or from asking questions about the nature and content of the mental events that fill her awareness. What, for example, is the meaning of her ideas? Why does she feel she is singled out to convert mankind to Christianity? Why is she preoccupied with thoughts about the difference between male and female? Why is she particularly bothered by these ideas in church? To provide her with the diagnosis of paranoid schizophrenia and then move on to the next patient does not help us to answer these questions, which are as much the concern of psychopathology as is the sorting and classification of mental disorders.

Let us approach the problem again with another patient. Toward the end of the last century Daniel Paul Schreber became president of the Superior Country Court at Dresden. Schreber was a lawyer of intelligence, ability and social position, who had led an active and useful professional life. Not long after assuming his new duties Schreber developed a mental illness. In the course of this he conceived the idea that through the intermediation of potent rays from God he was being turned into a woman so that he might give birth to a form of human life more glorious than that which then populated Germany. There was, however, one serious obstacle to the unfolding of this plan. An evil soul, emanating from the person of a Dr. Flechsig, was working counter to the nature of things. Flechsig was a neurologist whom Schreber had consulted some years earlier for an attack of depression; he is famous in his own right for his work on the myelinization of tracts in the brain and spinal cord and for defining the dorsal spinocerebellar tract named after him. As matters stood, Flechsig's soul in conjunction with other evil demons was trying to gain possession of Schreber to force him into being a prostitute to satisfy the lusts of a legion of hellish spirits.

This and many other autobiographical details Schreber published in a volume called in the English translation *Memoirs of My Nervous Illness* (46). He wrote the book, not as an illustration of schizophrenia (the illness from which he suffered), but because he thought the medical profession would be interested in the curious biological phenomenon of a man turning into a woman. His frantic family tried to buy up all the published copies, but fortunately for the science of psychiatry a few volumes escaped their zeal, and Schreber's *Memoirs* are now memorable mainly because Freud wrote his famous study of paranoid ideas based on Schreber's production.

Among the many torments that Schreber suffered at the hands of the Flechsig "soul gang," he described the following:

> All my *muscles* were (and still are) the object of miracles for the purpose of preventing all movements and every occupation I am about to undertake. For instance, attempts are made to paralyze my fingers when I play the piano or write, and to cause some damage to my knee-cap to make marching impossible when I walk about in the garden or in the corridor. Lately the effect has mostly been only to make such occupations difficult or cause only moderate pain on walking.
>
> My *eyes* and the *muscles of the lids* which serve to open and close them were an almost uninterrupted target for miracles. The eyes were always of particular importance, because rays lose the destructive power with which they are equipped after a relatively short time as soon as they *see something,* and then enter my body without causing damage. The object seen can be either visual (eye) impressions, which are communicated to the rays when my eyes are open, or images which I can cause at will on my inner nervous system by imagination, so that they become visible to the rays. I shall return to these events, which in the soul language are called the *"picturing"* of human beings, in another context. Here I will only mention that attempts were made early on and kept up throughout the past years, to close my eyes against my will, so as to rob me of visual impressions and thus preserve the rays' destructive power. This phenomenon can be observed on me

at almost every moment; whoever watches carefully will observe that my eyelids suddenly droop or close even while I am talking to other people; this never occurs in human beings under natural conditions. In order to keep my eyes open nevertheless, a great effort of will is needed; but as I am not always particularly interested in keeping my eyes open I allow them to be closed temporarily at times.

During my first months here the miracles on my eyes were performed by "little men," very similar to those I mentioned when describing the miracle directed against my spinal cord. These "little men" were one of the most remarkable and even to me most mysterious phenomena; but I have no doubt whatever in the objective reality of these happenings, as I saw these "little men" innumerable times with my mind's eye and heard their voices. The remarkable thing about it was that souls or their single nerves could in certain conditions and for particular purposes assume the form of tiny human shapes (as mentioned earlier only a few millimeters in size), and as such made mischief on all parts of my body, both inside and on the surface. Those occupied with the opening and closing of the eyes stood above the eyes in the eyebrows and there pulled the eyelids up or down as they pleased with fine filaments like cobwebs. Here too those concerned were usually a "little Flechsig" and a "little v. W." and sometimes in addition another "little man," who had originated from Daniel Fürchtegott Flechsig's soul which still existed at that time. Whenever I showed signs of being unwilling to allow my eyelids to be pulled up and down and actually opposed it, the "little men" became annoyed and expressed this by calling me "wretch"; if I wiped them off my eyes with a sponge, it was considered by the rays as a sort of crime against God's gift of miracles. By the way, wiping them away had only a very temporary effect, because the "little men" were each time set down afresh. Other "little men" were assembled almost continuously on my head in great number. They were called "little devils." They literally

walked around on my head, curiously nosing about to see
whether any new destructions had been caused on my
head by miracles. In a way they even partook of my meals,
helping themselves to a part, though naturally only a tiny
part, of the food I ate; it made them appear temporarily
somewhat swollen, but also less active and less destructive
in their intentions. Some of the "little devils'" participated
in a miracle which was often enacted against my head and
of which I will now say a little more. This was perhaps the
most abominable of all miracles—next to the compression-
of-the-chest-miracle; the expression used for it if I remember correctly was "the head-compressing-machine."
In consequence of the many flights of rays, etc., there had
appeared in my skull a deep cleft or rent roughly along
the middle, which was probably not visible from the outside but was from the inside. The "little devils" stood on
both sides of this cleft and compressed my head as though
in a vise by turning a kind of screw, causing my head temporarily to assume an elongated almost pear-shaped form.
It had an extremely threatening effect, particularly as it was
accompanied by severe pain. The screws were loosened
temporarily but only very gradually, so that the compressed state usually continued for some time. The "little
devils" responsible mostly derived from v. W.'s soul. These
"little men" and "little devils" disappeared after a few
months never to appear again. The moment of their departure coincided approximately with the appearance of
the posterior realms of God. It is true that miracles are
still responsible for opening and closing my eyelids in the
manner described, but for almost six years now it has no
longer been done by "little men" but directly by rays
which set the muscles concerned in motion. In order to prevent my closing or opening my eyes at will the thin layer
of muscle situated in and above the eyelids and serving
their movement has several times been removed by miracle. But again the effect was only temporary: the muscle
tissue so lost was always restored again.

In comparison with Joan A., it is both easier and harder to understand what Schreber is trying to tell us. It is easier because he is talking to us about somatic sensations—pain, touch, kinesthetic sensations, sight and hearing. As the very fabric of our waking life, we can share with Schreber his experience of these sensations; we can know directly what he felt.

On the other hand, it is difficult for most of us to comprehend Schreber's state of awareness when he saw and heard and felt "little men" scuffing and snuffling around on his scalp. Most of us, when awake, see and hear and feel only those things that are "really there," and that can be sensed in common with other people. Schreber's private and unsharable experiences are as alien to us as was the former patient's awareness that evil cosmic forces were obtruding sexual thoughts upon her mind. We call the phenomena that Schreber presents us hallucinations, and once again having named and classified them, we may feel that our job is done, and that we can turn our attention to other matters.

But once again, in ignoring the meaning of these events we have left many questions unanswered. Why should Schreber suffer such torments if there is no real reason for his pains? Why should he attribute his suffering specifically to Flechsig, to v. W., to the rays, to God? Why is he so sure that his head is cleft and deformed? Why does he feel that he is being changed from a man to a woman? What is the source of these literally crazy ideas?

Let us turn to a last brief clinical vignette. Each time Clarence B., a man of thirty, turned off a light, he would be seized with the thought "My father is going to die." "I *know* that this is a silly idea," he said. "I *know* that it couldn't possibly happen. But I can't convince myself that it's silly, and I get very nervous about it. I have to turn around, tap the switch three times and say to myself 'I take back that thought,' and then I feel all right until the next time. It's all such damn foolishness." He is *obsessed* with an idea which he combats with a *compulsive act* to allay his *anxiety*. In short, he is suffering from an *obsessive-compulsive neurosis*. Once again, we must not permit our ability to assign our patient a diagnostic label to distract us from important and relevant questions. Why does he have the thought of his father's dying? Why does he feel that his actions can cause or prevent tragedy? What is the source of these ideas so foreign and frightening to him?

Let us compare our three patients; the last shows a striking difference from the first two. The former regard their experiences as a true indication of the state of the world around them. The latter, on the contrary, is aware of the unreality of his ideas; he knows that they conflict with the real structure and working of the external world of objects. If we compare only the *content* of the ideas of each of these three, it is evident that no one of them has an exclusive claim to absurdity. It is quite as ridiculous to expect that turning off a light will kill one's father as it is to feel little men painfully compressing one's head or to dwell on lascivious thoughts in church at the devil's command. The nature of the content of the thoughts alone does not distinguish one patient from the other. The difference lies rather in the *form* in which the thoughts occur. A delusion differs from a hallucination, a hallucination from an obsessional thought. And both the delusion and the hallucination differ from the obsession in carrying with them a conviction of their intrinsic verity that is absent from the obsession. It is this latter formal difference that so strikingly distinguishes the last from the first two patients. It is his ability to separate inner thought from external reality that saves him from the insanity of the others.

It is evident that in assigning each of these patients to a diagnostic category we are concerned primarily with the *form* of his mental functioning rather than with the *content* of his thoughts. Our decision as to the diagnosis is based on whether the mental content is experienced by the patient as a belief, a sensation, or a troublesome thought; on whether it has for him the quality of being real or absurd. We are interested not in *what* the patient is aware of, but in the *manner in which* he is aware of it. We make no attempt to understand the information the patient is trying to communicate about his experiences.

Or, if we have noticed the specific content of an idea, we have done so in order to label it and place it in a more general category. For example, the belief of Joan A. that she was chosen to convert the world to Christianity is of interest because it enables us to classify it as a *delusion of grandeur*. We are less concerned with the specific, individual flavor of the thoughts of this particular patient than with the class to which they may be assigned. By focusing our attention on the general characteristics of such thoughts, we fail to explore the richness and uniqueness of the ideas in this singular human being.

Furthermore, in our diagnostic activity we make no attempt to compare our own mental functioning with that of the patient. Obviously there are many differences; few of us have felt called upon to save mankind; few have been tortured by "little men." It is these differences between the patients and ourselves, particularly with respect to the form of mental functioning, that make the schizophrenic an alien being. But there are many points of similarity, especially with regard to the content of our thoughts. Most of us have private sexual daydreams or occasional thoughts that someone dear to us will die. Whenever we direct our attention and interest to our inner, private, often unspoken imaginations—our world of *fantasy*—we find a wealth of imagery and ideas to rival the soliloquy of a Molly Bloom. Indeed, our initial judgment that we have not had the hallucinations or bizarre thoughts of the schizophrenic is not strictly true.

Those of us who dream, hallucinate. Our sleeping images are as real to us as Schreber's waking hallucinations. The strangeness of the events and moods and ideas of our dreams matches the bizarreness of the craziest madman. It is only when we are awake that we talk of "stuff that dreams are made on." Asleep we accept as real the world our dreams create for us.

It is noteworthy that we ordinarily dismiss our dreams and fantasies as meaningless and trivial. We pay little attention to our own and less to those of others. Our mental energies are ordinarily directed to the external world of things and people. Work holds the center of our stage, not idle dreaming. Our scientific endeavors (in physics, in chemistry, in biology) are aimed at explaining the nature and function of external objects. Mental events are looked upon as "epiphenomena," ultimately explainable in terms of the neurochemical and neurophysiological processes that are correlated with them. Or, if mental functioning is made an object of scientific scrutiny, the emphasis is on the form— the hallucinations, obsessions, delusions, the phobias, and the compulsions, which like external objects, can be described, sorted, and logically ordered into general categories. The multitudinous detail in the content of an individual dream or fantasy tends to be neglected as unworthy of scientific attention.

The task of the discipline of psychopathology is twofold: (1) to describe and classify the observed phenomena, and (2) to devise psychological concepts and theories that explain them. To ignore the content of fantasy and dream is to ignore the observations that lead to these explanations. It is *fantasy that gives the clue to the motivations,* the impulses and the feelings that lie hidden behind the clinical symptoms; it is the key to our understanding. Furthermore, a knowledge of the fantasy and other mental events that take place in ourselves helps us as observers to a better knowledge of the patient we are observing. He is not a specimen under the examining glass, a thing apart from ourselves. On the contrary he is another human being like ourselves, with the same basic needs, hopes, and fears, and the same fundamental psychology. A knowledge of our own mental life enables us often to *know* more immediately what is going on in the patient; it sharpens our powers of observation; it makes us a more sensitive instrument. Fantasy and dream and feeling cannot, therefore, be dismissed by the psychopathologist as froth. They are the stout ale of his discipline, and he must drink deep and seriously; he must make them the focus of his sober scientific endeavor.

In the discipline of psychopathology, therefore, *both* the form and content of mental functioning must be carefully studied. A knowledge of form, as we have seen, enables us to place patients in diagnostic categories; it furthermore allows us to describe and define normal and abnormal personality structure. A study of the content of dream and fantasy provides the means for understanding the psychological conflicts that lead to symptoms and abnormal behavior. Psychopathology without fantasy is the physiology of a corpse.

III

Thoughts, as we have seen, may exist in a variety of forms. Many of these, such as delusions, obsessions, and hallucinations are (except for the hallucinations of the dream state) manifestations of psychopathology. Daydreams, or fantasies, on the other hand, are universal and are not in themselves abnormal. Every fantasy represents an attitude and a concept of the world which arises not simply as a logical reflection on the facts of the outer world arriving in consciousness through the senses; on the contrary, the fantasy is the product of inner, personal, private psychological factors—of needs, impulses, and feelings. Furthermore, a fantasy is usually not a neutral, emotionless, pale, intellectual, logical thought; it is intimately tied to non-intellectual, non-logical mental processes—to hopes, fears, desires, emotions, and urges, even though these may often, as we shall see, be disguised or hidden from conscious awareness. The great value of fantasies to the investigator lies in the fact that they lead to the discovery of the motivations that are hidden behind them.

For the most part, we keep this inner life of fantasy to ourselves. It is a rare man who always says exactly what he thinks; he is guided by shame, diplomacy, and tact to be circumspect about many of his inner thoughts on people and things. A patient talking to his doctor is no different— he leaves much of his inner life hidden from view, even though the doctor explicitly asks him to disclose it. This poses a problem: knowledge of a person's fantasy is essential for an understanding of his mental functioning, and yet he tends to withhold just that essential information.

This is a surprising complication; one would expect a patient willingly to give relevant information to the doctor who is trying to help him; one would expect him to respond freely and openly to the doctor's direct questioning. In many instances he does; one can often successfully ask the patient to be an accurate witness of the physiological functioning of his own body. One can ask direct questions about the character, location, quality, duration, and onset of a pain, and get reliable answers. One can even inquire about the state of a person's bowels or about a woman's menstrual periods, and obtain accurate and straightforward replies, even though these are topics that shame and good manners might exclude from a drawing-room conversation.

But when a doctor asks a patient to observe and describe his own inner mental life, he is dealing with a more reluctant witness. For here the factors of reticence and shame and pride are often strong enough to overcome even a genuine desire on the patient's part to be honest and complete in his answers. All of us have thoughts that we would not tell another until we have grown to know and to trust him; all of us have thoughts that, except under the most unusual circumstances, we would *never* tell anyone else. Blunt cross-examination will not often elicit such thoughts no matter how valuable it may be as a technique for getting at the facts of physiological functions. It is quite valueless in getting at those fantasies and feelings of which the patient is himself unaware.

There are, however, ways of gaining knowledge of a person's inner mental life without directly challenging him to reveal it; and by the same methods of interviewing one obtains insight into the patient's manner of concealing and disguising his thoughts. The picture of the psychiatrist as a sphinx-like creature who stares, occasionally grunts, and mostly listens is a caricature, but like any caricature it has a likeness, though exaggerated, to the original. The psychiatrist *is* often silent, he *does* listen, because he wants his patient to talk freely and spontaneously. When the doctor asks a direct question (e.g., "Were you angry at your husband when he forgot your birthday?"), he asks it because he has a notion in his own mind as to what the patient is experiencing. He may be right, but it is also possible that his questions may slant and distort the patient's account of his own thought processes. With such a question, he abandons the position of a neutral observer who is watching and listening to discover what comes from the patient spontaneously. This should not be construed to mean that the doctor does not guide or control the interview. On the contrary, by his questions he focuses the patient's attention on the area he is interested in hearing about. But about that area he allows the patient to talk freely in his own way. For as the patient talks, he gives clues in his tone of voice, his phrasing, his pauses, his imagery, to important attitudes, feelings, and fantasies that he cannot directly talk about, and of which in fact he may not really be aware himself.

For example, a man in his forties seemed during an interview to be anxious and upset. He was restless, he sighed frequently, and the expression on his face was constantly troubled. When asked directly, he vigorously denied that anything was bothering him. He was, he said, not anxious, he was not depressed, he had no worries at home, and his finances were in an excellent state. Indeed, the more he talked, the more unbelievable his statements about himself became: he had *never* in his life been frightened, *never* in his life felt sad, *never* in his life been upset by the vicissitudes of living. He insisted that his life was completely serene and happy, despite the fact that he was now hospitalized, and had been out of work for over a year because of an injury to his back. In an hour-long interview, only one spontaneously uttered remark hinted at flaws in his utopia. Speaking of his wife, he said, "She and I get along just fine —she does what she wants to; I do what I'm told." This is a slender thread, but it is the sort of clue that designates an area of mental unrest, a point of tenderness, that provides the interviewer with an indicator of where and how to explore further for pathogenic attitudes and feelings.

The withholding of information about fantasies and feelings is the result of two factors. *Suppression* is the purposeful refusal by the patient to reveal facts of his mental life of which he is consciously aware. *Repression* implies that there are ideas and feelings outside the sphere of conscious awareness, and inaccessible to voluntary recall. Which of these factors was at work in the man we have just observed is not certain; presumably it was a mixture of both. Fortunately most patients are not so reticent; although they are unable to tell us *all* that they think, they tell enough to indicate the nature of their conflicts.

There is a further reason for using *indirect methods of interviewing.* Not only do they reveal individual fantasies of significance, but they permit one to observe the *train of thought* of a patient who speaks spontaneously and without interruptions. The importance of a train of thoughts derives from the principle of the association of ideas: thoughts, even during the most chaotic and fragmented daydreaming, do not come into conscious awareness simply by chance; their appearance, content, and sequence are causally determined. Seemingly disparate ideas are related to one another by their connection with a central underlying theme, motive, feeling, or impulse, which may not in itself be immediately apparent but which determines the nature of the conscious associations. If, therefore, one allows a person to *associate freely,* that is, to observe and to communicate all the ideas that flow through his consciousness, one can arrive eventually at an understanding of the central factor determining the ideas. If an interviewer interrupts a patient too frequently, or interjects too many of his own ideas into the flow of associations, that flow will be contaminated and distorted, and may not reveal the underlying motivating factor. In fact, owing to the normal reluctance of all of us freely to disclose all of our thoughts and fantasies, true *free association* is an ideal rarely achieved. Fortunately, even associations falling short of this ideal of completeness enable both the trained observer, as well as the patient himself to understand what motivates them. Moreover, the observation of where a patient seems to be holding back ideas, to be breaking the smooth train of associations, or to be resisting the unfettered flow of thoughts, provides important information about his whole personality structure.

These, then, are some of the basic reasons for using indirect methods of interviewing, especially in those situations where one wishes to gain information about a patient's psychological function. It is not our purpose to dwell on the details of the techniques of interviewing. This is a subject for a book itself, and indeed whole volumes have been written, directly or indirectly, about it (14-19). We shall restrict ourselves here to a brief discussion of the fundamental principles that form the basis for the more specific *tactics of interviewing technique.*

1. First and foremost the doctor must know how to *listen.* He often has to restrain himself from impatient interrupting, from premature counseling, or from personal reminiscence. He must know when to keep quiet even when the patient is silent—to allow the patient to say what he has to say in his own way, at his own pace. He must be able without premature generalizations to lose himself in the trees of the patient's associations until the pattern of the forest becomes clear. At the same time he must observe his patient's behavior—his movements, his gestures, his tone of

voice, the bodily dumb show of his affects—for clues to the regions of emotional conflict.

2. He must *know what to say and when.* The content of questions .depends on knowing what topics the patient is ready to discuss and the timing depends on knowing when the moment is appropriate for discussing them.

3. He must *know what not to say*—he must avoid asking questions that will bring about needlessly painful anxiety or depression in the patient, or will increase his resistance against communicating with the doctor.

4. And finally, as a part of his therapeutic measures, he must *know what information to give* the patient to help him to increased knowledge of himself, and must sense when the patient is ready for such communications; he must know when to reassure and support the patient to diminish intolerable anxiety, and when to provoke it in order to keep the therapeutic process moving. And he must know *when to give advice* and *when silence is wisdom.*

Like any skill, one cannot learn the art of interviewing by reading about it alone. To become proficient, one must watch others with experience as they talk with patients and do it oneself under supervision; in this way and gradually, with time and practice, the different techniques become second nature, and one develops a style of one's own. We may gain, however, some idea of the nature of interviewing by observing the various encounters between patient and doctor which are transcribed in the pages that follow.

Part II

Three Fundamental Concepts:

Psychological Conflict, the Unconscious,

and Psychogenesis

IV

Psychological Conflict

In our consideration of the nature of fantasies and associations, one fact has become apparent. Mental life is not a homogeneous stream flowing serene and unruffled, without crosscurrents, eddies, and backwaters. On the contrary, to switch metaphors in mid-stream, it has many aspects of a house divided against itself. Clarence B., for example, although he was obsessed with the thought that his father would die when he turned off the lights, vehemently disowned this idea; he was made uneasy by it and fought against it. Yet both the idea and his disavowal of it arose within the boundaries of his own mind. One part of his mind rejected another part; the one was in conflict with the other.

Here we come upon a concept that is central to the theory of psychopathology—indeed to the whole idea of dynamic psychiatry: the mind may be conceived of as having structure, and the parts of it as being in conflict with one another. Mind is an ever-shifting equilibrium of forces that may be manifest in symptoms or pathological behavior. This book is a gloss on that text; our purpose in this chapter is threefold: (1) to give a panoramic view of the structure of mind which we shall be subsequently examining in more detail; (2) to demonstrate the nature of psychological conflict; and (3) to show how a knowledge of fantasies and free associations provides the clue to the nature of the structure of the mind and of the conflicts raging within it.

Before we examine this structure as it unfolds before us in the details of an interview with a patient, let us first enumerate, name, and briefly define the major divisions of the personality. Basic to all human life are the impulses, drives, needs, appetites and desires—those energies without which the structure would be lifeless. Of primary importance are the sexual and aggressive drives, the source of which is termed the *Id*. The effect of these is experienced in consciousness as fantasy and feeling by a second part of the personality structure called the *Ego*. As the term implies, the ego has affinities to the *"I"-myself*, the person who is, lives, exists, experiences, does, senses, and feels, usually with an awareness of being a unit separate from other persons and things, with an identity and integrity of its own. The ego is the integrating organ of the personality. It perceives the object world through the senses, makes logical sense of it, and enables the organism to adapt itself to the environment.

An important element of this adaptation is the function of controlling the impulses which strive for unfettered satisfaction and expression. The ego manipulates the outside world to provide satisfactions for the impulses; at the same time it delays discharge of the impulses until the external circumstances are appropriate, so that the impulse may be satisfied without causing damage or destruction to the organism. In part the ego conforms to the demands of the physical environment; in part to the social structure surrounding it—the customs, sanctions, and prohibitions of society and individuals which determine when and how an impulse may be discharged, or that it may not be discharged at all. The *defenses* against impulses (and their derivative fantasies and feelings), which control, modify, and when necessary contain them, constitute a major function of the ego, and one that is especially important for an understanding of psychopathology.

As we have indicated, the ego must adapt the discharge of impulses to the demands of the external object and social world. There is, however, another internal mental agency which exerts strong pressures on the ego quite as stringent as those of the external world. The ego experiences the mandates of an inner voice, the conscience, which commands it to conform to certain modes of behavior, even though these may not be contrary to the demands of the external world. The conscience belongs to a part of the personality termed the *Superego;* to this organization also belong the *ego ideals,* those standards of behavior toward which we aspire.

In using the terms *Id, Ego,* and *Superego,* we have been speaking as if these, like objects in the external world, had form, substance, and location. This, of course, is not the case. The terms name mental organizations which can be immediately experienced, although their exact nature is hard to define. It is characteristic of the human mind that it is most at home in dealing with the objects of sense located in the outer world. Anyone conversant with the exuberant literature of allegory in all cultures and ages is aware of the human tendency to reify and objectify mental states. Psychologists are no different, and the substantive, objective quality of the terms we have just been defining reflects the fact that they are in a way allegorical. We must not be seduced by this into forgetting that what these terms refer to are the conscious, or potentially conscious, experiences arising in the awareness of a human being's inner, mental life.

Let us give these abstract concepts more color and meaning by observing the phenomena they name. The patient who helps us is Boyd C., a man in his thirties who had spent Christmas day in the hospital away from his family. In the opening minutes of an interview with his doctor on the following day he complained of being more anxious than he had ever felt in his life. His agitated behavior, worried facial expression, and trembling hands corroborated his testimony. As he entered the office he said:

Pt.   This is the roughest day yet, boy! Jesus, don't ask me why, because I don't know. Look—I can't even hold my hand still.

Dr.   Let's see when it began, and what it's all about.

Pt.   Gee, I don't know. I just think it's the aftermath of yesterday. Last night I lay in bed and bawled till about three or four this morning. It just hit me like that. I wasn't thinking about anything in particular, when, boom!, it just started like that. Yesterday after dinner I kind of thought of the kids and everything, and the wife. And looking at the football game I kind of wondered where the kid brothers are, and I knew one of them was home on furlough, and everything just seemed to come, and last night the dam just burst, that's all. Gee, I'm jumpy! I just don't know, I'm on edge.

Dr.   What is the feeling?

Pt.   Just jumpy. Criminy, I'm not only trembling on the outside. On the inside, I'm shaking all over. I can't seem to calm myself down.

Dr.   You're really quite anxious.

Pt.   I don't know whether it's anxious. I woke up shaking all over. Boy, it's an awful funny feeling. I wasn't thinking about anything. I just woke up that way. I've never experienced anything like this before, honest. I'll be doing something, like I was working on clay and I reached for something and gee, I just jerked like that, right out of a clear blue sky. This afternoon, getting some juice off the wagon there, the fellow was pouring it, and cripes, I gave a little jerk and spilled the glass of juice and everything. It's the awfullest feeling, not knowing what the heck is making me do it—why I should be that way. I feel almost as if I came off of a big drunk or something. It's that kind of a fluttery feeling. And, criminy, I threw up what dinner I ate.

Dr.   You did vomit?

Pt. Yeah, yeah, Jesus, just got the shakes, that's all.
Christ, I had to force myself to stay out where there were
people around. I guess I don't want to be around them
when I'm depressed. I'd just like to go in that room and
close the door and stay there all day today. I actually had
to force myself to get out ... I didn't get out of bed till
eleven-thirty. I wouldn't have then, but I knew it wouldn't
have done me a damn bit of good to lay there. There's no
sense in just laying there feeling sorry for yourself. I had
sense enough to know I had to overcome this thing one
way or another. As I say, I laid there and I tried to figure
out what the hell was making me that way, and I can't find
the answer for it. Just whether it's a kind of a reaction
from yesterday, or just what the hell it is. One time I
wrecked my car, and I was just as calm and everything
until it was all over, and then when everything was all over
I trembled and shook, and that's just the way I feel today.
It's the funniest damn sensation ... At first I thought it
was because I didn't get much sleep, and then, Christ, I
said it couldn't be just that, because I've gone nights without sleep and it didn't bother me like that. I was really
concerned about it. I wanted to know *how* and *why* and I
haven't been able to put anything together.

Dr. What thoughts *did* you have?

Pt. It's something new that's never happened before.
What happened to me? What has transpired to make me
this way? Am I sick, or am I coming down with a bug? The
first thought was whether I had caught something, if I
was sick, or is it just this place that's getting me down? Is
it the atmosphere, or what the hell is it? All those thoughts
went through my head, and I couldn't pick any one of
them up to make it click into that puzzle. Someone dropped
something in the Occupational Therapy Shop, and I think
if I could have jumped, if I could have pushed with my
legs, I think I would have jumped straight up in the air.
But as soon as it was over with, I was trembling like a leaf,
and sweating—sweating like hell.

It is apparent from what the patient says that he has experienced both a sense of sadness and depression, and a feeling of anxiousness. All of us are familiar with these feelings and can through introspection understand what the patient is experiencing. Both of them are basic and important feeling states experienced by the "I," the Ego, and both of them, as indicated by the patient, are acutely painful states of awareness. We shall later on be examining these two phenomena at greater length; they are important and common symptoms of emotional illness. Let us here briefly focus on the anxiety.

As is so often the case with feelings, the patient has some difficulty in describing his anxiety. He says it is a "fluttery feeling," a sense of trembling inside as well as outside, and he likens it to the aftermath of a drunk or to his sensations after wrecking his car. For the most part he describes the physiological processes that accompany it: trembling, sweating, an increased reaction of startling to external noise, abrupt and jerky movements, and vomiting.

Particularly striking is the patient's perplexity over the reason for his anxiety. He assumes that there must be a cause for it, he wonders whether he is sick, or is "fed up" with the hospital, but these explanations do not really satisfy him, and a part of the painful quality of the anxiety lies in the mystery about its origin—as he says, ". . . not knowing what the heck is making me do it—why I should be that way."

The patient's mystification is no greater than ours. There is no obvious reason why he should have become so acutely anxious. Nothing that we should ordinarily consider sufficient reason to produce a reaction of fear and anxiety has occurred. It is here that fantasy and the means of eliciting it through the technique of interviewing help to provide an answer. We notice that so far in the interview, the doctor has said very little. For the greater part he has been listening to the spontaneous flow of the patient's speech; he has asked few questions, and those he has asked have been aimed primarily at eliciting from the patient an elaboration of his feelings and thoughts (fantasies); the doctor has directed the interview to particular areas of interest, but he has not slanted the specific content of the patient's thoughts in any certain direction by asking direct questions about fantasies and feelings that he thinks may be in the patient's mind.

Finally, it should be noted that in the first few sentences which the patient uttered he mentioned that he had thought about his wife and children celebrating Christmas at home. Let us simply make note of this fact here without further elaboration as we return to the process of the interview. When the patient described his reaction to the noise in the Occupational Therapy Shop, the doctor asked him:

Dr.　How did you feel when they dropped that?

Pt.　I don't know. I was ready to—I almost felt like picking up something and throwing it.

Dr.　You did really?

Pt.　Yes.

Dr.　What was this feeling?

Pt.　Well, just for an instant, just when that sound hit, I felt like grabbing something and throwing it. That's an awful funny way to feel, but that's how I felt for that instant.

Dr.　You got mad momentarily?

Pt.　Yes, I guess it was mad. Like, Jesus, throwing something! I mean it—oh, Jesus, it's an awful feeling for me, it really is! And if I could understand it, I'd feel different about it, but I'm way out in left field about it ... Look at my hands. Honest to God, I can't hold them still at all! And that's how I feel inside, trembly, almost a throw-up feeling. I go into my room, I stay there a minute, and I have to leave the room. I go outside to do something, and I got to do something else.

Dr.　It's a very restless feeling.

Pt. Oh, it's awful! It's the type of feeling if I had it at home, I'd walk it off. I'd work it out of me, bang things, chop wood, saw wood, anything—run around the block.

At the start of this section the patient introduces a new element. Whereas before he had been describing sensations and feelings, he suddenly mentions an urge, an impulse to do something actively, as indicated by his momentary fantasy of throwing something. The doctor at once, and prematurely, tries to translate this into a feeling of anger, to suggest that there was something aggressive in the patient's impulse. The latter only half-heartedly agrees, and then reverts to describing his painful anxiety, ending again with his inner urge to do something strenuously active. He then continues:

Pt. I was on the irritable side, and it wouldn't take much to set off the spark. Little things rubbed against me there and I had to hold myself together. I probably would have started a row and got everyone upset. I was holding back on it, and yet I didn't want to. I wanted to let loose and say some mean things.

Dr. What did you want to say?

Pt. Oh, there's a girl there who is griping all the time and pitying herself and she's always needling someone and I wanted to say to her—I could be mean and say something that would hurt like hell, but it wouldn't do any good. What was the sense to it? She gripes me plenty, and I guess I'm not the only one. Everyone over there is sick of her. When she started in, I had this answer on the tip of my tongue, and well, I kind of thought it over—she's one of the alcoholics over there, and she'd start her ranting and raving. I might blow off my steam, but still it would cause a bad situation all around, so I just got the hell away and went into my room. I tried to read. I'd read two or three minutes and stop and work on a toy animal; then I'd drop the animal and go to something else. Jesus, I couldn't do anything! And I got a hell of a headache. Jesus, my head has been pounding! . . . It aches like a son of a gun, like your eyes are coming out of your head. Like a steam-boiler: You figure that the needle has hit the top and you're ready to pop off steam. Something's got to give one way or the other. I don't know what's going to happen. I'm either going to go to bed and bawl all night, or I'm going to say something and blow my stack and get someone arguing and start a fight. That's a heck of a feeling to have! . . . I think that at the moment if someone took a couple of swings at me and I could swing back I'd feel damn glad about it. I don't know if you can understand that type of feeling I have, but that's just the way I feel. I'm not mad, it's not mad. I have to get that damn feeling out of me, that's all.

Here we begin to see the usefulness of fantasy as it pours from the patient in the images and thoughts of what he wanted to do: to "say something mean" to another patient that would "hurt like hell," to "blow his stack," "start a fight," "take a swing" at someone. These indicate to us a quality in his emotional state different from the anxiety of which he just complained. Furthermore, he introduces a new symptom—not this time a disturbance in the emotional sphere like his anxiety, but a somatic symptom, his headache. And again, the imagery he uses to describe it is revealing about his inner state. Our knowledge about what this patient is experiencing has been considerably expanded. Not only is he anxious and depressed, but we find that he has a headache, and is filled with violent, aggressive impulses. It appears as if he were angry.

Curiously, however, although the patient begins by saying he is irritable and talks about wanting to fight and hurt, he ends by saying, "I'm not mad." Although it seems obvious to an observer listening to the patient that this must be so, the patient is himself reluctant to admit it. And, indeed, throughout this section of the interview we can detect a conflict within the patient: He is filled with aggressive impulses which appear to him in the form of fantasies. At the same time he is self-critical of these fantasies and the impulses behind them. He is moved to say something to hurt the woman patient, but on reflection, realizes that it would "cause a bad situation," and therefore refrains. He comments that "it's a heck of a feeling to have" to want to "take a swing at someone." As a result, he controls his impulses. Here we can observe the *ego* experiencing an *impulse* (the aggressive impulse), judging it wrong as measured against certain personal standards (*superego*), and exercising *controls* over the impulse and the behavior it threatens to produce, even to the extent of apparently excluding from consciousness an awareness that he is angry.

Through all of this runs the theme of anxiety: noting the train of associations linking the anxiety to the active aggressive impulses, we ask ourselves, "Is the anxiety related to the aggression? If so, how is it related?" It is clear that the patient does not like being aggressive. He would much rather not be that way; he tries to disclaim his anger. Again, we have to ask, "Why?"; anger and aggression are universal; why does the patient try so hard to avoid these feelings and impulses?

Before we can find answers to these questions in the unfolding of the patient's associations in the interview, he momentarily veers off on another tack:

Pt. I felt all right last night when I went to bed. I wasn't lonesome. I was a little sad, you know what I mean. Then I got to thinking about the wife and the kids, and then we watched TV and there was kids on it, and it just kind of made a lump in your throat. So I went to bed and said my prayers, and I got to thinking about home, and the first thing you know I started to cry and I bawled and I bawled. I couldn't seem to stop. My God, it came out of me in buckets! It wasn't a loud cry, but I couldn't stop the tears from coming. It was a sad and choked up feeling, you know. Then finally it eased off, and the nurse came in and asked me how I was, and I said I just couldn't sleep. I thought, "Why bother her with my troubles?", so I just told her that I couldn't sleep. She said it was pretty late and I said, "Do you want me to put the light out?", and she said no, not if I want to read and maybe get tired by reading to go ahead and read. Then I read and read and I couldn't even get interested in the books, so I went out to get me a drink of water and I seen it was quarter to four. So I went back in and turned the light off and I don't know how long I lay there, but I did get choked up again, my thoughts wandering back home to the wife and the kids, and then I dozed off to sleep. I heard the orderly come in at seven o'clock. This morning when I come to I went to put my feet over the side of the bed and reach for the chair, and when I did I started to shake inside of me.

Here the patient turns from his aggressive impulses to his feelings and thoughts of the night before. Again, as in the opening measures of the interview, he briefly mentions his wife and children. This digression is short, however, and he reverts at the end to the acute anxiety, before continuing as follows:

Pt. But I've just been shaky all day. Cripes, just the way we're talking now, nice and soft, I could, well—I could holler! I really can't explain it. At lunch time there, the craziest damn urge hit me: there's a pitcher on the table there, and I was pouring a glass of milk, and, Christ!, I just wanted to pick that pitcher up and heave it! I've heard of people having thoughts like that, and I really had to make a conscious effort to keep from doing it. If I had done what that feeling at that particular moment told me to do, I would have heaved it out the window or something, or thrown it in someone's face. I don't know what I would have done. But looking at the pitcher, I had the damndest urge to heave it . . . I'm scared of what the hell it is. I have this feeling, and I wonder what the hell is going on. What am I doing? What makes me this way? I think at the present time if I went back over there and someone would say something and I let myself—my feelings get away from me a little bit, I would enjoy having a fight with someone or banging something, or Christ!, going in and tearing my bed all to pieces or some crazy thing like that. I don't know how the hell to express it.

Dr.   You're afraid you'll let it get the best of you.

Pt.   Yeah, afraid I'll let the damn thing get hold of me—because I can't understand what makes me feel like this.

During all of this recital, the patient had been growing more and more anxious and agitated. He began to talk fast, tripped and stammered over words, gestured more violently, and his voice, perceptibly higher in pitch, rose to a near shout. And then suddenly at this point he burst into tears and for a minute was so choked up with emotion that he could not talk. In a moment, he quieted down, and the interview continued.

Dr.   This is what is making you so scared.

Pt.   That I won't be able to hold myself back. Like that urge I had at noon—for cripe's sake, a man in his right mind—who the hell is going to be getting a feeling like that? Why should I feel that way? What if my sense of balance should go the other way—should give ground to these feelings I have of banging somebody or throwing a pitcher or some damn foolish thing like that?

Dr.   Is it a feeling that no one else ever had these feelings?

Pt.   No, it isn't that. It's a feeling of being scared of what I'm apt to do. If I got hold of someone, I don't know if I'd just be satisfied to smack him in the face, or if I'd really have to do a job on him. Or, if I threw something, it would end there or just build up into something—go berserk. Jesus! It's an awful feeling!

Here are even clearer signs of psychological conflict. The patient's ego is experiencing strong impulses to violent action. It judges these impulses as wrong, as crazy, as being unworthy of his ideal of what a man in his right mind would do, or of what he himself wants to do; he struggles valiantly to control himself from translating the impulses into action. Furthermore, what he is afraid of, and why, is now evident; we have discovered the source of the anxiety that floods his ego. He sums it up himself in the sentence, "It's a feeling of being scared of what I'm apt to do." In other words he is frightened of his own aggressive impulse lest it escape from his control. Furthermore it is the violence and destructiveness of the aggressive impulse that makes it so frightening to him. His fantasies indicate the quality of the impulse— to throw a pitcher of milk, tear his bed apart, smack someone in the face, "really do a job on him," "go berserk." The patient's emotional equilibrium is being strained to the breaking point, and the result is the acutely painful anxiety that mounts as he talks about his feelings until at one point it momentarily overcomes him.

We should take note of how much we have learned about the patient by allowing him to talk and by listening to his account of what he is experiencing in his inner mental life. At the start of the interview we were confronted with his acute anxiety, for which we had no adequate explanation; now his aggression has appeared openly and distinctly before us as an important causal element. But it is not only we, the observers, who have learned something. The patient's own awareness of himself has increased as he has talked under the doctor's guidance. At the start of the interview the patient was quite as perplexed as we as to the reason for his being so anxious. He tried to explain it to himself, but was not satisfied with the thought that it might be because he was "coming down with a bug"; his inability to understand his anxiety further heightened the painfulness of the emotion. Now, after talking freely about himself, he too can see that he is frightened of "what he is apt to do." We had conjectured this earlier in the interview before the patient himself was aware of it, but now he confirms the truth of our inference in his open recognition of his own inner experience.

Let us pause to re-emphasize a basic principle of the technique of interviewing. Had we asked the patient directly, "What are you anxious about?", he would of course have answered truthfully, "I don't know." If we had asked him specific questions based on our own conjecture (for example, "Are you anxious because you are angry?") the patient would have given a negative answer. In fact, in the interview itself, when the doctor did prematurely raise the question of anger, the patient disclaimed it. Were we to have been satisfied with these early negative answers, and to have turned to other topics, we should have deprived ourselves of important information about the patient and his anxiety. We could uncover the relevant facts only by listening quietly but alertly to his report of his fantasies and feelings. The patient had to be given the floor; he had to be helped by relatively neutral questions and remarks to keep his stream of talk focused on the area under investigation.

Thus far we have been able to uncover the connection between the patient's anxiety and his aggression. But there is still an important question unanswered: Why is he so angry? What has aroused this violent, destructive rage in him? We know that he was startled by the noise of an object dropping in the Occupational Therapy Shop; we know that he was annoyed by a troublesome woman on the ward. But were these causes, or was his reaction to these stimuli perhaps determined by an anger that was already rising in him from another source?

At this point let us turn to his wife and children, who were home celebrating Christmas while he remained in the hospital. As we have noted in passing, he mentions them twice in association with his sadness and his anxiety. Is the association significant? Does it indicate a connection between this external event and the patient's inner feelings? We must ask the patient; we must direct his attention to the topic, and allow him to talk about it. The interview continued as follows:

Pt. We had dinner in there on the ward, a good dinner and everything, but to me it went down like lead. And I don't know, just knowing the kids and the wife are home, and I was halfway hoping I'd get a phone call from them. There was nobody on the ward and it was lonesome as hell —only three of us over there, three or four, I guess. It was quiet. It was like being in a tomb—just no activity at all.

Dr. They didn't call?

Pt. No, they didn't call. It was just a remote spark of hope I had. I didn't expect it, but I thought there was the possibility they might. It was something I would have welcomed.

Dr. And you were disappointed when they didn't?

Pt. Well, in a way, yes. It wasn't as though in her letters she said she'd call and have the kids talk. There were people there—her sister and mother, and they were so busy they didn't think of calling. They had other things on their mind. It wasn't that they put me in a corner, but they did have a lot of things to occupy their mind, and they didn't bring themselves to calling, that's all . . . It didn't dwell on my mind. After the football game I told the nurse that I was going to my room to make an animal, and I said, "Maybe the wife will call. I don't hardly expect it, but she might call, and could they put the call up here on the ward?" And she said she thought so, and I didn't think another thing about it until I told you just now. I thought that because it was Christmas and she knew where I was, there was the possibility she would call. For all I know, she may not have planned to call, but come down tomorrow. I really don't know. I don't expect her, but I won't

be disappointed if she comes down. I'll be damn glad if
she does. It's the same type of thing I had about the phone
call.

Dr.   There are a lot of feelings here.

Pt.   I would say so, yeah. Probably every type of emotion you could experience—the wondering, hoping, and
then maybe when Saturday comes, and then Sunday, and
I don't see her, maybe there will be a disappointment. It
won't be a big issue. But a week gone and I haven't seen
the wife; a couple of letters, but "what the hell good is a
letter"—that type of feeling . . . It seems to me, and I
know there's no getting around it since I got hurt, what
grows more and more important to me everyday is the
wife and the kids. I don't dwell on them in my mind. I'm
not anxious for them. I'm not worried about them, but to
me they get more important because I've got to get on my
feet quicker. They are the only damn things that I have to
strive for. They are like the guy reaching for the 64-dollar
question.

Dr.   I wonder, though, if there weren't an awful lot of
feelings—not only that you weren't home with them and
that you were alone and lonesome, but somehow feelings
about the fact that they didn't call, and that you felt quite
left out.

Pt.   It could have been, but it went in one ear and out
the other. It didn't stick there . . . When I was on the other
ward she used to call pretty regular there, and I got to look
forward to it. There were days every time the phone would
ring my heart would pound and I'd get anxious: "Is that
for me? Is that for me?" Well, yesterday I didn't have that
feeling. I just had the thought she might call, and then I
thought no more of it . . .

Dr.   But your thoughts were, "There they are at home
and why are they so busy that they can't think of calling
me?"

Pt.   No, I didn't think of it like that . . . Not the meaning of "They just don't think of me; they don't want to call
me; they don't think of me." I thought of it in the sense

that she was too busy keeping the kids and all that stuff. I could have done the same thing myself. Had the situation been reversed, I'd have done the same thing. It wasn't a hurt feeling, "For Christ's sake, why don't you call up? You had all day to do it!" I didn't think of it in that attitude. Christ, I don't know. After the game there I just had the fleeting thought that maybe they'd call up. But later on when I started watching TV the old lump started coming up, and Christ, the kids on the screen there, and it was one of those sad things anyway—someone was off to war or something like that. It gets you thinking; you can't help yourself. Instead of dropping it right there, I carried it to bed with me and thought of it there, and the first thing I knew I was crying. I really got worked up about it.

In this section of the interview the patient tells us clearly that his sadness resulted from his lonesomeness on the ward during Christmas day, from thoughts of his family celebrating the holiday at home, and from the sentimental television program that apparently was in harmony with the tone of his own mood. But we also observe him doing a strange thing: he is telling us of a number of feelings and thoughts that he did *not* have. He half hoped his wife would call (to the extent of alerting the nurse on the ward to this possibility), but he really *didn't* expect her to. His mind *didn't* dwell on it. He was *not* hurt when she didn't. It was *not* that they just put him in a corner and forgot about him. He did *not* have the attitude, "For Christ's sake, why didn't you call up? You had all day to do it!" The doctor's few attempts to suggest that maybe the patient did have such feelings only strengthened the insistence of his negations.

If we consider only the content of the patient's imagery, his fantasy, without for the moment being concerned with whether it is positively or negatively qualified, we see that he is preoccupied here with his family, with how much he needs and misses them, with thoughts about their calling him to remember him on the holiday, with explanations as to why they didn't call, with feelings of disappointment and anger at their failure to phone, with his eagerness to hear from them, etc. If he had confessed to having had all these thoughts and to having suffered all these feelings, we could quite understand why he experienced them; we could readily sympathize with him for being upset, alone on Christmas and apparently forgotten by his family. But he does not make this open confession; he says only, "Here are many thoughts and feelings about this situation, but I didn't have them. I was not disappointed and angry."

It is said that during the gloomy days of American prohibition it was possible to buy grape juice which came with a notice reading in essense, "WARNING! Do *not* add two cups of sugar to this grape juice. Do *not* let stand for 12 weeks at 72 degrees Fahrenheit. For if you do, you will make wine, and that is illegal." Perhaps our patient protests too much.

At this point we must make an *inference*. We shall disregard the minus sign the patient places before his fantasies, and shall infer that they tell the truth about at least a part of the patient's mental apparatus: that he did very much want his wife to remember him on Christmas by calling him; that in fact he was very much disappointed and hurt when she did not; that it appeared to him that they *had* shoved him off in a corner and had forgotten about him; and finally, that he was not only saddened by this, but seized by a fury of rage. This wealth of feeling and fantasy, however, came into conflict with that part of him that loved and needed his wife, who, with his children, was the "only thing he had to strive for." As a consequence, he could not allow himself to become aware of his true state of mind— that is, he *repressed* the fact that he was angry at his wife, and *negated* the fantasies and feelings that still forced themselves into his mind. Despite this the feelings and fantasies did not thereby become inert and neutral. On the contrary, they strove for expression, and threatened to emerge on the ward when he almost lost his temper at the woman patient, was tempted to throw the milk pitcher, and so forth. The object of his wrath was changed now from his wife to a casual woman, to inanimate objects, or to indefinite people —e.g. "someone." That is, his anger was *displaced. Repression, negation,* and *displacement* are all *ego defenses,* but they did not function entirely adequately, for as we have indicated his aggressive impulse still threatened to overwhelm him, which resulted in his experiencing a painful anxiety.

Let us look for a moment at the nature of the inference we have made. In reality, during the interview we made two. The first was that his anxiety was the result of an underlying anger and aggressive impulse. This inference was validated, as we have seen, by the fantasies and feelings that subsequently poured from the patient. The second inference, based on an association of ideas, was that the anger really was the result of the patient's reaction to the fact that his wife had not called him. Our attempts to validate this during the interview merely led to further behavior on the patient's part (what we have named his negation) which strengthened our faith in this second inference, but did not actually validate it, since the patient did not in the end produce actual fantasies and feelings of anger directly expressed toward his wife. If our second inference is true, it simply means that the *resistance* on the patient's part to admitting to himself and others that he was disappointed and angry at his wife was greater than his resistance to admitting that he harbored feelings of anger toward other objects. The latter we were able to uncover; the former still remained hidden. To validate the second inference (or possibly to show it wrong), we need more information than we have.

An inference of this sort is a paradigm of the type of logical operation that one uses constantly as one listens to patients and tries to understand what they are saying. Because this operation deals with the more intangible phenomena of thoughts and feelings, rather than with the tangible objects of the "real" external world, it often appears mysterious and suspect. In reality, it is a type of inference that is, logically speaking, elementary, and one that is constantly made in the daily round of internal medicine. Consider for a moment the examination of an abdomen. The physician, palpating deep in the right upper quadrant, feels a sudden "flip" of something riding up over his probing fingertips just below the costal margin as the patient inhales deeply. He at once asserts that the patient has an enlarged liver. This is not necessarily so. All the doctor can really state as fact, as observation, is the sensation in his fingertips as the patient breathes in. The statement that the liver is enlarged is an *inference* based on the observations made on and through the outside of the patient's body. It is, however, an inference that represents the true condition of the patient's inner organs with a high degree of accuracy: it is based on the many times the doctor has previously found similar signs in his examination of an abdomen, and has correlated his findings with other observations concerning liver function and anatomy, and with *seeing* directly at postmortem examination a liver enlarged as he had predicted. Most of the judgments that we make about patients' insides from observations on their outsides are based on such inferences. We are so accustomed as physicians to thinking in this way that we often forget that our conclusions involve a logical operation; we tend to assume that our physical examination gives us *direct* knowledge about inner organs that are actually hidden from view. The inferences we have made here about our patient's psychological state are comparable; they are based not only on external signs, but on knowledge of what does lie below the surface of patients' initial thoughts and feelings when with time and the proper technique one comes to know a person more intimately.

As we have been observing our patient we have been evolving a picture of psychological conflict which can, *mutatis mutandis,* serve as a model for understanding human behavior and its disorders. A stimulus in the environment arouses an impulse to action. Expression of the impulse involves danger to the integrity of the physical or psychological structure of the organism, which therefore experiences anxiety. To avoid the pain of the anxiety a part of the psychological organization of the organism erects psychological defenses against the impulse (and its derivative feelings and fantasies) which tend to remove the impulse from the sphere of conscious awareness. Furthermore, the defensive operations of the organism may themselves be unconscious —defenses may be raised without the person's being aware that this is occurring. The character of the stimulus, of the impulse, of the anxiety, and of the defenses determines the character of the conflict and of the symptoms and behavior that result from it.

In the form in which we have just stated it, our model is incomplete. We have been considering only the *dynamic* aspect of conflict, that is, the contemporary stimuli and reactions of the organism that constitute the conflict. We have, so to speak, been examining the machine in cross-section, seeing how the parts are put together, what forces they exert on one another, how they react to external pressures, and what results from the summation of these forces. We have not concerned ourselves with how the organism has come to be what it is today, that is, with the factors in early life that influence development and determine the characteristics of the adult—the *psychogenetic* aspect of conflict.

The concepts of unconscious mental processes and of psychogenesis are fundamental to our understanding of psychopathology. We must therefore now examine them both in more detail.

V

The Unconscious and Repression

That feelings, fantasies, attitudes, and impulses may be unconscious is, as we have indicated, a central concept in our theoretical structure; it is essential to our understanding of mental functioning. We have used the word "unconscious" here as an adjective, but it is employed also as a noun, the *unconscious*. Like the terms *ego, id,* and *superego,* the word *unconscious* does not refer to a tangible object with form and spatial location. It is a theoretical construct that helps us to order our observations.

Before discussing the nature of this concept, let us first turn our attention to the type of phenomenon that leads to an introduction of the construct into the theoretical structure. In his essentially autobiographical work, *Remembrance of Things Past,** Marcel Proust provides us with a detailed description of an experience that occurs in less dramatic form to many persons—the return to consciousness of previously forgotten memories.

> And so it was [he writes in *Swann's Way*] that, for a long time afterwards, when I lay awake at night and revived old memories of Combray, I saw no more of it than this sort of luminous panel, sharply defined against a vague and shadowy background, like the panels which a Bengal fire or some electric sign will illuminate and dissect from the front of a building the other parts of which remain plunged

---

* *Remembrance of Things Past,* translated by C. K. Scott Moncrieff, Random House, New York, 1934.

in darkness: broad enough at its base, the little parlour, the dining-room, the alluring shadows of the path along which would come M. Swann, the unconscious author of my sufferings, the hall through which I would journey to the first step of that staircase, so hard to climb, which constituted, all by itself, the tapering 'elevation' of an irregular pyramid; and at the summit, my bedroom, with the little passage through whose glazed door Mamma would enter; in a word, seen always at the same evening hour, isolated from all its possible surroundings, detached and solitary against its shadowy background, the bare minimum of scenery necessary . . . to the drama of my undressing, as though all Combray had consisted of but two floors joined by a slender staircase, and as though there had been no time there but seven o'clock at night. I must own that I could have assured any questioner that Combray did include other scenes and did exist at other hours than these. But since the facts which I should then have recalled would have been prompted only by an exercise of the will, by my intellectual memory, and since the pictures which that kind of memory shews us of the past preserve nothing of the past itself, I should never have had any wish to ponder over this residue of Combray. To me it was in reality all dead.

Permanently dead? Very possibly . . .

Many years had elapsed during which nothing of Combray, save what was comprised in the theater and the drama of my going to bed there, had any existence for me, when one day in winter, as I came home, my mother, seeing that I was cold, offered me some tea, a thing I did not ordinarily take. I declined at first, and then, for no particular reason, changed my mind. She sent out for one of those short, plump little cakes called 'petites madeleines,' which looked as though they had been moulded in the fluted scallop of a pilgrim's shell. And soon, mechanically, weary after a dull day with the prospect of a depressing morrow, I raised to my lips a spoonful of the tea in which I had soaked a morsel of the cake. No sooner had the warm liquid, and the crumbs with it, touched my palate than a shudder ran through my whole body, and I stopped, intent upon the extraordinary changes that were taking place. An exquisite pleasure had invaded my senses, but individual, detached, with no suggestion of its origin. And at once the vicissitudes of life had become indifferent to me, its disasters innocuous, its brevity illusory—this new sensation having had on me the effect which love has of filling me with a precious essence; or rather this essence was not in me, it was myself. I had ceased now to feel mediocre, accidental, mortal. Whence could it have come to me, this all-powerful joy? I was conscious that it was connected with the taste of tea and cake, but that it infinitely transcended those savours, could not, indeed, be of the same nature as theirs. Whence did it come? What did it signify? How could I seize upon and define it?

I drink a second mouthful, in which I find nothing more than in the first, a third, which gives me rather less than the second. It is time to stop; the potion is losing its magic. It is plain that the object of my quest, the truth, lies not in the cup, but in myself. The tea has called up in me, but does not itself understand, and can only repeat indefinitely, with a gradual loss of strength, the same testimony; which I, too, cannot interpret, though I hope at least to be able to call upon the tea for it again and to find it there presently, intact and at my disposal, for my final enlightenment. I put down my cup and examine my own mind. It is for it to discover the truth. But how? What an abyss of uncertainty whenever the mind feels that some part of it has strayed beyond its own borders; . . .

I retrace my thoughts to the moment at which I drank the first spoonful of tea. I find again the same state, illumined by no fresh light. I compel my mind to make one further effort, to follow and recapture once again the fleeting sensation. And that nothing may interrupt it in its course I shut out every obstacle, every extraneous idea, I stop my ears and inhibit all attention to the sounds which come from the next room. And then, feeling that my mind

is growing fatigued without having any success to report,
I compel it for a change to enjoy that distraction which I
have just denied it, to think of other things, to rest and
refresh itself before the supreme attempt. And then for a
second time I clear an empty space in front of it. I place in
position before my mind's eye the still recent taste of that
first mouthful, and I feel something start within me, something that leaves its resting-place and attempts to rise,
something that has been embedded like an anchor at a great
depth; I do not yet know what it is, but I can feel it mount-
ing slowly; I can measure the resistance, I can hear the
echo of great spaces traversed.

Undoubtedly what is thus palpitating in the depths of
my being must be the image, the visual memory which,
being linked to that taste, has tried to follow it into my
conscious mind. . . .

And suddenly the memory returns. The taste was that
of the little crumb of madeleine which on Sunday mornings
at Combray . . . when I went to say good day to her in her
bedroom, my aunt Léonie used to give me, dipping it first
in her own cup of real or lime-flower tea. . . .

And once I had recognized the taste of the crumb of
madeleine soaked in her decoction of lime-flowers which
my aunt used to give me . . . immediately the old grey
house upon the street, where her room was, rose up like
the scenery of a theatre to attach itself to the little pavil-
ion, opening onto the garden, which had been built out
behind it for my parents (the isolated panel which until
that moment had been all that I could see); and with the
house the town, from morning to night in all weathers, the
Square where I was sent before luncheon, the streets along
which I used to run errands, the country roads we took
when it was fine. And just as the Japanese amuse themselves by filling a porcelain bowl with water and steeping
in it little crumbs of paper which until then are without
character or form, but, the moment they become wet,
stretch themselves and bend, take on colour and distinc-
tive shape, become flowers or houses or people, permanent

and recognizable, so in that moment all the flowers in our garden and in M. Swann's park, and the waterlilies on the Vivonne and the good folk of the village and their little dwellings and the parish church and the whole of Combray and of its surroundings, taking their proper shapes and growing solid, sprang into being, town and gardens alike, from my cup of tea.

What characterizes this experience produced for us by Proust's genius for introspection? There is first of all the fact that after a lapse of many years he remembered scenes and events that had occurred in his childhood. But these memories were not at the beck and call of his voluntary recollection. No amount of conscious effort and concentration on his part could raise them once he had an inkling that something was trying to push its way into his awareness. On the contrary, he felt an inner resistance against their recall; he was finally able to retrieve them only by the indirect maneuver of "clearing a space" in front of his mind and allowing the ideas to come spontaneously into his awareness; conscious volition had nothing to do with their return.

Once the memories had leaped into his mind, he recognized them as a part of his long-ago past. Before he tasted the tea-soaked madeleine, he had not the faintest idea of the vivid memories that lurked somewhere within him; he had a pale remembrance of a few aspects of his childhood, but the repertoire of images was small, and always came to him in the same garb whenever he reflected on his earlier life. He knew, of course, that he had seen and heard and done many things in this period of his life, yet all these experiences appeared to be completely forgotten; he had no memory of them.

Completely forgotten? Obviously not, in the sense of being totally eradicated from his mind, even though he could not by an act of will recall them. For under the stimulus of his taste they suddenly crowded in upon him. Where had they been, these memories, during all the years Proust had reflected on his childhood without recalling them? We can say only that they had been *unconscious* (or in the *unconscious* mind); they had been preserved in some manner that we cannot qualify further—out of reach of conscious voluntary recall, yet with the potential of returning to awareness with a startling clarity.

An experience such as that which Proust describes happens only under unusual circumstances or to unusual people. Most of us, however, have known it in a lesser way in the common phenomenon of forgetting a name or a word. Try as we may, we cannot recall the name; no amount of conscious effort can bring it back, even though we are sure that it is there somewhere just below the surface. We sense a resistance working against our attempt to force it into the light of consciousness. Eventually we give up the struggle, and turn our minds to other things. Suddenly, unbidden and unexpected it leaps into awareness as if it had a life of its own. Immediately, with a sense of relief and pleasure, we recognize it as the name we had forgotten.

Where had the name been during the time it was beyond our knowledge? Again, as with Proust's memories of his childhood, although inaccessible to consciousness, it had not been totally eradicated from our mind; it was preserved somehow, somewhere, as its eventual return to our awareness attested. It was temporarily *unconscious*.

The word "unconscious" is perhaps not the happiest choice as a term to designate the phenomenon we are observing. The German, *unbewusst,* of which it is a translation means literally "unknown," and describes simply and unequivocally the observed fact about the absent thought. It avoids the logical and semantic difficulty of understanding how a thought or a feeling (which are almost *ipso facto* conscious) can be "unconscious." It also avoids the confusion resulting from the other uses of the same word: a man who has been felled by a blow on the head is described as "unconscious"; a person whose attention is absorbed in a task is said to be "unconscious" of unrelated stimuli impinging on his sensorium; if we are now paying strict attention to what we are reading, we are not aware of the memory of what we ate for breakfast, although presumably we can recall this if we wish; this memory, at the time it is out of conscious awareness, is characterized colloquially as being "unconscious," technically as "preconscious."

We are clearly not using the word in any of these ways. In our meaning, a mental event (thought, memory, feeling) is "unconscious" when it is out of the awareness of a person who is alert and observant of his surroundings; it cannot be brought into conscious awareness by a voluntary act of recall; it is not irretrievably eradicated from the purview of mind, but is preserved in a poorly understood state, with the potential under proper circumstances of returning to consciousness. The term "unconscious" as we employ it is a *dynamic* concept— it implies that mental forces are actively countering the entrance of certain mental events into consciousness. Although there are objections to the use of the word, custom has made it a part of our scientific vocabulary; we should be able to avoid confusion if we keep in mind the manner in which we use it, and the phenomena it denotes.

We must here turn to a consideration of the term *repression*—the name given to the processes involved in the force countering the entrance of mental events into consciousness —a force comprising the basic ego defense mechanism. Like the Unconscious, *repression* is a theoretical construct devised to explain certain observations (for example, the conscious experience of a resistance against the recalling of a forgotten name) and to account for the fact that mental events may be out of awareness and beyond voluntary recall

—i.e. unconscious. Theoretically, if repression were completely effective, what was repressed would not only be unconscious, but would be without effect on conscious thought processes and behavior. This is presumably the case in many instances; but as we shall see when we come to discuss symptom-formation, there is often an uneasy equilibrium established between the unconscious elements striving for conscious awareness and the repressive forces countering them. The former tend to escape the latter and to emerge into consciousness in distorted disguises resulting in part from the additional ego defenses called up as auxiliaries to aid in repression.

Before going on to other examples of the *dynamic unconscious,* let us make explicit two further characteristics of the material we have been examining. A remarkable aspect of Proust's memories is their striking clarity and freshness; it is as if the events they portrayed had happened days, not decades before. The realm of the unconscious appears to have a timelessness about it that is absent in our ordinary consciousness, where memories fade and pale. Furthermore, we should note the sense of exhilaration that accompanied the return of the long-lost memories to awareness; in a lesser way we find the same thing in the pleasure and relief that go with the recapture of a temporarily forgotten name. This sense of pleasurable excitement, of discovery, is frequently felt when the boundaries of conscious awareness are expanded to include previously unconscious mental events— whether these be the intuitive hunch of the scientist, the insight of the patient in psychotherapy, or the vision of the artist.

Proust's account dealt mainly with the return of memories of by-gone events and objects. Feelings, too, may arise out of the buried past. Stanley T., a man in his late twenties undertook psychotherapy for chronic anxiety and an inability to form any lasting relationship with a woman because he was afraid of being deserted; he consequently held himself aloof from permanent ties, although his casual sexual promiscuity was noteworthy. His mother had died suddenly when he was five years old; he was told only that she had gone away for a while. As his father subsequently informed him, for a period of months he had expected his mother to come back and had repeatedly asked about her return before he was finally told the truth about her death; he remembered none of this directly. His father had been very dependent on his wife. After her death he failed to remarry, hired a housekeeper, and became a recluse. As the patient eventually came to realize, his father maintained an attitude of mistrust and bitterness toward women for their "inconstancy."

As therapy developed, the patient's associations indicated that his mother's sudden disappearance had an important bearing on his subsequent expectations of being deserted by women. It was impossible, however, to get him to talk much about her, because, as he pointed out repeatedly, he had few memories of her before she died, and his mind was a complete blank about his reactions following her death. His own memory of that period was that he had never thought of her again; he was himself surprised at how completely devoid his mind was of thoughts and feelings about her. Furthermore, it was noticeable that he never referred to her in anything other than dispassionate, emotionless tones, and always spoke of "My mother." He never called her "Mom," "Mum," or any of the familiar names that one usually hears when patients speak of their parents.

One day the patient was discussing his father's attitude of distrust and bitterness to women, and his apparent fear, like the patient, of forming any close, lasting relationship with any one of them. The doctor remarked that it seemed to be hard for him to give up his father's attitudes. At that the patient suddenly and surprisingly burst into a flood of tears that momentarily prevented him from talking. Finally, between sobs, he blurted out, "I know it—my father was so bitter toward women—I was surrounded by that when I was little, and I was just waiting for my Mummy to come back."

It is hard with the mere written word to conjure up the moving quality of this outburst as it came from the patient, or to re-create the effect it had on the listener. It appeared to be an upsurging of pure emotion appropriate to the time of his mother's death, without a revival of memories. His use of the word "Mummy" for the first time in two years of therapy, as well as the quality of the tone of his voice, which was that of a sad, bereft, despairing little boy indicated that this was the reappearance after many years of a feeling which the patient had once experienced and had forgotten. It was at least an emergence into his conscious awareness of feelings about his mother which the patient could not remember having had before, and which surprised him considerably as he experienced them.

It not infrequently occurs in dreams that thoughts and feelings arise which appear new and strange to the dreamer as he reflects on them when awake. Here, for example, is the dream of a patient in therapy, which revived an almost totally forgotten childhood scene which was later confirmed by an independent observer. Rosalie M., a woman in her early thirties, dreamed that she was at a railroad station with a little girl, waiting for the arrival of a man whose identity she could not place. For some reason the train did not arrive, and after four hours of waiting she gave up and went home. When the patient awoke, her first thought in connection with the dream was to recall that as a little girl of five she had been allowed to stay up late one night to meet her father, who was coming home from a trip. She had always been aware of this bare fact, though she remembered none of the details of it. Later on that morning the patient saw her mother. Out of curiosity she asked her if she remembered this episode. "Remember it?" exclaimed her mother. "How could I forget it? The train was snowed in by a blizzard, and after waiting four long hours I finally had to take you home."

In her waking state, even with the dream image before her, the patient could not directly remember the four hours in the station. To her waking consciousness it still appeared to be unconnected with her own life and the experiences that were a part of her image of herself. She could not feel it as part of her own past history; she still could not directly "remember" the event. In the state of dreaming, however, the boundaries of her awareness and her memory were enlarged; asleep she could revive an experience that had remained for years alive and vivid somewhere in her mind; there was a momentary return of memories from her unconscious.

The three examples we have observed so far have been drawn from experiences that occurred unexpectedly in a natural setting. The same type of phenomena can be observed under the artificial experimental conditions of hypnosis. The older literature, written at a time when hypnosis was more in vogue than currently, has many reports of mental events, ordinarily unconscious, revived by this procedure. In "The Unconscious" (22), published in 1914, Morton Prince describes a hypnotic experiment with a woman who suffered from an intense phobia of cats, especially of white cats. She could not consciously or voluntarily recall memories of frightening experiences with these creatures. Under hypnosis a pencil was put into her hand and she began automatic writing—that is, her hand, seemingly without her conscious attention or direction began to write, a peculiar but well-known form of what is called mental *dissociation*. She, or perhaps better, her hand wrote as follows:

I think I know about cats. I can remember myself, a little child playing on the floor with a kitten, and it began to run about the room and had a fit I think, and it jumped on me, and I was alone, and I screamed and cried and called my mother, but no one came, and I was very much frightened. I do not believe I ever told anyone. It was a white kitten. It ran out of the room and after a bit I went on playing.

Prince then asked the hand to describe the furnishings of the room and the plan of the house, in order to test the extent of the conserved memories. The hand continued:

There were two windows on the side of the room. The shades were gray, I think, with a border of grapes, or something of that color. The carpet was green or gray with green figures. There was a large old-fashioned sofa between one window and the door which led into the dining-room. A bookcase and desk-combination, you know. There was a mantel, I think between the windows. It was the ground floor.

Prince comments: "This childhood episode and the furnishings of the room were completely forgotten by B.C.A. in the sense that they could not be voluntarily recalled. Even after reading the script she could not remember them. She had not seen the room since she was six years of age, the family having removed at that time from the town where the incident took place. As to the accuracy of the 'Automatic' account and the possibility of fabrication, the description of the room has been corroborated by the independent and written testimony of an older member of the family. It was not possible to confirm the incident of the kitten as there were no witnesses."

Here, appearing in an altered state of consciousness artificially produced by hypnosis, we observe a hypermnesia— that is, an ability to remember beyond the ordinary limits of the conscious, volitional recall of the subject. Events that had occurred many years before, some of which were corroborated independently, returned to consciousness with a striking vividness and minuteness of detail that is again evidence of the apparent timelessness of the unconscious, which preserves memories and images without the attenuation that bleaches most of our conscious memories. The similarity of this experience to the dream of our earlier patient, Rosalie M., is also noteworthy—including the fact that "even after reading the script" the subject could not consciously recall the events. In certain states of altered awareness such as dreams and hypnosis the boundaries of memory are enlarged over those of our normal, conscious waking mental life.

We must note one important feature of this experiment. The incident of the kitten could not be corroborated by other observers, but if this was a recall as accurate and as vivid as that of the furnishings and plan of the house, it suggests that an unconscious mental event (here a memory) can unbeknownst to the person involved influence conscious mental life and behavior—in this case contributing to a phobia of cats. The observations arising from experimental post-hypnotic suggestion provide evidence that this is indeed so.

H. Bernheim, the famous French psychiatrist of Nancy, reports a number of such experiments in *Suggestive Therapeutics* (20), published in 1880. Under hypnosis the subject is instructed that when he awakes he will perform a specific act, but that he will have no memory either of the instructions or of having been hypnotized:

> On another occasion [he writes] when my colleague, M. Charpentier, was present, I suggested to him when he first fell asleep that as soon as he waked, he should take my colleague's umbrella, which was lying on the bed, open it, and walk twice up and down the piazza on which the room

opened. It was some time afterward when I waked him. Before his eyes were open, we went quickly out of the room so that the suggestion might not be recalled by our presence. We soon saw him coming with the umbrella in his hand, but not open (in spite of the suggestion). He walked twice up and down the corridor. I said to him, "What are you doing?" He answered, "I am taking the air."—"Why, are you warm?"—"No, it is only my idea; I occasionally walk up and down out here."—"What is the umbrella for? It belongs to M. Charpentier."—"What! I thought it was mine. It looks like mine. I shall take it back to the place I took it from."

Sometimes the subject tires himself out trying to find a reason for the ideas in his brain. One day I suggested to the same subject that as soon as he waked, he should go to a certain patient in the same room and ask how he was. He did so as soon as he awoke, and when I asked him why he did it, and whether he was especially interested in that patient, he replied, "No, it was just an idea." Then after thinking a moment added, "He would not let us sleep last night." Thus he tried to explain the idea to himself by the wish to know, whether the sick patient would allow them to sleep that night or not.

On another occasion I suggested that as soon as he waked he should put both thumbs into his mouth, which he did. He connected this necessary act with a painful sensation in his tongue owing to his having bitten it the day before in an epileptic attack.

In all of these experiments we find the existence of an idea and an urge to action that is unconscious. We know that it exists because it has been supplied by the experimenter. And the subject, although he is unaware of the command, or its source, carries out the command as if it were his own idea. Indeed, he even provides reasons for doing what he does, which to him seem logically sufficient. The experimenter, who knows differently, can see that the subject's explanations are not the real reasons for his actions, but *rationalizations* which satisfy the subject's need to explain to himself and others why he has behaved in a certain way. The subject's action has in fact been determined by unconscious ideas and commands to action of which he knows nothing.

These actions and the experimenter's commands that led to them are of course in themselves trivial. But the principle that not only actions, but symptoms may be caused by unconscious ideas, fantasies, feelings, and impulses, and that symptoms may be removed by making the unconscious factors conscious was the great contribution made to psychiatry by Breuer and Freud late in the nineteenth century. Their discovery led to the ultimate development of psychoanalytic methods and theories, which are the basis of all contemporary dynamic psychiatry. Their volume *Studies on Hysteria* (21), published in 1894, presents both their clinical observations and the theoretical formulations derived from their data. The case of Fräulein Anna O. whom Breuer treated in 1880-81 by hypnosis for multiple hysterical paralyses and sensory defects is not only interesting historically, but provides us with an excellent demonstration of this principle.

Breuer writes as follows:

When this happened for the first time—when, as a result of an accidental and spontaneous utterance of this kind during the evening hypnosis, a disturbance which had persisted for a considerable time vanished—I was greatly surprised. It was in the summer during a period of extreme heat, and the patient was suffering badly from thirst; for, without being able to account for it in any way, she suddenly found it impossible to drink. She would take up the glass of water she longed for, but as soon as it touched her lips she would push it away like someone suffering from hydrophobia. As she did this, she was obviously in an absence for a couple of seconds. She lived only on fruits, such as melons, etc., so as to lessen her tormenting thirst. This had lasted for some six weeks, when one day during hypnosis she grumbled about her English lady-companion whom she did not care for, and went on to describe, with every sign of disgust, how she had once gone into that lady's room and how her little dog—horrid creature!—had drunk out of a glass there. The patient had said nothing, as she had wanted to be polite. After giving further energetic expression to the anger she had held back, she asked for something to drink, drank a large quantity of water without any difficulty and woke from hypnosis with the glass at her lips; and thereupon, the disturbance vanished, never to return. A number of extremely obstinate whims were similarly removed after she had described the experience which had given rise to them. She took a great step forward when the first of her chronic symptoms disappeared in the same way—the contracture of her right leg, which, it is true, had already diminished a great deal. These findings—that in the case of this patient the hysterical phenomena disappeared as soon as the event which had given rise to them was reproduced in her hypnosis—made it possible to arrive at a therapeutic technical procedure which left nothing to be desired in its logical consistency and systematic application. Each individual symptom in this complicated case was taken separately in hand; all the occasions on which it had appeared were described in reverse order, starting before the time when the patient became bed-ridden and going back to the event which had led to its first appearance. When this had been described the symptom was permanently removed.

The initial enthusiasm for the therapeutic maneuver of arousing pathogenic memories and feelings under hypnosis was dampened when it failed to work in all patients or with a variety of different neurotic manifestations. But the underlying principle of symptom formation had been demonstrated and much of the later theories and practical operations were modifications of this initial discovery—modifications resulting from subsequent observations and clinical experience.

It is important to recognize that we cannot know by direct experience exactly what the unconscious is. For by the time we have become aware of whatever *was* unconscious, it has already become conscious as part of the conscious ego which experiences it. The notion of the unconscious is, as we have said, a theoretical construct inferred from observations of the sort that we have been examining in this chapter. It is, however, a construct of the most far-reaching implications for the study and understanding of mental phenomena. The field of action has been immeasurably widened. We can no longer be satisfied that we have obtained all the relevant causal factors in any behavioral phenomenon by simply surveying the experiences initially found in the field of a subject's awareness. We must assume that many factors are unconscious, and that they will come to light only through patient observation and skillful investigation. With the notion of the unconscious thus acting as our guide, our task of exploring the nature of mental life becomes far more complex, but infinitely richer. The theories we arrive at provide better explanations for the facts, and a more logical rationale for the procedures we employ in treating patients.

It is clear that a great deal of our mental life is unconscious. Certain aspects of it have probably never been conscious, nor ever will be—the deepest biological roots of our impulses, for example. These appear in consciousness only in derivative forms, i.e. in urges to action, feelings, and fantasies. But a great deal of what is unconscious in an adult has at one time or another been an object of conscious knowledge and experience which has subsequently been pushed into the unconscious by the forces of repression— forces as we have seen, and shall see later in more detail, that operate continuously, manifest themselves as resistance when one tries to uncover unconscious mental events, and lead us to the notion of a *dynamic* unconscious.

We must re-emphasize here that portions of all the mental institutions may be unconscious. The ultimate source of impulses in the id is always unconscious, as well as many of the feelings and fantasies deriving from them. But we may also be quite unconscious of many of the operations of the ego—of, for instance, the defense mechanisms the ego employs. Boyd C., for example, was not only unaware of the feelings aroused toward his wife by her failure to call him, but he was also not conscious of the mechanisms of negation and displacement which formed a part of the defenses his ego employed to keep his feelings and impulses unconscious. Similarly many operations of the superego remain hidden from conscious awareness.

Finally, a noteworthy fact has emerged from our observations: the unconscious harbors not only the feelings, impulses, and fantasies that arise as a reaction to the current environmental stimuli in the life of the adult. On the contrary, mental events that have been a part of a person's childhood experience exist in an unconscious state; under proper circumstances they may emerge into consciousness with a clarity and freshness that is surprising in view of their antiquity. Of particular importance is the fact that these early experiences now unconscious, may significantly affect and determine the mental life and behavior of the adult. This is the basis for the psychogenetic propositions to which we must now turn our attention.

VI

PAST IN PRESENT: THE CHILDHOOD ROOTS OF EMOTIONAL DISORDERS

Man, says Proust, is "one of those amphibious creatures who are plunged simultaneously in the past and in the reality of the moment." We must now turn to the sorts of observations that have led the scientist, as well as the poet, to frame genetic propositions which describe "how any condition under observation has grown out of an individual's past, and extended throughout his total life span" (24).

A young woman, Martha O., undertook psychiatric treatment because of a chronic depression which was related to a marked feeling of personal inferiority, especially in comparison with men. "Men," she said, "get a better deal out of life." They were bigger, stronger, smarter, and more logical than women; they were free to come and go as they wished without the restrictions that curtailed a woman's actions. The social structure confirmed a man's superior status—it was the accepted convention that his sexual expression could be freer; the important professional and business jobs were given to him; many professions were completely closed to a woman. The "frail sex" was a second-rate citizen.

The patient resented the fact that she had been born female, and was aware that she engaged in a continuous angry competition with men—a competition that she knew was doomed to failure because of the male's innate superiority. The only times she felt she had the best of it was in the act of sexual intercourse; here, at the point of the man's orgasm, she would have the fantasy that she had drained her partner of his strength, and had made his powers her own by taking his genital organ from him and swallowing it up inside of herself.

This resentful envy of hers that poured forth in therapy was nothing new in her life. In fact, she had consciously felt this way from the age of five. A neighbor's boy, slightly her senior, had one day shown her his penis and had demonstrated his ability to void standing up. That evening she attempted to do the same thing and was distressed at her dismal failure. She began to pray every night that she would wake up in the morning a boy with a penis, and was bitterly disappointed and resentful when this, of course, failed to occur. Her envy and her wishes continued openly from that time on; as an adolescent she would wear pants and try to walk and stand like a man; in young adulthood it was the attitudes enumerated earlier that contributed to her depression, dissatisfaction, and sense of inferiority.

What is noteworthy about the patient's history is the fact that the attitudes she exhibited as an adult extended back into her early childhood. At the age of twenty-five these were pathogenic attitudes, since they led to profound unhappiness, social isolation, and an inability to love, marry, and have a family. They first arose as a part of her experiences at the age of five, and the patient never outgrew them. The child was mother to the woman.

Let us examine another woman who is similar to Martha O., with one important difference. Sarah J. was thirty-one when she began psychotherapy for attacks of overwhelming anxiety. These occurred most commonly when she was in the company of men, and the patient was at a loss to explain them: she knew of no reason why she should be afraid of men, and was aware of no frightening attitudes or fantasies about them. But despite the fact that she chided herself for "being a fool" to react in this way, she could not control the panic; as a result she had so limited her activities to avoid being near men that she not only declined all invitations from them, but was barely able to get to work each day.

In the course of therapy the patient's anxiety abated and she began occasionally to go out with men once more. One day she reported to her doctor that the night before as she was driving home with a casual friend she had suddenly thought that he might attack and rape her. Although aware of the absurdity of this idea, she reacted with intense fright in a typical attack of anxiety. She was puzzled by the episode and insisted that she had never had a thought like this before.

It was not until a few weeks later that the subject came up again, following a short visit to her parents' home. One afternoon family friends had come to call with their three-year-old daughter. As she watched her father playing gently with the little girl, the thought abruptly occurred to her that her father might sexually attack the youngster. She was perplexed; the idea felt utterly foreign to her; it was in marked contradiction to her image of her father as a mild and loving man. As she talked about this, she suddenly remembered something she had forgotten for years: that as a little girl of five she had often had the fantasy that her father roamed the countryside, sexually attacking little girls. Later in her therapy she recalled fantasies from childhood that her father might attack her as well. As the memory of these fantasies emerged into consciousness she became acutely anxious and for a few days thereafter all of her anxiety with men returned.

Here again, as with Martha O., we find an adult mental phenomenon (in this instance a fantasy) which has a forerunner in childhood. But there is a difference between the two patients. Martha O.'s attitude toward men was always a part of her store of conscious thought processes; its origin in childhood and its subsequent life ran as a continuous and visible thread throughout her personal history. In Sarah J., on the other hand, the fantasy was unconscious during the greater part of her life. It was only during therapy that it became conscious, first as a fear of attack in her adult life, then as a memory of having initially had the same fantasy in childhood. The fantasy was an important element in her difficulties with men; although unconscious, it had an important influence on her adult feelings and behavior; its origin was rooted in childhood, where it had first arisen, gone underground and remained hidden for years, finally to make itself felt as a pathogenic source of the adult patient's symptoms. As these memories, long buried in her unconscious, reappeared in her conscious awareness, the present merged with the past.

In both of these patients the pathogenic idea responsible for their emotional disorder had its origin in childhood. Our investigation of the psychopathology of adult symptoms has been broadened to include its genetic roots in the early development of the growing child. In both of these patients our attention was directed to the earlier phases of their lives by the adult memories they had of that period. Their associations indicated that children, like adults, have fantasies and concerns about sexual differences or being sexually attacked.

The direct observation of children themselves confirms the truth of these indications—the child has a wealth of feeling and fantasy that includes, but goes far beyond the thoughts and fears we have been concerned with here. A young lady of five, for example, had just finished having a bath with her younger brother. As she was rubbing herself down with a towel, she said to her father, "Daddy, I wish I had a bottom like Charlie's." Her father, half amused, replied, "Why is that? You have a nice bottom yourself." To which she answered, "Because I like those kind of bottoms better." Here, direct and without adornment, is the little girl's envy of the male genital and her wish to have the same for herself. Not long after, the same little girl recounted at breakfast a dream of the night before: "Mummy," she said, "I dreamed last night that some men were trying to hurt me with pistols and you chased them away with your sword." Here again is the theme of attacking men which loomed so large in Sarah J.'s fears. In this instance it was not a waking fantasy, but a dream—the product of the sleeping youngster's inner life of imagination and fancy.

It is not mere accident that the memories of our two adult patients and the experiences of the little girl refer to the age of five. If one investigates children systematically, it becomes apparent that fantasies of this nature are characteristic of the period of from three to six, with a peak of intensity in the fifth year of life. A two-year-old does not have such preoccupations and concerns. They appear as a part of the process of the growth and development of the maturing child, and characterize that phase of the child's development known as the Oedipal period.

This is a time of life for the little girl when she dwells on the basic facts of human life and relationships. She is curious about the relationship between her mother and father; she experiences strong desires to possess her father and to eliminate her mother ("Wouldn't it be nice, Daddy," said a young lady cheerfully, "if Mummy died, and you and I were married?"); she is fascinated by babies and the idea of pregnancy; she notes the difference between the sexes and is concerned because, unlike the boy, she has no visible genital; she resents the difference and is envious of the boy for what she considers his superior equipment. As she tries to explain these mysteries to herself, the answers come in the form of the common fantasies of childhood—that, for example, a man's attack has injured her genitals, or that she has harmed herself by masturbation.

The key words in our discussion here are *"phase of development."* In order to illustrate the principle of the childhood origins of adult emotional disorder, we have focused on only a tiny part of the richness of the ubiquitous life of fantasy that is found in child and grown-up alike; we have directed our attention to only a small segment of the entire process of human development from birth to death. We have, furthermore, considered only the girl, ignoring the fact that the boy passes through comparable stages of growth. Unlike most other creatures, the human being is slow to reach maturity; his long dependence on his parents makes the early years of his life an important period for the formation of the personality he will have as an adult. It is during this time that there unfolds a regular development of his libidinal and aggressive impulses, his ego structure, and the type of relationships he makes with the people in his environment.*

The complicated process of early human development takes place under the guiding influence of two factors: (1) the innate, inner thrust to maturation characteristic of living organisms, in part at least determined by hereditary factors, that unfolds as the child grows; and (2) the shaping and molding pressure of the external physical and human environment that surrounds the child.

The innate thrust to maturation determines the potential rate of growth, the age at which developmental phases appear, and the characteristics of those phases. In its most obvious form this may be seen in the motor development of the growing child, who begins to sit, then to walk and talk

---

* Although we shall consider in more detail certain aspects of these developmental streams in later chapters, it is beyond the purpose and scope of this book to present a complete account of this process. The reader should consult Brenner (7), Glover (10), or Hendrick (12) for a systematic discussion of the phases of development.

at certain specified ages, as his nervous system matures. There is a similar, if more subtle and complex progression in the psychological sphere, which determines the timing of the appearance and character of impulses, ego functions, and fantasies. As we have indicated, the fantasies that we examined earlier belonged to a specific phase of the child's development; they made their appearance only after a certain stage of maturation had been reached.

If the innate maturational forces supply the inner potential for development, the environmental influences determine whether that potential is achieved, and the manner in which it is achieved. The end result of development is a *combination* of these factors of inner maturation and outer environmental influences. The age, for example, at which the child develops the capacity to learn to talk is determined by the inner maturation of his cerebral speech centers; the language he speaks—English, Russian, or Chinese—is determined by his cultural environment. The importance of environmental influences lies in the power they have to warp and pathologically distort the normal processes of maturation. The effect these outer influences will have is determined in part by the nature of the influences themselves, but also by the phase of maturation of the organism at the time when the external event impinges on it. The death of a child's mother will have a different effect when the child is one from what it will have on a child of six. This may be likened to the differential effect of mechanical trauma on the growing embryo; the result of the trauma depends on the phase of the embryo's maturation.

Given an adequate environment (in particular, a good emotional climate provided by mature parents), the maturational phases normally succeed one another as the child grows into an emotionally healthy adult. The little girl, for example, gives up her resentment and envy of the boy, and succeeds in developing a healthy pride and pleasure in her femininity and her ability to bear children. If, however, through adverse environmental influences her normal maturational progress is blocked, the child may not outgrow this envy; like Martha O., she carries into adulthood an attitude of resentment and aggressive competitiveness with men that keeps her from the fulfillment of normal adult love, marriage, and motherhood.

The fact that Martha O. could remember and connect her early attitudes with her later feelings toward men was unusual. Generally the line of succession is not so evident until therapy has helped to uncover previously hidden mental events. Most of us remember little other than isolated experiences before the age of seven or eight, and it is a rarity to find memories of the period before three. This is the natural result of the normal process of maturation: ordinarily during the seventh and eighth years of life, the events of the slow prior phases of development are repressed —the fantasies, the feelings, the impulses, the memories of experiences are mostly made unconscious. If there have been abnormal developmental arrests, these too now ordinarily disappear from awareness. But because unconscious, they do not lose their potential for causing difficulties. As foci of distorted development, they remain as scars or sensitive areas of weakness in the individual's psychological structure. An event in later life that has affinities with this buried, unresolved childhood conflict tends to activate and bring into consciousness the old, unconscious feelings and fantasies and impulses that were never laid to rest in the earlier years of development. As these repressed mental events press to emerge into awareness, the individual experiences anxiety—in part the anxiety that originally accompanied them in childhood, in part the anxiety that results from the threat they pose to the integrity of the adult personality structure. Thus the psychopathology of Sarah J.'s anxiety with men became clear only when, first her adult fantasies about men, and then their origin in a phase of her childhood development were uncovered. It was then apparent that although she was largely unconscious of it she was living "plunged simultaneously in the past and in the reality of the moment." The full understanding of her illness was based on knowledge of the dynamic structure of her adult psychological conflict, and of the shaping experiences in the past of her childhood, which, still living and fresh in her unconscious, exerted their influence on her present.

Part III

Symptom Formation

VII

Ego Structure and Anxiety

The symptoms of psychological illness are grouped into somewhat loosely circumscribed clinical syndromes. The patients whom we shall meet in the chapters that follow fall into the more common of these diagnostic categories: anxiety neurosis, obsessive-compulsive neurosis, hysteria, phobic reaction, depression, and schizophrenia. Our primary concern, however, is not with the natural history of the syndromes (their incidence, onset, course, clinical characteristics and treatment), but with the individual symptoms that comprise them. Our purpose is to examine the psychological factors that give rise to the latter—in short, to discover the psychopathology of symptom-formation.

We shall begin this task with an exploration of two feeling states which we have already come upon in the clinical material we have examined before. *Anxiety* is a fearful anticipation of something unpleasant to come in the future. *Depression* is a reaction to loss—that is, to an unpleasant event that has occurred in the past. Both are the inevitable, if unbidden, companions of man's life on earth; both are prominent symptoms in the whole spectrum of psychiatric disorders; both are acutely painful states of being. In order to avoid the pain that attaches to them, the individual employs a variety of psychological defensive maneuvers that themselves contribute to the formation of symptoms. Both anxiety and depression are experienced in the ego, which is

likewise the site of the defensive operations; we must, therefore, include a consideration of the ego in our discussion.

We have already had the opportunity to observe these
defensive maneuvers at work; when we examined the nature
of psychological conflict, we noted that the anxiety from
which Boyd C. suffered on the day after Christmas occurred
in a situation where an impulse pressing for expression
came into conflict with other countering forces—the ego
defenses. The latter form part of that complex psychological
organization, the ego, the structure and function of which
is to guide and canalize the impulses in such a way that,
where possible, they may be expressed, but expressed within
the limits imposed by the demands of the physical and social
surroundings; otherwise, their expression might bring the
individual into difficulty. If Boyd C., for example, had
allowed himself actually to attack one of his wardmates,
he would have antagonized the ward personnel and other
patients, and might have run the risk of physical injury to
himself; both of these results would have had serious consequences for him. It was in part because he could antici-
pate these possible consequences that he imposed controls
on his aggression.

Before we consider in more detail the nature and the
function of ego defenses and in particular the part they
play in symptom formation, it is important for us to become
familiar with the concept of the ego as an organized structure interposed between impulses and their expression in
action. The brief biographies of two men enable us to see
concretely what is meant by the term "ego structure." The
one, acting on impulse, raped and killed a woman. Found
sane by legal criteria, he was sentenced to life imprison-
ment. The other, an official state executioner, killed 397
people during his life and earned his livelihood by so doing.
Looking at the bare fact that each of these men took human
lives, one would call them both killers. In the light of the

respective nature of their actions and ego structures, there is a vast difference between them.

At the time that Charles L. was a patient on the psychiatric service he was in his mid-twenties. He had a long history of troubles. His parents were both severely addicted to alcohol; because of the difficulties that arose from their drinking, the home was frequently broken up, forcing the patient as a boy into many different foster homes. At an early age he developed severe temper tantrums which persisted beyond the time of their normal occurrence. On several occasions he ran away from home. He did poorly in school because of inattention and truancy and finally left after being made to repeat several grades. He fared little better in his work. He repeatedly had difficulties with his fellow employees which led to his being fired or quitting before he could be discharged. He had held almost more jobs than he could remember. A part of his difficulty resulted from his frequent unfounded fears that his fellow employees were going to attack him or hurt him, or that he himself might lose control of impulses and assault them. There was some justification for this latter fear, for he had already on several occasions attacked and badly beaten members of his own family in uncontrollable, impulsive rages. His eventual marriage brought no improvement in his behavior. He was intensely jealous of his wife and frequently abusive. When she was seven months' pregnant with their first child, he threatened to kill her with a butcher knife; this led to his commitment to a state hospital for a brief period of psychiatric observation. His wife then divorced him, and he began to drink heavily. Twice more he was admitted to the state hospital as a result of brief periods of hallucinations resulting from a combination of excessive drinking and taking benzedrine. He was twice in jail for nonsupport of his divorced wife and child, and served a third sentence for robbery. During his last incarceration he developed in-

somnia and acute anxiety, the latter centering around his
fear that he might again seriously assault and harm someone. On the day following his release from jail he was found
collapsed in the street and was brought to the hospital complaining of a sore throat.

Because of his symptoms and past history he was admitted to the psychiatric ward, where he readily adapted
himself—too readily, in fact. He spoke constantly of how
much he liked the shelter of the hospital; he felt safe, protected, and comfortable there. He wanted to stay indefinitely and be taken care of, since he found the thought of
fending for himself in the outside world unsupportable. He
became as helpless and as dependent as a small child, and
whenever his doctor raised the question of his being discharged, the patient became acutely anxious, and insisted
that people were following him. From the way he behaved
it seemed to the doctors that this fear was not a true paranoid delusion, but that, in imitation of patients he had observed during his prior experience in state hospitals, he was
feigning severe mental illness in order to keep his foothold
in the hospital. Because it was judged that his increasing
dependency was jeopardizing his eventual chances for rehabilitation and adult self-sufficiency, he was discharged
from the hospital to be treated in the out-patient clinic instead. Four days later he was back on the psychiatric ward;
he had come that day to the clinic in a tremulous, anxious
state, again insisting that he was being followed and spied
on. He was admitted to the ward while arrangements were
made for his re-entry to a state hosptial for more prolonged
treatment.

It was one month later, while he was away from the second hospital on a leave of absence that he passed a strange
young woman on a lonely road. On a sudden impulse he
grabbed her, raped her, and in the process strangled her to
death.

By contrast, let us look at the man who became an executioner. This was not the vocation he had originally planned to follow. His training and earlier work was that of an electrician, but long before he took up his official duties there were inklings of the interest that was later to guide his choice of profession. While a young man, as he tells us in his memoirs,* he found himself strangely interested and excited by the first recorded electrocution in history—that of William Kemmler on August 6, 1890, in Buffalo, New York, for killing his mistress, Tilly Zeigler, with a hatchet.

Not long after this, another murderer was to be executed.

> I was [he writes] talking with George T———, son of a local druggist, when the papers reached us that S. was to be electrocuted. Strangely enough, my thoughts turned from the doomed man to the one who, by the mere closing of an electric switch, would dispatch S. into the next world.
>
> "Think of the executioner's great responsibility," I declared. "That's a job I'd like to have."
>
> An expression of horror spread over T's face. He looked at me unbelievingly, as though he had not heard correctly. Then the full significance of what I had said dawned on me. I hurriedly changed the subject, and I guess he did not take my statement seriously. Surely neither of us ever dreamed that the day would come when I was to be engaged in such work.
>
> What impelled that remark, I do not know. Often I have tried to explain it to myself, but without success. Perhaps I entertained the opinion that a high degree of science was required to kill human beings painlessly; that the man who served as executioner must be a clever electrician.

It is clear that he is surprised by the wish that suddenly leaps into his awareness. His momentary desire to be the

* Elliott, Robert (with Albert Beatty), *Agent of Death,* E. P. Dutton & Co., New York, 1940.

person who kills another seems to come from realms alien to his usual consciousness. He cannot understand its motivation or its source.

Thereafter for some years this desire remained in abeyance as he underwent his apprenticeship as an electrician. A part of his training took place in state prisons, and for a short period of time he acted as the assistant to the official electrocutioner. He soon gave this up, however, and started a small, private electrical business in which he was engaged for a number of years. One day he learned that the official state executioner had died, and that the authorities were having difficulty in replacing him. After considerable self-examination he decided that it was his duty to offer his services to the state, in view of his previous experience with electrocutions while attached to the state prison system. Unbidden, he volunteered to take over the job and was accepted.

His description of his approach to his new duties is interesting. He was notably conscientious and thorough:

> I never permit myself to relax for a second during an execution . . . I do my work deliberately and carefully, hurrying only when I see that the person to be executed is particularly nervous or apparently on the verge of collapse . . . Certain information about the condemned is necessary if I am to guard against mishaps. I must know his general physical specifications, such as his size and height . . . The chair will accommodate people of all sizes, but extremely tall or short persons require special preparations. For the regulation of the head electrode, I find out the size of the hat worn by the doomed prisoner. I also inquire whether his hair has been cut short in the back. I did not make it a point to ask about this until after an experience . . . in 1935. On that occasion, three young men . . . were brought to the chair, and, for some reason had not had their hair clipped. All had bushy, oily hair . . . As a consequence, the head electrode could not come in con-

tact with the flesh, thus burning the hair and causing considerable smoke.

He was meticulous and skillful in performing the actual
process of electrocution:

> Five seconds after the initial shock of two thousand
> volts, I decrease the current to 1000 volts or somewhat
> under. The purpose of this is to avoid sparking and need-
> less burning. At the end of half a minute, I increase it to
> 1800 or 2000 volts, and after another few seconds, cut it
> down again. This is repeated at half-minute intervals. As
> the current is increased and lowered, the body in the chair
> rises and sinks. Finally after the fifth shock, I reduce the
> current gradually.
> Lowering the current slowly following the final shock is
> my own idea. I believe that it effectively weakens the heart
> and stops the action. Perhaps this is a fallacy, but once or
> twice when I have not done it, the heart has continued to
> beat after the current was turned off.
> I time the process by a wrist watch, a gift from my wife.
> It is like those used by nurses, being especially equipped
> with a large second hand.

During the execution, he was usually able to maintain a
dispassionate objectivity that enabled him to see and describe accurately the details of the phenomena of death by
electrocution:

> I have kept a careful record of all my cases. A page—
> sometimes more than one—is devoted to each. There are
> noted the name of the individual, the nature of his crime,
> and how he went to his death. This information is set
> down while the facts are still fresh in my mind. From these
> accounts I have been able to reach various conclusions . . .
> Before sending the lethal current on its journey of de-
> struction, I glance again at the chair. I want to be sure that
> no one is too near it. Then I throw the switch . . . The figure
> in the chair pitches forward, straining against the straps.

There is the whining cry of the current, and a crackling, sizzling sound. The body turns a vivid red. Sparks often shoot from the electrodes. A wisp of white or dull gray smoke may rise from the top of the head or the leg on which the electrode is attached. This is produced by the drying out of the sponge, singed hair, and despite every effort to prevent it, sometimes burning flesh. An offensive odor is generally present . . . The heat which the electricity produces in the electrodes and in the body is almost unbelievable. There was a night in my experience when the copper in the leg electrode was actually melted. The average body temperature after the current has been on for two minutes is one hundred and thirty-eight degrees.

In addition to performing his work efficiently, he was interested in trying to improve the apparatus he used:

As an instrument of death, today's electric chair is efficient and quick. I would suggest only two improvements. One is that an electrode be placed over the prisoner's heart, thus stopping the action of this vital organ almost as soon as the current is applied. The other is the employment of clamps instead of straps to hold the person in the chair. This would expedite the process of preparing the condemned for the current, and the resulting reduction of a few seconds would make the method even more humane.

Moreover, he took pride in his work:

Since assuming the role of official executioner . . . I have thrown the switch which has hurled into eternity three hundred and eighty-seven occupants of the electric chair. This is the largest number of human beings that any executioner has put to death by the lethal current.

These people, who it was decided had forfeited their right to live, have represented all strata of society. Some have come from the slums; others from the mansions of the rich. Five of them have been women. Most of them have been unknown, except for the brief notice which their trials and subsequent executions brought them ... The names of a few ... have been on the lips of millions.

Away from his work, his private life was usually quiet and uneventful:

> I believe I have a number of friends— -real friends. Among them are men of prominence. One of my good friends is the pastor of the church of which [my wife] and I are members. He frequently calls on us, and sometimes comes for dinner, on which occasion my wife prepares his favorite dish—Boston baked beans ... I spend a great deal of time in my flower garden. I am particularly proud of my roses and gladioli, which have been the envy of the neighborhood. Children often gather round me when I appear in the back yard, and sometimes accompany me on a short stroll ... In the evenings my diversions are varied. Although we are not avid movie fans, my wife and I go to the theater occasionally. She enjoys romantic pictures and musicals; my choice is comedies.

The contrast between these men is striking. There is, however, one point of similarity—in each the aggressive impulse is evident. The patient's tempers and the executioner's startling youthful fantasy of being the man at the electrocutioner's switch attest to its presence. In both it led to the killing of human beings. But there the similarity ends.

The patient's impulse was sudden and resulted immediately in an action that led to his being sentenced to prison for life. There was no premeditation; there was no thoughtful consideration of his impulse to see whether it was right or wrong, no speculation as to the consequences, no careful planning how to go about doing what he was impelled to do, no restraining himself from action until he had had time to reflect on what it was that his impulse urged him to do. The action followed immediately and inevitably on the impulse with no intervening thoughts or controls.

The situation with the executioner is quite the opposite. It was many years between the time when the impulse to kill suddenly emerged as a fantasy in his consciousness, and the time when he first actually fulfilled his fantasy by executing a prisoner. Furthermore, each actual electrocution was not an act of violent, explosive, uncontrolled passion, as was the patient's attack on the woman he killed. On the contrary the executioner went about his work carefully, slowly, methodically, and with a measure of dispassion that allowed him to do his job efficiently and skillfully. Moreover, the job of executioner became very much a part of his life and his image of himself as a person. He took pride in the official position he held. He reflected on the work he was doing: he observed carefully the effect of electrocution on the victim; he attempted to improve his techniques; he invented new methods to make the process more humane. Like any conscientious worker in other fields, he accepted his job as something worthy of careful attention to details and self-improvement. What is more, although (as in the patient) the aggressive impulse enters into his actions, unlike those of Charles L., the executioner's actions are permitted and approved of by society. Far from being imprisoned for taking the lives of others, he is paid for it. The act of killing follows a socially acceptable pattern.

The difference between these two men may be stated thus: in the executioner the aggressive impulse achieves expression in an external act of killing only after it has passed through an elaborate and complex psychological structure that controls it, delays it, attenuates the passion attached to it, ensures that it conforms to the behavioral requirements of society, and makes it acceptable to the person himself. At the same time the intellectual functions of this structure help the impulse to a successful expression by enabling the individual efficiently and intelligently to use the means provided by the world around him to achieve the goal he desires. In the patient, on the other hand, there is little or no psychological structure interposed between the impulse and the expression of it. No sooner thought than done. His behavior is an impulsive act resulting from a *defective ego structure* that imposes no controls or modifications on the raw impulse.

From the standpoint of symptoms, we may state this distinction somewhat differently. We have consistently called the first man a "patient," implying that he was sick. From the psychiatric point of view that is true; the symptom of his illness is an impulsive act, which results from a *defect* in his ego structure. It is a "symptom" because it deviates from what we expect normal social behavior to be. On the other hand, the similar behavior of the executioner is not considered a symptom because, by the same criteria, it does not run counter to socially acceptable action.

Before examining further the details of the structure of the ego, let us return to our consideration of anxiety, which, as we have said, plays an important part in setting into motion that portion of the ego structure known as the *ego defenses,* which in their turn contribute significantly to the formation of the symptoms of emotional illness. In their experience of anxiety there is yet another distinguishing feature between these two men. The patient exhibited considerable *anxiety*—he was afraid of what he might do; as it turned out he was justified in taking his own potential aggressiveness more seriously than did any of the doctors who cared for him. The symptom of anxiety was not present in the executioner; he was not afraid of his impulse. On the contrary, he used it to his own advantage and accepted it as a part of himself. The patient, on the other hand, was aware of the intensity and violence of his impulse; he was aware of the weakness of his controlling mechanism; he was *afraid* of what might occur as a consequence. We should note here that this very concern over and distaste for his own aggressiveness indicates the presence of a certain degree of ego structure, which was in operation during periods of relative calm. It was only when the patient's impulses were aroused to an intensity which he could not control that the defect in the ego structure could be seen. It was either the intensity of the impulse, or the weakness in the controlling mechanism, or both, that differed from the normal— that were, in other words, pathological.

It is time for us to examine the phenomenon of anxiety in greater detail. Here is the description of an attack of acute anxiety given by a patient in treatment:

> I had been feeling sort of tense all day—nothing out of the ordinary. My hands had been perspiring, and my head felt a little full and tight, and I didn't feel so comfortable and relaxed and in contact with people as I often do now.
>
> I wasn't really prepared for what happened during the evening. I was sitting around with a small group of friends talking casually about this and that, when somebody mentioned something about homosexuality. Suddenly I began to sweat hard and my heart began to race; I could feel it pounding uncomfortably. I lost contact with everyone there and could pay attention only to myself and what I was feeling. I knew it was that homosexual business that had triggered it off, and I tried to get my mind off it, to tell myself not to be silly—there was nothing to be so scared about.
>
> By sheer will power I seemed to get control of myself, but I realized that I was more nervous now, even though I was talking with the group and trying to appear relaxed and at ease. I'm sure I looked relaxed enough and that no one knew what I was feeling inside. Somehow, I was afraid now of being afraid again; I was getting more and more anxious that someone was going to mention homosexuality again and set me off once more. To make a long story short, someone did and it really got me going. My heart began to race and pound; I began to sweat and felt as if I couldn't

get enough air into my lungs. I can't quite describe that to you; it was as if something were expanding inside my chest and crowding everything else there out of the way; it made me want to take deep, rapid breaths—or to get to the window for fresh air. It was a feeling partly physical and partly of panic.

I don't know what I was afraid was going to happen. It was partly a fear that the other people there knew what was going on inside of me and that I'd make a fool of myself. But somehow during all of it I knew that people couldn't really know what I was feeling, and they really wouldn't care if they did. But that didn't help; this unnamable terror just seemed to take hold of me and I had the feeling I just *had* to get out of that room. I had to move; I had to do something; I just couldn't sit there any longer. I really can't tell you what I was scared of; not knowing was one of the worst parts of the whole thing. Well—I didn't move. I just sat there sweating it out, and pretty soon things began to quiet down. For the rest of the evening I was sort of tense, but I didn't have any more of those terrible, panicky feelings.

In this description we should note the mixture of physical manifestations and subjective emotional feeling. Many of the physical symptoms are indications of a widespread autonomic discharge—in particular here the tachycardia, the palpitations and the sweating. Other common complaints associated with acute anxiety are trembling, gooseflesh, hot and cold sensations, dizziness and faintness, dry mouth, nausea, and urinary urgency. The frequent appearance of a sharp precordial pain often leads to a mistaken diagnosis of a myocardial infarction. The hyperventilation that results from the feeling of "air hunger" may lead to numbness and tingling in the fingers and toes, stiffness in the extremities, and even tetany as a consequence of respiratory alkalosis.

These bodily signs are a significant part of the unpleasantness of this experience. Even more painful is the subjective sense of terror and panic, which many find more agonizing than any severe bodily, physical pain they have known. The quality of this, like other subjective sensations, is hard to describe or convey to someone who has not himself experienced the same thing. The closest that most of us have come to it is in the state of *fear* of something from outside that threatens us with actual bodily injury, or the common sensation of anxious discomfort in the face of stress, such for example as taking an oral examination or making a speech to a large audience.

There seems to be little in the patient's environment for him to fear, and he is not sure himself what it is that frightens him. He suggests that it may have been the topic of homosexuality, or his fear that other people would know what he was feeling. But even to him these are not sufficient reasons for the terror he has experienced. As he says, he told himself "not to be silly—there was nothing to be so scared about." The patient's suggestion that the subject of homosexuality was related to his anxiety proved to be correct. In the course of treatment it became evident that the conversation had touched on an underlying homosexual impulse that emerged into consciousness in the form of fantasies and feelings as this episode of anxiety was examined with him. When he first touched on these feelings in his therapeutic hours, he once again became acutely anxious; he (and his doctor) then saw that it was his wish for homosexual experiences that was so frightening to him. His panic derived from these inner fantasies, not from any real danger in his external environment.

What we have just said about anxiety should not, however, be construed to mean that it may not be referred by the sufferer to external objects. In the first place, as with the patient, some relatively innocuous event in the environment may act as a precipitant; it may, by touching us in a sensitive spot, stimulate impulses and fantasies which then produce anxiety. Moreover, certain objects or situations, in reality quite harmless, may be endowed by the individual with special meaning, and thereafter regularly induce a reaction of anxiety. The confrontation with heights, crowds, closed spaces, open spaces, a variety of animals, and many less common objects * precipitates an acute attack of anxiety, and the sufferer soon learns to avoid those things that have the power to make him so uncomfortable. We shall examine the dynamic structure and formation of such *phobias* later on.

We must make one more observation about the nature of anxiety before turning to an examination of its role in the formation of symptoms. We have so far been talking about the acute, overwhelming anxiety that was so striking in the experience which our patient described for us. But he mentioned also a state of uneasiness of less intensity; he referred to it as being *tense.*

This latter condition is a milder form of anxiety, with which most of us are familiar from our own experience. The sensation of mild uneasiness, of vague apprehension, of restlessness, of being somewhat unpleasantly "keyed-up" is usually bearable, if uncomfortable. In both states there is a central anticipation of some unpleasantness that one expects in future time. In the panic of acute anxiety, this painful anticipation has reached major proportions. It threatens to overwhelm the person who experiences it; he feels in danger of losing his identity as a person, even of dying. The victim feels helpless in the face of a relentless, crushing, menacing force. Such dread permeates the account that Rilke † gives of a number of bizarre phobias.

---

* Cf. G. Stanley Hall (42) for an exhaustive list of phobic objects and situations.

† Rainer Maria Rilke, *The Notebooks of Malte Laurids Brigge,* trans. by John Linton, Hogarth Press, London, 1930.

The fear that a small, woolen thread that sticks out of
the hem of my blanket may be hard, hard and sharp like
a steel needle; the fear that this little button on my night-
shirt may be bigger than my head, large and heavy; the
fear that this crumb of bread that is falling from my bed
may be shattered like glass when it reaches the floor, and
the oppressive anxiety lest therewith everything break to
pieces, everything forever; the fear that the torn scrap of
an opened letter may be something forbidden that no one
ought to see, something indescribably precious for which
no place in the room is secure enough; the fear that if I
fell asleep I might swallow the piece of coal lying in front
of the stove; the fear that some numeral may begin to grow
in my brain until there is no more room for it within me;
the fear that it may be granite I am lying on, grey granite;
the fear that I may shout and that people may gather at
my door and finally break it open; the fear that I may
betray myself and tell all I dread; and the fear that I might
not be able to say anything, because everything is beyond
utterance, and the other fears . . . the fears.

This quality of helpless passivity and dread is missing
from the experience of lesser forms of anxiety. One feels
that one can keep the latter under control, that one can
function despite it, and, furthermore, that one can get rid
of it by appropriate maneuvers. The anxiety acts as a warning that danger is impending, but the danger is one that the
individual is capable of coping with; it is not yet overwhelming or inevitable. It is this lesser *signal anxiety* that is so
importantly related to symptom formation, to which we
must now turn our attention.

VIII

ANXIETY AND SYMPTOM FORMATION:
OBSESSIONS AND COMPULSIONS

Chester B., aged 41, was admitted to the psychiatric ward of a general hospital because of a variety of anxieties and disturbing thoughts. As the doctor was taking him to his office for the first interview, he casually asked the patient whether he would mind walking down the stairs instead of taking the elevator. To his surprise the patient enthusiastically agreed, replying with great vehemence that he certainly did *not* want to take the elevator. It was for this reason that the doctor opened the interview with the following request:

Dr. Tell me about the elevator—how that bothered you.

Pt. Well, I was an elevator operator, and I've never had no accidents. But still, lately, the last six months or so, it's been bothering me. Where I live . . . there's a self-service passenger elevator, and I don't use it; I walk upstairs . . . When I go by it, I make sure the door is closed. It's funny—I walk by to go out and I have to pass it to go outside, so I make sure the door is closed. I dream I'm driving an elevator and falling down in it. That sort of got me scared, but I've never had any accidents in an elevator . . .

At the outset we find the patient describing mild anxiety: he has been scared by a dream of a falling elevator, and he hints in a vague way at his concern that something bad may happen in them; they are in some way dangerous. His response is to avoid them in order to remain free of anxiety. In other words, he has developed a *phobia* of elevators, but controls the anxiety attached to the object by a *phobic avoidance* of it. Both the anxiety and the avoiding behavior are, from the clinical point of view, symptoms of a *phobic reaction*.

The statistical chances of his really having an accident in an elevator are almost nil. There is in reality little likelihood of injury, and it is puzzling why the patient should have developed this fear of them. Furthermore, we cannot understand why he has to make sure that the elevator door is closed. We must turn to the patient for the answer to these riddles by listening to what he can tell us further about his fears and his fantasies.

The patient went on to say,

> Since I've been nervous, everything seems to bother me. Like this morning. This fellow was taking a sponge bath in the sink. See, he's got a bandage around his head. He's had an operation, so it seemed to bother me, so I used the other sink . . . He is washing his feet, and he has athlete's feet. So he washes himself in the sink, and he'd rinse out the towel in the sink—so that's what I'm scared of: diseases . . . If anybody should talk that they have a disease, they're sick, I'm ready to run. I'm so afraid that I'm going to catch it from them. I know I'm healthy. I shouldn't be so scared. The last time I was here—I was here for five days, and this girl said she had cancer. So it upset me so much I had to leave the hospital . . . As soon as she mentioned that, I didn't want her touching me. I had this shirt on; she touched my back when I was sitting down playing cards . . . I know if she had cancer, she wouldn't be on that ward. If only I could tell my mind that. I mean, it keeps going around.
>
> *Dr.*   How does it go around?
> *Pt.*   Well, I mean, I knock it off for a while. I'll say

to myself, try to convince myself that if she had cancer, she wouldn't be in this ward. So I'd be all right for a few seconds. Then it would come back to me again, and I'd say, "Ooh!—maybe she has"; and then I'd say, "No" and try to convince myself again, and that's all I would be doing all day long, until I couldn't stick it out any longer ... I wouldn't stay in the hospital near her.

The patient had in actuality left the hospital, and came back only when he was assured that the patient he was afraid of was no longer on the ward. His behavior was controlled by the varied fears that beset him. Furthermore, he introduces us to a new type of phenomenon: in addition to the irrational fear of getting cancer is the fact that the fear forces itself upon him as a recurring thought that constantly hounds and plagues him. He tries to deal with this *obsession* by reasoning with himself, but each time he is only momentarily successful, and the thought hurls itself back on him. He is preoccupied with this repetitious process all day long, as long as the phobic object, the woman, is present. He can avoid the anxiety only by leaving the hospital—by an act of avoidance. We should note that the patient is himself entirely cognizant of the absurdity of his fear. But his intellectual knowledge is no help; the idea has a life of its own and infests the patient against his will.

As the patient continued to talk, he mentioned an increasing number of things that bothered him. He had once enjoyed going to the local gymnasium and taking steambaths, but:

... the past two years I stopped going to the gym. We have steam cabinets, and I've heard that they urinated in the steam cabinets; when they had to go to the bathroom, a fellow would just do it right in the steam cabinet. I would wash them out. Before it didn't bother me, but the last couple of years it bothered me.

... My main concern is I'm afraid to touch things. I

mean I'm afraid to open doors ... Like we go out at night, five or six of us, so they'll open the door, and I always try to manage to get in without opening the door knob ... I try to hold the door; I try not to hold the door knob ... so many people handle the door knob, and I'm afraid of getting disease. I wash my hands a lot. That's one of my main troubles. I wash my hands too much. I try to keep clean.

... I seem to jump from different things. I mean, I don't stick to one thing. Like before going to the hospital, it was just glass and the batteries from a car—acid from the battery of a car. Any time I would see something white under where a car would be parked, I'd think it was acid from a car, and I would walk around it and try not to step in it. Then I walked by a factory where they make batteries, and I took the shoes off, and I still have them in the house, and I'm undecided what to do with the shoes. I'd like to throw them away because I walked by the factory, and it's a shame to throw the shoes away because it bothers me in such a way; that if I touch them—if I put the shoes on, it bothers me. I don't know what to do with them.

... And I can't wrestle. I used to do a little wrestling, and I can't do that now because the sweat from somebody else's body would come on my body. And even though I'd take a shower, I can't do it. It would bother me.

Dr.   Are there any other things you are afraid of?

Pt.   I'm afraid of sewers in the street ... I know that the sewer—if I walked over the sewer, I couldn't fall in. But still, when I walk over the sewer—I know it would take two or three men to lift the sewer, but still, when I walk and see a sewer, I try to walk around it; I'm afraid of it ... I wouldn't want to fall down a sewer ... That's what comes to my mind: the sewer is liable to tip; I'm liable to fall down a sewer.

Nor did this complete the repertoire of the patient's fears. Because other people had used it, he could not sit down on the toilet seat to move his bowels; he would always defecate half standing up. When he flushed the toilet he would hold the handle with a paper towel. He would not touch the pottery clay in the Occupational Therapy Shop, or pick things off the floor when he dropped them, because they had been dirtied. He had given up using a reconditioned razor when it suddenly dawned on him that another man had shaved with it before he had bought it.

What is striking about all of these fears is how much the patient is preoccupied with dirt: he is afraid of getting dirty and he is afraid that somehow harm will come to him from it. He also mentions one new phenomenon—the act of washing his hands in order to keep clean. We shall see in a moment how he elaborates on this.

Let us stop for a moment and consider what a world it is this man lives in. Everything is dirty, dangerous, and harmful. He cannot rid his mind of its constant preoccupation with the dangers that lurk in every corner. No matter what he does to prevent disease and injury, such as washing his hands or avoiding situations, the beneficial effects of these actions are only temporary; new terrors spring up to replace the old. His task is as herculean as cleansing the Augean stables. His whole day is so taken up with watching out for dangers and trying to prevent them that he has little time for the ordinary pursuits and pleasures of life. And the worst of it all is that intellectually he knows that his fears, and the things he does to prevent the evil consequences as well, are utter foolishness. Yet the knowledge does not help rid him of his concerns—he is trapped in a sticky web of fears and doubts, of "do's" and "don'ts," none of his own volition.

These symptoms of his emotional illness are crippling. His life is as effectively shattered as if he were suffering from the most debilitating of physical illnesses, without the hope of an early release by death from his suffering that at least accompanies a lethal disease. And yet no one, nor any external physical restraint, is forcing the patient to live such

a life. The restrictions seem to be of his own doing. What is
the reason for this self-constructed prison? Why is he beset
by these inane, crippling fears? As we listen to the further
associations and fantasies, we begin to find some of the
answers. The patient continued:

> Like the last time I was here, that girl scared me so
> much I went home. I took this shirt off and this pair of
> pants ... And I didn't wear it for about three or four
> weeks because that girl touched me and I sat in the chair
> she sat in. So I had my pants steam cleaned and my shirt
> steam cleaned. I'm wearing it now. It's a fight to wear it.
> I would rather throw it away ... At home I had them on
> a chair for about three or four weeks. My mother wanted
> to take them to the cleaners, and I'd say, "No, let them
> stay there." I didn't want my mother to touch them.
> *Dr.*   Why?
> *Pt.*   Because I was scared she might get cancer.

Suddenly the patient introduces an interesting new note.
Up until this point in the interview, he had been talking
only about his concern that he *himself* might be hurt. All
at once, he indicates that he was afraid that harm might
come to *another person*—specifically that his mother might
get cancer. The doctor, noting this new element, focused
the patient's attention on it by asking him:

> *Dr.*   Are you worried about other people the way you
> are worried about yourself?
> *Pt.*   Yes. I'm worried about other people very much.
> I make sure my hands are washed very thoroughly before
> I handle the food on the table, because if I take something
> and dirt or something from my hands should fall on the
> milk or something—whatever I'm handling—it upsets me.
> *Dr.*   How does it upset you?
> *Pt.*   Well, I wouldn't want any dirt to fall in the milk.
> It upsets me. I try to tell myself, "My hands are washed,
> my hands are washed." I shouldn't worry about it ... I

have to convince myself. I have to keep fighting with myself. I have to say, "No—your hands. You washed your hands, Chet. There is nothing on your hands." And I have to keep doing that most of the day—telling myself that I washed my hands and nothing would go into the milk to harm anybody.

Or again he says,

There was something else I wanted to tell you. I didn't want to go do shopping for my mother, because I figured the dirt from my shoes—well, you know, they're crowded about as far down as those books on your shelves are— are shelves crowded with food, canned stuff and so on. Well, I was scared to go in the supermarket on account of I figured dirt might—from my shoes—might go on the canned stuff. But if everybody felt like that, the store would have to close up, because how would they do their shopping? And that's what I try to convince myself of. I'm no different from nobody else. I walk on the street like everybody else does. They don't clean their feet before they go in there. So why should I be any different? So that's what I keep saying to myself.

As the patient tells us thus about his thoughts that other people may be harmed, we see that he feels that something *he himself does* may be injurious: among the dangerous things in his dangerous world is himself. Grammatically speaking there are two voices to the danger: the *active* and the *passive* voice. Either he harms others, or is harmed himself. The content of the ideas, regardless of the voice, is the same. As when the ideas were in the passive voice, we find the same emphasis on dirt and destruction; we see the same obsessive preoccupation with the thoughts and the same sense that they are foreign to him—that he is not really the author of the thoughts, that he does not voluntarily think them, or himself desire the consequences of his acts. They are *ego-alien*. Indeed, he fights against the thoughts—he tries to convince himself, without success, that they are silly. And he takes another precaution against possibly harming anyone—he washes his hands. He had mentioned before his need to keep clean; we now discover that it is stimulated by the fearful thought that he might harm someone else by having dirt on his hands. This *compulsive act* of hand washing is an attempt to rid himself of the anxiety aroused by the *obsessive thoughts* about dirt. The same factors are present in his self-imposed restriction on his activities: he *avoids* the supermarket so as not to contaminate the food with the dirt on his shoes.

We have now a partial explanation of why the patient's life is so crippled, apparently by his own doing. It is an attempt on his part to prevent the harm which he fears he may cause others. But this only raises a further question for us. His fear that he may harm others is quite as absurd and needless as the measures he takes to counteract it. What, then, is the reason for the fear and its source?

Let us return to the patient. His doctor said to him:

> *Dr.*   Now part of this trouble is being afraid that other people will get hurt too.
>
> *Pt.*   Yes it is, Doctor. There are quite a few ways I'm afraid of it. If I'm walking in the street, like at night we go out for a walk, and we walk by a sewer, and I know there is five or six of us. So I count the six of us, or the five of us, to make sure nobody got hurt, or that we are all there. And then I hate to walk by the elevator. If somebody is there, I'm afraid they might fall down. Not that I would push them—I wouldn't harm nobody. Gosh, I have enough troubles without harming anybody.

Once again, he mentions the sewer and the elevator, now not as instruments of damage to himself, but to others. And then, at the end, there abruptly appears his curious, spontaneous, seemingly unnecessary disclaimer that he would push anybody down the elevator shaft. In this fantasy he is more actively involved in hurting people than in the fantasy of dirt falling from his hands into the milk. In the latter, the harmful agent works without his taking a really active part; the dirt drops into the milk of itself without his really causing it to do so, although he *is* the carrier, and, therefore, feels himself to be responsible for the harm. But in pushing someone down the elevator shaft, it is necessary for him to make an active movement to accomplish this; it could not just happen by itself.

A moment later the doctor asked him about "pushing." The patient replied,

> It's just that that thought comes into my mind—that somebody fell down the elevator even though I didn't push them. It's just maybe somebody fell in the elevator well ... It bothers me; I have to convince myself I didn't do it. I would never do it. I don't know why I think like that ... I wouldn't ever hurt anybody. I liked to do favors; I felt good when I done favors. It would give me a good feeling. I don't drink or smoke. I never spent my time in the bar room.

Here there appears a new obsessive thought, that he *has* pushed someone down the elevator shaft. And it brings with it the anxiety we have noted before, as well as the same desperate attempt to convince himself he has done no such thing. Judged by the fantasy alone, this act has a violently aggressive and destructive quality, and we wonder at this point whether it is related in some way to the patient's own aggressive impulses. This he spontaneously disclaims—he disavows any such desires; in fact, he tries almost pathetically to tell us what a good person he is; far from hurting other people, he does favors for them, and enjoys it; he doesn't smoke, he doesn't drink, he doesn't waste his substance in the bar rooms.

However, despite his disavowal of any aggressive intentions, the patient behaves as if he didn't trust himself. As he said,

> I would walk around on the other side [of the elevator] to go to the bathroom, but Dr. E. says you have to do things you don't want to do, so I walked by it. I forced myself to walk by it . . . If there is anybody standing near the elevator, I won't walk by, but if there is nobody there, I'll walk by.

Again we observe a defensive act of avoidance, not so much of a situation where he might be hurt himself, but of one in which he might harm others. The reasons for his concern about the elevator which were obscure at the start of the interview have now become clear. Can we gain further light on the patient's potential aggressiveness? Again from the interview:

> *Dr.*   In what other ways do you feel you hurt people?
> *Pt.*   Well, going on streetcars. If I'm going on a streetcar and there is a crowd—especially if there is a crowd—I'm afraid somebody might fall underneath the streetcar. Like last year, my sister took me to her house, so I went on the streetcar with her. And it was kind of crowded, so I thought I accidentally pushed somebody . . . under the streetcar wheels. So it took me about two or three weeks to convince myself I didn't do it. I was even going to call up the streetcar company and find out if any accidents had happened there. My sister was right along there aside of me . . .
> *Dr.*   How do you think you have pushed them?
> *Pt.*   I don't know. It just comes into my mind—it just comes into my mind, "Did you harm anybody, Chet? Did you push anybody?", and I say, "No—I didn't push anybody. I had my hands in my pockets to make sure I don't push anybody." I hold myself like this (the patient demonstrated how he held his arms tight against his body), and I stand alongside my sister. It makes it awfully hard for

me. I can't even go by streetcar. If I want to go in town or
something, I can't even go by myself. It's an awful feeling ...

Dr. You're terribly scared you are going to hurt
people.

Pt. Accidentally I might. I figure maybe accidentally
you get in crowds going on the streetcar. You *accidentally*
might bump into somebody and push them underneath the
car tracks, but that's an accident. I mean, not that I want
to do it. I mean—but gosh, you can't take somebody and
throw them under the streetcar unless you really took him.
And he's not going to stand there to let you throw him
under a streetcar. He's going to put up a fight. And I'm
sure with so many people around me—I'm sure they're not
going to stop me ... I'd rather not go on the streetcar so
it wouldn't happen to me—I mean, wouldn't occur in my
mind. I never harmed nobody in my life, Doctor.

The patient's language and imagery are noteworthy. He
speaks about an "accident"; the word occurs four times in
three short sentences. And yet it is a strange "accidental"
push. In his fantasy he talks of "taking" somebody and
"throwing" them under the streetcar. He keeps his hands in
his pockets, or pressed tightly against his body so that this
won't happen. The other person is "going to put up a
fight." Other people are not going to stand passively by;
they will enter into the affair and try to stop it—at least that
is apparently what the patient was trying to say, although he
makes what seems to be a slip of the tongue, which we shall
examine in a moment.

Looked at only from the point of view of the patient's
fantasy, we glimpse a scene in which the patient grabs a
bystander on the station platform and struggles violently
to throw him off the edge under the car wheels. The victim
fights back, and the surrounding crowd enters into the fray
to restrain him. And this is what the patient insists is an

"accident"! An "accident" implies something that occurs seemingly by chance—that there is no volition, intent, or purpose on the part of the person who "accidentally" causes something to happen. Yet this is just what the patient's fantasies belie; they are images of highly co-ordinated actions that seem to have aggressive intent and purpose behind them. Nevertheless the patient strongly protests that any such violent intention is utterly foreign to him.

Let us for the moment ignore the patient's protests and postulate that in actuality there exists within him a strong aggressive impulse. Let us assume that he is driven by an inner furious anger to commit violently murderous acts, but that the anger and the impulse to aggression are *unconscious;* that he is not aware that such forces exist inside him, and that he does not want to be aware of them or accept the fact that such impulses and emotions are his, because they run counter to his ideal of himself as a person who "never harmed anyone," who "liked to do favors for others," who was in all respects a model citizen.

Despite his disavowal of their meaning and significance, the patient does have murderous fantasies. They come from him and we discover them only because he tells us about them. What he disclaims is that they in any way designate what he feels or what he wants to do. There is a discontinuity in his mental processes. Unfettered and unrestrained the aggressive impulse produces a feeling of anger, an urge to act, and fantasies of action that then lead to the action itself. In the patient we find only a fragment of this chain of events. The anger and the impulse, that is the *affect,* the feeling component, and the volitional component have disappeared; they have lost their connection in the patient's consciousness with the images; the action has been curtailed. All that remains of the total process is the fantasy which, though aggressive in content, is relatively pale and innocuous compared to the rest and persists only as a vestige of the whole. In technical terms the affect and the impulse have been rendered unconscious by the defense mechanism of *isolation* from the fantasies. But though unconscious, these forces still strive for expression; they constantly exert their influence on the patient's conscious mentation; they require a continuous effort on his part to keep them contained.

With this inference we can pull together and understand many of our observations. The quality and violence of the fantasies are now seen to be an expression of a feeling and impulse to which they are appropriate. It is the violence of the impulse and the constant threat that it will escape control and impel him to murder that provoke the patient's anxiety; it conflicts with his image of how he should and wants to behave. The segments of his total personality structure are at war with one another, which leads to the anxiety that stimulates him to employ the various ego defense mechanisms. These are manifested as symptoms—his phobias, his obsessions, and his compulsions. The final result is a severe clinical neurosis which completely disables the patient from leading a reasonably active, happy, and normal life.

Let us return briefly to what appeared to be a slip of the tongue. When describing his fantasies of what might happen on the streetcar platform, the patient says of the bystanders, "They're *not* going to stop me." From the context of all that has gone before it seems that the patient should have said, "They *are* going to stop me"—that is, not only would the victim whom he is "accidentally" pushing to his death beneath the streetcar wheels fight back, but the people around would also grab him and restrain him. As the patient's words pour out, he states exactly the opposite: they will stand passively by and allow him to attempt murder. It looks as though the aggressive impulse had suddenly made a direct appearance. Despite the patient's conscious thoughts and wishes to the contrary, despite his reiterated disavowal that he wants to harm or that he is responsible for his actions, he makes a statement directly contrary to his disclaimers. In this small, almost unnoticed way the impulse is able to sneak by the cordon of defenses and against his better judgment make the patient say something that he consciously does not want or mean to say. From the point of view of behavior this is a minor event; in fact the patient's doctor did not notice it until he was later reviewing the transcribed copy of the recorded interview. And yet it is a further indication of the nature of the underlying impulse, and demonstrates the constant pressure it exerts to erupt into consciousness and expression.

We have so far been examining material from the patient which has enabled us to infer unconscious anger and aggression. There is as yet nothing to tell us why he should be so angry; furthermore the people who in his fantasies suffer harm at his hands are for the most part either vague, unnamed persons, or casual individuals like other patients on the ward. It is hard to see what real importance or significance they could have in the patient's life and relationships. The one exception is the fact that when he first mentioned harm occurring to someone other than himself he named his mother as the object. In all that he says, the patient talks very little about direct, open, explicit feelings of anger and aggression, but it is interesting that when he does, his mother again comes into his associations. At one point he said:

> *Pt.* . . . Things bother me so much that even if somebody hit me, I don't think I could hit them back.
> *Dr.* Really.
> *Pt.* Unless I got very mad. I mean I have to get awfully mad to hit somebody back.
> *Dr.* And if you got awfully mad?
> *Pt.* Well, I mean, it never happened. See, I've never had a fight except when I was a youngster, and that's

maybe thirty-two years ago. Maybe when I was ten years
old I had a fight, but I haven't had any fights since.
    Dr.   But if you got awfully mad now?
    Pt.   I don't think I could hit anybody.
    Dr.   Well, what would happen if you did?
    Pt.   If I did—if I hurt them, it would bother me some-
thing terrible. I mean, I get mad—I get awfully mad. At
home I get mad that I'm this way. Sometimes I blame my
mother, because my mother has been a sick person for the
last twenty-five years. She has always been sick. She has
high blood pressure. And I was like her favorite son because I would help her; I would take her out; any time
she didn't feel good I would wash the floor for her; I would
do the shopping for her, I would just let her lay in bed,
and I would do everything for her. So I was her favorite
son.

The patient's anger is like an object in a thick fog, appearing and disappearing as the fog lightens or deepens
from moment to moment. He speaks about being "awfully
mad," and then in the next breath says it "never happened."
He talks about fighting in the present, and at once says he
hasn't had a fight for thirty-two years. And we should note
that for him being "mad" means at once translating it into
the action of a fight, in which he fears hurting somebody,
which would "bother him something terrible." And finally
there is the reference to his mother. He mentions "being
mad" that he is "this way" and says he sometimes blames
his mother; for the moment he allows himself to be slightly
critical of her, but at once turns to telling us how *good* he
has been to her all of his life.

As the interview continued, the doctor asked him to describe his anger.

    Dr.   When you were a little boy and got mad, what
would happen?
    Pt.   When I got mad? Well, I'll tell you one way I

would get mad. If I would come home and find my mother
not home and the lock was on the door, I would kick the
door because my mother wasn't home. I wanted her home
—I wanted her. And when she would go to her club (she
would go and dance with people—I was eight, maybe ten
years old), I would hold onto her dress; I wouldn't want
her to dance . . . I wanted her to stay with me.

A short while later, speaking about the present, the
patient said,

When I go out for a walk I like to go with my mother.
Well, it's like a security, I think you'd call it; sort of, well,
if you had—like you had a policeman with you. I can
walk with her. I feel free and easy. Walking by myself I
wanted to make sure I didn't step on glass or didn't step
on dog shit.
Dr. Does that bother you?
Pt. It does—yes, it does, Doctor. As a matter of fact
when I came here to the hospital, I got out of the taxi, and I
just accidentally touched a little with my shoe, and gosh,
it bothered me something terrible. Nothing went on me,
but it bothered me. Every time I went out in the grass, I
wiped my shoe to make sure nothing went on me. But
that's the feeling I have. When I'm with somebody, I feel
good; it's a good feeling—I don't know—that I'm not
scared of things so much. Like I go for a walk with my
mother or anybody, I don't feel so alone in the world. For
instance, when I'm alone I feel if I step on glass, if I step
on oil, grease, or anything like that—if I'm with somebody
else, I ask them, "What's that? Grease, Joe?" He'll tell me,
"Yeah, it's grease, Chet," or "It's oil," and I feel better
about it.

Let us focus our attention briefly on his relationship with
his mother. His father had died before he was born and his
mother had raised him and his sister alone. He had never
married, but had chosen to remain at home with her. Be-

cause of his illness he had not worked for ten years, and at forty-one was now financially completely dependent on her. His emotional dependence is a solid bondage too; he wants her and needs her; he does not feel safe when he goes out of doors unless she accompanies him. We observe the same dependence in the childhood vignette he reveals of clinging to her skirts to keep her near him and to have her for himself. Even for an eight- or ten-year-old this is an unusual attachment; it is more characteristic of the infant in his first two or three years of life. It is certainly an abnormal and pathological dependence for a man of forty-one. He has failed to develop beyond the normal infantile maternal ties into an autonomous, self-sufficient, and responsible adult.

When we come later to examine the problem of abnormal dependence in more detail, we shall find abundant evidence that aggression is a significant element in this type of relationship. The dependent person is not only more demanding of the attention and affection he needs; he tends to react with rage when it is denied him. Chester B. was no exception to this pattern, at least in his childhood; we saw how he would kick the door in fury when his mother was not home to be with him. When we look for a similar anger toward her in his adult life with her, we are unable to find it. The closest that he comes to a direct, open expression of resentment toward her is in his mild comment that he "sometimes blames" her for his sickness. But he hastens to point out what a good, dutiful, helpful, and loving son he has been to her throughout his life. On the other hand, he does not want her to touch his clothes for fear that she will get cancer. Although he knows that this is in reality an absurd idea, he behaves as though he really believes she will contract a cruel, lethal, painful disease; he refuses to have her take his clothes to the cleaner. His mother is, therefore, intimately bound up in his phobias, his obsessions, and his compulsions. If we interpret this phenomenon in the light of our previous analysis of his symptoms, we should infer that beneath lies hidden a direct, destructive aggressive impulse toward his mother, more overt in his childhood, but now unconscious and capable of achieving expression only in the indirect, distorted, symptomatic form imposed on it by his ego defenses. Furthermore, in view of the primacy of his relationship with his mother, we may postulate that his aggression was and is in the first instance directed toward her; the inclusion of other less important, more casual people in the web of his fantasies is the result of *displacement* of his aggression, a further defense against open expression of this impulse toward his mother.

We have as yet taken no notice of a prominent feature of the patient's symptoms—his preoccupation with and fear of dirt, waste, sewers, and feces. Let us approach an elucidation of this through our knowledge of early development derived from the observation of children. At the age of two to three the child is in a phase of growth from the earlier passive, helpless dependence on his parents to the later Oedipal, genital stage of development which we touched on briefly in discussing the childhood roots of adult conflicts. This intermediary period is known as the anal phase of maturation, owing to the fact that the child exhibits a heightened pleasurable preoccupation and interest in his anal orifice and its products. This is seen in his tendency to anal masturbation, his pleasure in passing and retaining stools, and his delight in playing with or displaying feces, toward which he exhibits no disgust. At the same time his aggressive impulse has reached a phase of destructive violence against which adequate ego controls have not yet been entirely developed. This is the age of violent temper outbursts, which fail to be destructive and murderous only because the small size of the child prevents him from carrying out his fantasies. The aggression is seen in the child's willfulness and stubbornness in the face of parental discipline, particularly in the area of bowel training. In the normal maturational process, the erotic sensitivity of the anal zone subsides and gives way to the primacy of the genital zone as the source of physical sexual pleasure. In like manner, the destructive aggressive impulse diminishes as the growing child develops his capacity for the altruistic, giving, unselfish love that eventually characterizes healthy adult relationships. In the face of unduly harsh and demanding parental discipline, the child's anal and aggressive impulses may disappear from view, not as a result of normal maturation, but because they have been pushed underground by defenses devised by the developing ego to force them out of consciousness. The child develops traits of behavior which are the exact opposite of the underlying impulses; he becomes exceptionally clean and fastidious; he is disgusted by dirt and excreta; he is excessively "good" and unaggressive; he may even develop compulsive rituals indistinguishable from adult symptoms. Even in uncomplicated growth, such *reaction formations* may to a lesser degree form a part of the normal development of the maturing ego.

Though lost from sight, these underlying impulses are not without their effect. They are rarely seen directly in the adult, especially the anal erotic component. Occasionally, however, they appear in practically pure expression, as for example, in the stool-smearing and eating of feces by adult schizophrenic patients, the anal intercourse which the passive male homosexual finds the most satisfying form of sexual expression, or in the sexual aberrations in which sexual satisfaction is obtained by being defecated on by the sexual partner. In these instances, the behavior carries clearly the stamp of its origins.

More commonly it is the early defenses erected against the impulses in the course of development that appear in the behavior of the adult. This is the source in part of adult patterns of behavior characterized by excessive fastidious-ness, cleanliness, and perfectionism and by an inordinate emphasis on control of feelings and behavior, especially anger and aggression. If in therapy one explores these patterns with adult patients, one arrives invariably at the anal and aggressive drives and fantasies that lie behind them, and can often trace them back to their childhood origins.

Finally, as a manifestation of ego defenses, one sees the clinical obsessions and compulsions that so cruelly plagued our patient. In him we found no direct wish and impulse either to be destructively aggressive nor to find pleasure in excrement and waste. On the contrary, we observed only an excessive and absurd concern to avoid being dirty and destructive. On the one hand he vehemently denied such impulses; on the other he behaved as if they were leaking out all over the place. Before either the dynamic or genetic aspects of the patient's illness could be fully explored he again fled from the hospital. He did not confess to desires of his own to hurt and kill in anger. That these impulses existed in him or that they had their origin in his childhood remained in the realm of inference, although from the content of his fantasies as well as from the knowledge derived from the observation of other similar patients there seemed little doubt that the inferences would prove to be correct. As inferences, their value lies in providing us reasonable guideposts pointing to important areas of conflict that need further exploration to uncover the relevant dynamic and genetic factors.

One important general principle arises from our observation of this patient. The symptomatic constellation of defenses and impulses is in a delicate state. The aggressive impulse is not merely pushed out of awareness by a single defensive act, to remain thereafter forgotten and inert. On the contrary it seems constantly to strive for expression and to require an ever alert vigilance on the part of the ego, which exerts the continuously operating psychological forces of the defenses to keep it unconscious. Even so the impulse makes itself felt; this is seen not only in the small slip of the tongue we have commented on, but more importantly in the major symptoms themselves. It determines the content of the fantasies, and it supplies the motive force of the obsessions; the patient has to convince himself over and over again all day long that he has *not* harmed anyone—he has to maintain a constant guard against his actions' being destructive, and to attempt by repeated compulsive acts to undo or prevent the damage he fears doing. There is a continuous struggle against the anger and the aggressive impulse which, without his being aware of it, makes itself felt. In other words, the symptoms of obsessions and compulsions are the end-product of the mixture of elements from both an unconscious impulse and the ego defenses directed against it. The symptoms are a compromise formation, the result (to use a spatial, physical analogy) of vectors of forces showing the summated effects of all the elements. This is the process of *symptom formation*. It is apparent from this that symptoms may be viewed from the outside in clinical, descriptive terms, or from the inside, as the consequence of causally related psychological forces. We come again upon the two functions of the discipline of psychopathology—to describe and to explain.

Finally let us note the important role that anxiety plays in this patient's life and symptom formation. At no time does it reach the intensity of panic, but at no time does it completely disappear. The patient is chronically troubled by anxiety; it rises and falls all day long. It is, however, kept at a level of intensity below panic by the defense mechanisms we have examined. The overwhelming anxiety that occurred, for example, in Boyd C. when his violent aggression began to appear openly in consciousness is avoided in Chester B. through the agency of the obsessions; these isolate the aggressive impulse and keep it out of the patient's awareness. The maneuver is not entirely successful, however. There is still a quality of aggressiveness in the content of the obsessions which continues to arouse anxiety in the patient. This in turn acts as a signal to the patient for a further defensive operation, the compulsion, which combats the dreaded consequences threatened by the obsessive thought. In other words, it is the anxiety that goads the patient to a defensive maneuver to avoid the discomfort produced by the anxiety.

There is yet another aspect of Chester B.'s anxiety that we must comment upon. Boyd C., as we noted when we observed his acute distress on the day after Christmas, was made anxious by an impulse that threatened to cause him to perform a destructive act in the *future*. This was true also of Chester B. when, for example, he avoided subways lest he accidentally push someone onto the tracks—again, an action that he anxiously anticipates as occurring in the future. There were, however, times at which he was obsessed with the idea that he had already caused damage in the *past;* on one occasion, as he tells us, he feared he *had* knocked someone under the wheels of a streetcar and felt under a compulsion for several weeks to call up the transit authorities to find out whether this had actually happened. Or, when he walked by a sewer, he would have to count his companions to make sure that none of them *had* fallen down the manhole.

Realistically he knew that his obsessional thoughts about damage past were absurd, and yet his anxiety would rise if he could not reassure himself by checking to make sure that nothing had happened; the compulsion to check acted as a defense against his anxiety. Although he knew better, he acted and felt as if he were really guilty of his imagined crime. In other words, his conscience (the punitive, critical agent of his superego) took his destructive fantasies at face value and, acting on the assumption that he had committed mayhem, filled him with remorse. His ego was beset not only by the impulses striving for expression, but by the pressures of the superego as well. His compulsions were an attempt to ward off the fear of the punitive superego. Moreover, this same *superego anxiety* was a motivating force in his attempts to avoid and prevent destruction before it occurred —he was afraid of the painful guilt that would ensue under the influence of his constantly monitoring conscience.

Again, we should note that the patient is suffering from a conflict of *internal* forces that play out their roles with little regard for reality. It is typical of patients with obsessions and compulsions to have a superego structure characterized by a heightened vigilance and severity as compared with more normal people. When we come to examine the problem of depression, we shall find that there too the superego plays an important role in symptom formation, but with a difference: in the case of obsessions and compulsions, the ego does not completely accept the judgments of the superego; it knows that in reality there is no truth in the fantasies and no reason for feeling guilty. In severe depressions, on the other hand, the patient is overcome by guilty remorse; he feels and is convinced, in the face of a contrary reality, that he is bad, sinful, and guilty; his ego accepts the judgments of an overweening conscience.

In Chester B., as we have seen, although his anxiety goads him to defensive maneuvers devised to avoid the pain of anxiety, this process is not entirely successful. The ghost of aggression is never entirely laid. The impulse, as we noted a moment ago, is constantly striving for expression; it comes momentarily closer to the surface, anxiety increases, and a defensive maneuver aroused by the anxiety temporarily dispels it. But there is no final resolution of the process. Like Sisyphus the patient must be constantly at his never-ending task. He suffers from a chronic and crippling psychoneurosis, the clinical manifestation of his underlying psychopathology.

IX

ANXIETY AND SYMPTOM FORMATION: CONVERSION AND PHOBIA

In most of the patients whom we have so far examined, anxiety has been an obvious and important symptom. Despite the fact that defenses have arisen to protect the patient from this painful affect, these maneuvers have not been entirely successful. The patient we are now to consider controlled his impulses in a manner that enabled him completely to avoid anxiety, but at a considerable cost to his whole way of life.

Francis S. came all the way to America from New Zealand for neurosurgical relief of persistent pain in his back and left leg. He had suffered for many years. A previous operation for a ruptured intervertebral disk at the lumbar 4-5 interspace had been no help. Despite this chronic burden of pain the patient managed courageously to carry on with his work and to support his wife and three children. A year before he came to this country, in a further attempt to relieve his suffering, he underwent a second operation on his back. Not only was he not freed of his symptoms, but following surgery he became totally incapacitated; his old pains were far worse, and he developed new symptoms of pain in his arms and neck, as well as generalized weakness of such severity that he could no longer get out of bed. From being an active wage-earner he turned into a totally helpless, bed-ridden invalid.

The patient's pattern of behavior in the years before his

second operation was in striking contrast to his present incapacitation. He had prided himself on his capacity for hard, active work; he spent twelve hours a day at his regular job as a mechanic; at night he kept himself busy either working around his house or helping friends with their household repairs; he was unhappy if he could not be always physically active; he had taken no vacation in years. He emphasized how much he needed to be self-sufficient and independent: he liked to do everything for himself without help; he never asked other people for advice or assistance; he never borrowed or sought favors. On the other hand, he was always ready to lend a hand to anyone who needed it. He never felt exploited or resentful when others availed themselves of his altruism. On the contrary, it pleased him to be of use to others, and he prided himself on being an even-tempered person who was never upset nor angry, however trying a situation might be.

His wife spontaneously and independently corroborated his comments. "Doctor," she said, "he is famous in our town for being good-tempered, exceedingly generous, and independent. Sometimes I think he's too much that way." She went on to complain mildly that she sometimes resented his willingness to help other people—his readiness to replace a broken window pane or to repair a leaky faucet for his neighbors. She emphasized, however, what a courageous man he was; before his final collapse, he had kept up his arduous schedule even when it meant dragging himself around in great pain. His fortitude had so impressed his many friends and neighbors that they had collected a goodly sum of money and had persuaded him to accept it toward defraying the expenses of his trip to America.

During his hospitalization extensive examinations confirmed the diagnosis of a ruptured lumbar disk, and indicated that his continued pain following his first operation was the result of scar tissue involving the spinal nerve roots in that area. The extent of his symptoms, however, went far beyond what could be explained by his physical findings, and observations of his behavior gave evidence that emotional factors were important both in increasing old symptoms and producing new ones. The patient was very much concerned about his disability. He insisted over and over again that he "had to get going," that the "inactivity was killing him," that he would "rather be dead than a hopeless cripple." Although he seemed to be quite sincere in making these statements, his behavior belied his overt attitudes. During his entire stay in the hospital, he lay passively and helplessly in bed. He would not make the slightest move to do anything for himself, even when it was possible for him to do so. He was excessively demanding of the nurses' attention and help, and organized the other patients on the ward into a squadron of personal servants to take care of his wants. It was hard to say exactly how he had achieved this, but he had managed somehow to arouse the sympathy and admiration of his fellow patients so that they catered completely to his whims; furthermore, they were critical of the staff of doctors and nurses for not responding to all the patient's demands and for trying to make him exert himself within the limits of his actual physical capacities. The patient himself did not appear overtly to resent these attempts on the part of the staff, but he effectively countered them: whenever he was made to stand up, he slumped and wobbled and drooped and writhed and struggled and groaned and panted and contorted his face as if he were trying his utmost to succeed, but at the cost of great agony in the struggle. All of this was utterly out of keeping with the considerable degree of physical strength and ability which objective examinations showed him to possess. His attitude, expressed in every groan and movement, was one of "This is agony, Doctor, but I'm a courageous man; I'm doing my

best to make it"—a type of behavior that induced one observer to entitle him "the hobbling hero."

As a result of these detailed observations and examinations a complex clinical diagnosis was made. It was judged
that the patient was suffering from a mild arachnoiditis involving the lumbar nerve roots, as a result of the irritation
from his previous ruptured intervertebral disk and surgery.
His extensive paralyses, however, could not anatomically
be attributed to this disease process alone. It was clear that
he was also suffering from the psychoneurosis *conversion
hysteria*, which produced not only the paralyses of his upper
extremities, but accounted as well for the exaggeration of
his leg symptoms and for his general pattern of behavior.
This latter diagnostic label was a description, not an explanation of the etiology of his illness. To understand the
reasons for his condition, it was necessary to carry out a
more extensive psychiatric investigation.

Because his total collapse had occurred after his second
operation, the focus of psychiatric interviews was directed
to this event in the hope of uncovering relevant emotional
problems. The patient stated in a matter-of-fact way that he
had not really wanted the second operation. He had been
afraid that it might make him worse; and furthermore, although he did have pain, he was satisfied with his ability to
work and function despite the limitations imposed by his
condition. His doctors, however, had strongly recommended
a second operation to try to relieve the pain, his family had
urged him to have it, and, therefore, against his own better
judgment, he had complied. When he was asked if he had
resented the pressure brought to bear on him to undergo
surgery, he denied having had such feelings. He spoke very
quietly, calmly, and without show of emotions about the
entire matter.

In an attempt to diminish what appeared clinically to be
an inhibition of his expression of affect the patient was given

the sedative sodium amytal intravenously. It was hoped thus
to uncover aspects of the patient's psychological life which
would aid in confirming the impression that emotions were
important in the formation of many of his symptoms. The
effect of the drug was striking; as the patient now discussed
the second operation, he told with considerable show of resentment how his doctors had called him almost daily to
urge him to enter the hospital immediately for an operation.
His family's pressure was even greater and more insistent.
His mother told him he "owed it to his family to get completely well" and that he was "only being selfish to refuse
the operation." His wife added her urgent persuasion and
finally threatened to divorce him if he did not go along with
her wishes. When he finally agreed to the operation he was
told that the procedure would take three hours; in actual
fact, he was in the operating room for eleven hours, because
"the specialists left in the middle for lunch." He was "boiling
mad" about this, but felt he could make no complaints because "it might make a breach with the surgeons." As the
patient described these pressures and his attempts to with-
stand them, he began to express greater and greater anger
at everyone involved, both family and doctors, of whom he
said vehemently, "They stink!" Suddenly, speaking of at
last deciding for surgery, he said, "So I finally decided if
I had to cut my throat, I *would* cut my throat—and here I
am; the family needed a lesson."

After this comment, the patient went to sleep. When he
awoke he had no memory of the interview, of the rage he
had expressed, or of the details of his family's and the doctors' behavior which he had recounted while under the influence of the drug. Instead, now that he was awake again,
he spoke without anger or feelings, and described the circumstances of his surgery exactly as he had done before
being given the sodium amytal. He was aware of none of
the details that he had revealed while drugged. Nevertheless

the observations of his behavior and associations while nar-
cotized gave a partial clue to his paradoxical behavior—that
although he professed a strong urge to get on his feet, he
behaved quite the opposite by lying passively in bed when
unstimulated, and by resisting with dramatic contortions of
his body and agonized facial expressions all attempts to mo-
bilize him. His behavior gave the impression that he was
emphasizing in pantomime to all observers how desperately
crippled he was and how much he suffered from pain. The
observations made under sodium amytal indicated that
there was a *motivation toward illness* beneath the surface, of
which the patient was not consciously aware—a motivation
stronger than his conscious wish to become active; beneath
the surface was the wish to show his family that he was right
after all when he had refused surgery, the wish to make them
suffer for their behavior and for having forced him into
something he had not wanted to do. "The family needed a
lesson."

When the patient was fully alert and conscious he showed
and expressed no anger or resentment toward his family; he
was consciously aware of no such feelings. When the inhibi-
tions imposed by his ego defenses were rendered partially
inoperative by the artificial means of sodium amytal narcosis, he expressed and felt great resentment toward his
family and his doctors; furthermore, he indicated that his
being paralyzed and totally invalided was a means of expressing this. His condition was a constant, living reproof
to his family for having forced him into further surgery. His
paralysis was *not* the result of damage to his central nervous
system, peripheral nerves, or musculoskeletal apparatus.
The disturbance lay in higher functions which can best be
understood in psychological, motivational terms. His anger
and resentment were translated into, were *converted* into,
and expressed by a malfunctioning of his physical body.

The patient was not aware of this mechanism of conversion. He was not aware of the motivation for these symptoms, or of the anger expressed in them. All he knew was that he was sick: he was paralyzed; he could hardly move his arms and barely lift his head off the bed; he was totally incapacitated. The symptoms were something foreign to him; they had afflicted him, like any sickness, from causes outside of himself and beyond his control; he was not aware of the role of his unconscious feelings and motivations in producing them. He did not, therefore, have to assume responsibility for the action (or perhaps better, inaction) of his body, and all the expense and grief it was causing his family. Furthermore, through this mechanism of conversion, he remained unaware of his anger toward his family; he could continue to think of himself as a loving, giving, altruistic, and co-operative and friendly person, free of anger and resentment. He was spared the anxiety that would ensue from the emergence into consciousness of an anger and an impulse to aggressive action which would be in conflict with these ideals for himself. Unlike the patients we have observed who became anxious as their anger obtruded into consciousness, Francis S. remained free of anxiety. The impulse and the feeling were directly converted into the symptoms; these protected him from the anxiety and at the same time allowed him to express his real feelings and wishes without having to be aware of the aggressive nature of his actions and without having to take responsibility for them. The cost, however, of this defensive maneuver to his ability to lead a normal life was incalculable.

Once again we discover that a psychoneurotic symptom is the result of a compromise among inner psychological forces. Both Chester B.'s obsessive-compulsive neurosis and Francis S.'s hysteria prove to be the end result of a conflict over the aggressive impulse which if expressed would lead to anxiety. To avoid the latter, the ego erects defenses against the impulse (and its associated feelings and fantasies), which control the impulse, keep it out of conscious awareness, and at the same time permit a distorted expression of it, which in this disguised form is acceptable to the ego. It is clear that the difference in the type of symptoms results not from the nature of the impulse but from the kind of defense employed against it; *conversion* leads to hysterical paralysis; *isolation* and *undoing* to obsessive thoughts and compulsive acts. The structure of the ego determines the form of the psychological illness.

It is important to note that aggression was not the only factor which entered into Francis S.'s symptoms; as is often the case there were multiple determinants in the production of his illness. The symptoms served another function: they allowed him to be completely passive, dependent, and cared for by others. His needs to be dependent, which he repudiated since he consciously wanted to be an active, independent person, could be gratified without his having to accept such needs as his own or to assume responsibility for them. Dependency needs and aggression are both important elements in the human being's reaction to injury and physical illness, which we shall be considering later in greater detail.

In Carol E., a woman of 28 with a phobia of boats, we again find overt anxiety as a prominent symptom. Her treatment extended over a period of nearly two years of weekly interviews, and it was therefore possible (in contrast to Chester B. and Francis S., who were seen more briefly) to watch in the development of her therapy the emergence into consciousness of childhood memories which provided a genetic basis for her symptoms. Like Chester B., she suffered from irrational fears but, unlike him, she had no obsessions or compulsions, and her personal life and relations had been more nearly normal. A survey of the main themes which appeared during the progress of her treatment will enable us, therefore, to examine in more detail the elements that enter into the formation of a phobic symptom, and at the same time to see the complex nature of a psychoneurotic illness.

Her fear of boats, which had started abruptly some years before she began treatment, was an inconvenient symptom. Whenever she caught sight of a boat of any size or shape, she would be seized with an attack of acute anxiety; gradually even pictures of these, in the newspaper, on television, or in the movies, would produce the same effect. She could prevent the anxiety only by avoiding the sight of the object she feared; her husband and young son were her staunch allies—they systematically cut out pictures of boats from the papers and magazines that came into the house, and hurriedly switched off the television set whenever a ship appeared on the scene. They were unable, of course, to do anything about real boats, which was unfortunate, since the patient lived in a small harbor town. As her illness progressed the patient began to avoid places where it might be possible to see the boats in the harbor or at sea; her life and her activities finally became so restricted that she was forced to seek psychiatric help.

In the early interviews of her treatment, as she talked about her phobia and her anxiety, her spontaneous associations turned to her fear of men. It soon became apparent that this was another major fear in her life; she sensed in almost any man who looked at her a bid to sexual intercourse. When her husband was not with her, she was filled with fearful fantasies of seduction and sexual attack. An insurance salesman, for example, came to her house one day when her husband was away; when he sat down on the couch beside her with a contract and started to run over the clauses in small print, she was frightened he was going to attack her. She was similarly scared of the milkman because he on occasion made familiar remarks when he delivered the morning milk. She was afraid of one of her husband's friends because he had once complimented her on her hair. She saw and feared sexual lust in almost any man she met.

Gradually there emerged from these associations ideas with a new quality: not only was she afraid of aggression *from* men; she harbored *toward* men strong aggressive impulses of her own. These too were connected with sexuality; she was enraged at men for their sexual interests and behavior. She described, for example, having had one day an almost irresistible impulse to break a chair over the head of a traveling salesman who came to her door and made what she felt was a suggestive remark. She complained that sexual relations with her husband were disgusting and intolerable; when he approached her she would react with a feeling of fury, and often feigned a headache to avoid him. She was particularly angered at his habit of wandering around their bedroom dressed only in his pajama tops, naked from the waist down. She could not tolerate any indication on his part that he had sexual interests; she found him on one occasion looking at some pornographic photographs and lost control of herself; in a sudden fit of destructive rage, she began to run around the living room pulling pictures from the wall, dashing table lamps to the floor, and hurling loose crockery at her husband as he hastily retreated.

The wealth of associations of this nature that poured from the patient indicated how closely sexuality and aggression were intertwined within her. Her comments about men were characterized by acrid remarks about their dirty, disgusting sexual behavior; she was impelled to hurt them, to fight them, to drive them off; at the same time she expected a brutal assault from them. Sexuality had for her a violent sadistic and masochistic coloring that filled her with anxiety whenever the subject arose, within an interview or without.

Gradually, as she talked in this vein over the course of a number of therapeutic hours, she began to recall long-forgotten memories of childhood, which shed light on the early history of her adult anxieties. She remembered as a little girl of five or six being very much frightened of a man who had made an aunt illegitimately pregnant. He was and remained for her a "gruesome character," and she was filled with fantasies in childhood that he would climb in her bedroom window at night and attack her. She recalled an old man who lured her into a small shipyard one day and to her horror exposed himself. She would often run all the way home from school in terror lest a strange man dart out from a dark corner and grab her. As these memories emerged, she began to recall similar feelings about her father. She suddenly remembered in one therapeutic hour how when she was four or five her father had carried her around in the morning in his arms; he was clad only in his pajama tops, naked from the waist down (like her husband, later) and she recalled her disgust when she saw his genitals and how she "hated the closeness to him." On another occasion she had been shocked and disgusted when she had seen him put his hand inside her mother's dress to fondle her breast. She looked upon him as a brutal man, who philandered and was "cruel to my poor mother." These attitudes survived into her adulthood in attenuated form: her father, she felt, was a selfish, tyrannical, hot-tempered old man for whom she had no affection.

As the patient unburdened herself over the weeks in therapy of these memories and fantasies, her acute fear of boats lessened. However, for a while she became more generally anxious and uneasy, and in particular her fear of sexual attack from men became almost continuous. She began to find it hard to walk on the street because she expected men to jump out at her and rape her; at home she was in constant anxiety when her husband was away from the house lest someone force entry to harm her in this way. At the same time an interesting new note crept into her associations: she began occasionally to express a positive interest and desire for sexual experience. She developed romantic fantasies of going out on dates, of picking up men in a bar, of going to a fashionable resort and having a passionate affair. At first, as these ideas emerged into consciousness, the patient was disturbed by them and tried to repudiate them. Gradually, however, she became less concerned about having such desires and began occasionally, for the first time in years, to want and to enjoy sexual intercourse with her husband.

It should be kept in mind that the patient was always well aware of the imaginary nature of all of her ideas; she was able to look at them with considerable objectivity as they appeared in her mind, and to distinguish them from the reality of her actual life, which except for rare temper outbursts and the restrictions imposed by her anxiety, was quite proper and orderly. The ideas were important, however, in that they gave the first clues about the function of her phobia and the nature of her conflict: it was her own outgoing, positive, direct desire for sexual love which was primarily responsible for her anxiety. This impulse had been unconscious until it emerged with the help of therapy: it then became clear that the patient had kept it hidden from herself behind her wealth of sado-masochistic fears. In diagrammatic form we may conceive of her defensive maneuvers as having the following steps: (1) "I do not want and love men (the frightening impulse); on the contrary, I hate them" —an ego defense called *reversal of affect;* (2) "Men lust after me and are going to hurt me in a sexual attack"—a *projection* of both her sexual and aggressive impulses onto outside objects. These defenses kept men at a distance, and helped to keep her own frightening positive desires from entering into her relationship with them. But this solution to her conflict over her sexual impulse only created new problems, for now she was faced with her fear of men as a substitute for her fear of her own desires. The next and last step in the erection of her defenses resulted in the phobia:

(3) "It is not men I am afraid of, but boats." She *displaced* her anxiety from men onto boats in an attempt to control the anxiety. Theoretically this should be an effective defense: men are ubiquitous and hard to avoid; boats are less prevalent and one may more readily keep away from them, thus avoiding the stimulus to anxiety. In actuality, her phobic symptom was not an adequate protection; she was not able successfully to avoid seeing boats, nor was she able completely to displace all of her anxiety over men onto the phobic object. Her fear of men was constantly erupting into her feelings and ideas.

These formulations do not as yet explain for us many aspects of the patient's illness. In particular we need to understand why in the first place her sexual impulse should cause her anxiety, and how boats came to be chosen as the phobic object. The further unfolding of her fantasies and feelings as they emerged in the continuing therapy provided at least partial answers to the questions.

In addition to her own sexual desires, the patient began to talk about pregnancy. This too had always been a frightening aspect of a woman's life. As an adolescent she had developed very disturbing notions of the process after reading a description of parturition in a medical text; it seemed to her that giving birth to a child left a woman painfully and irretrievably ripped, torn, and mutilated. A previously unconscious memory emerged in this context; she recalled that when she was five, her brother Bill was born at home. As she sat in the living room aware of the bustle and confusion upstairs, she had the idea that the doctor painfully broke her mother's legs to extract the child; she was convinced that if she did not keep out of the doctor's sight, he would do the same to her. When, shortly after her marriage, she became pregnant herself, she was seized with a paroxysm of fear at what was ahead of her, and tried unsuccessfully to abort herself by drinking hot wine. After an anxious nine months she was uneventfully delivered of a healthy boy; at that time she developed a transient phobia of boats, which disappeared spontaneously in a few weeks. From then on she refused to get pregnant again, despite the fact that her husband wanted more children.

As these memories and fantasies took the stage, the patient developed a consuming interest that puzzled her. She found herself irresistibly drawn to reading every story about illegitimate pregnancies and abortions she could find in the pulp magazines that open their pages to the confessions of wronged women. Her interest was a mixed blessing; she was fascinated by these accounts, but often became so anxious in the course of reading them that she would have to put down the magazine. She said of this one day, "It's just like the boats—I always wanted to look at them, but I always was so frightened that I couldn't."

The connection of boats with her sexual conflict became more understandable as she developed another and related theme. During the course of one hour, she mentioned that when she was seventeen "something awful had happened" with a boy of whom she was then very fond. As she said this, she became acutely panicky, jumped from her chair, ran to the window, threw it open, and stuck out her head gasping for air. For many weeks she could say nothing more about this, but would become overwhelmed with anxiety whenever the doctor introduced the topic. Gradually, however, she began to talk about it. Jim, her friend, had a boat on which they spent many initially happy hours together alone. As their romance developed and Jim became increasingly insistent, she allowed herself one day when they were far from shore to indulge in an episode of minor sexual play. Initially she maintained that she had found this disgusting, and that she had been so angered by Jim's behavior that she had broken off her relationship with him. Suddenly, however, in the middle of a therapeutic hour, accompanied by panic and another rush to the window, she blurted out, "The awful thing was that I *liked* it." In the context of this same episode she exclaimed, "Supposing I had got pregnant —it would have killed my mother." She then went on to describe how she had felt that her mother knew and utterly disapproved of her relationship with Jim. When she would come home after a day on the water, she could sense her mother glowering at her, and could only lower her eyes and sneak off to her room. It was in reality because of these feelings about her mother that she had felt forced to give Jim up.

This reference to her mother opened up a whole new area for psychiatric exploration. Up to this point she had always thought of and presented her mother as a sweet and loving woman who had protected her from the harsh discipline and cruelty of her father. Now, as she said, she "suddenly realized for the first time" that this was not completely true. Her mother was in reality a strict, critical, rigid moralist who disapproved of many things that the patient did or wanted to do. She had not only been opposed to Jim, but had several years later been against her marriage to her husband. The patient, with some misgivings, in this case defied her mother's disapproval, but remained convinced that her mother had frowned on her choice of a husband and was bitterly opposed to her having children. She felt that her mother resented her and was jealous of her because she was attractive, had pretty hair, nice clothes, and a husband who helped her around the house. She remembered, too, long-forgotten memories of difficulties in childhood. She recalled feeling anger and resentment toward her mother immediately after her brother Bill was born. Though only five, she was delighted with the baby and in a motherly way wanted to help take care of him. In particular she was fascinated by his genitalia and like to peep at them under his diapers. Her mother strictly forbade all these activities and one day, when she caught the patient peeping, chastised her severely. As she recalled this in the interview, she was suddenly filled with anger mixed with intense, anxious guilt and said that "even now" she felt as if she had "committed the worst crime in the world." These memories were linked with recollections of how her mother in times of personal stress and unhappiness would threaten to kill herself or to run away and leave the children to fend for themselves. The patient still felt anger and frightened longing as she reflected on her mother's outbursts.

At the same time as her image of her mother changed, she became aware of new, previously unconscious feelings toward her father. She now remembered that as a child there had been a period during which she had been very close to him. He had obviously been very fond of her, had many pet names for her, and had given her a lot of loving attention. She recalled a long-lost episode from her fourth or fifth year: her mother was sick in bed; her father on the sly gave her a piece of candy, forbidden her by her mother, and hid with her under a bed while she half-fearfully consumed it. She remembered feeling that her mother resented her close tie to her father.

During the time that the patient was struggling to talk about these disturbing ideas and feelings, two interesting events occurred. One day she came to her interview acutely depressed and in tears over a minor, but to her important crisis. She had asked her mother for one of the kittens which her mother's cat had recently produced. She had suddenly become convinced that her request would not be granted because in a small fit of pique she had refused to do her mother a favor. She expected her mother to retaliate, and on the assumption that her fear was reality, was filled with a sense of sadness and longing for her mother's favor, affection, and largesse. Her mood improved only when a few days later she was after all given her kitten.

In this context the patient had a dream that made a great impression on her: she had (she dreamed) a new baby whom she loved with tremendous poignancy and tenderness. The feeling was intensely real and pleasurable, but it thoroughly perplexed her, because her conscious attitudes toward pregnancy and babies had always been so completely contrary. After reporting the dream she came to her hour a week later in acute anxiety because she was convinced she was pregnant, although this was in reality impossible. Gradually, over the succeeding weeks there emerged through her fear and anxiety over pregnancy a growing positive desire for more children, which coincided with an increased feeling of conflict with her mother. It was, moreover, very hard for her to discuss her mother with her doctor, because the topic often made her acutely anxious; on one occasion she cried out, "I'd rather see a boat than talk about my mother!"

At length, her wish for a baby won out, and for the first time in ten years she intentionally conceived. By now, after nearly a year and a half of therapy, she was in many ways improved: her phobia had disappeared, she was generally less tense, her sexual life had improved, and her social activities and relationships with her friends were comfortable and pleasurable for her. The full force of her anxiety was focused on her mother and this mounted as her pregnancy drew closer to term. She was in particular concerned over her mother's questions about her plans for the new infant and her offers to help. The patient feared in ways she could not specify that her mother wanted to do harm to the child, or to take it away from her. Somewhat to the doctor's surprise, the patient accepted his comment that maybe her mother's intentions were friendly, and that perhaps she might do well to share her interests and pleasure with her mother. The patient, acting on this, began to see her mother more frequently, to shop with her for clothes for the expected infant, and discovered that both she and her mother despite her mixed feelings and fantasies shared warm affection for one another.

Therapy was ended shortly before the baby was born, and the patient informed the doctor by letter about his arrival.

> You'll be happy to hear that I had my baby. A little boy and he weighs 7 lbs. 10½ oz. . . . I have never felt better in my life. I'm so relaxed . . . I never dreamed having a baby could be so enjoyable. My mother thinks I'm nuts but it doesn't bother me in the least. She said she's glad it's me and not her that's having a baby. I just looked at her and laughed. She doesn't know what she's missing. I didn't realize what I was missing either . . . By the way my mother and I are the best of friends and she's been a great help to us while I was in the hospital before and after I came home. This also makes me happy.

Now that we have followed the patient through the twistings and turnings of her path toward health, it is time to see what further light her associations cast on the questions we earlier asked ourselves concerning the choice of her phobic object and the reason for her fear of sexuality. It would be well to remember that our answers are in all likelihood incomplete—that further relevant factors lie unavailable to us in that part of the patient's mental life that did not come to light in the course of her therapy.

The choice of boats as the phobic object seems clearly related to her experiences with Jim. It was with him that her first serious adult love affair occurred against a background of sea and ships; and it was with him that she ran aground on her anxiety and her sexual conflicts. Given the tendency of her ego to use the defense mechanism of displacement, it is not surprising that her conflict was displaced onto the boats so intimately tied to her sexual experiences. What is not clear from our material is why she chooses the mechanism of displacement in preference to some other common defense—isolation, for example, or conversion.

The reason for her anxiety over her sexual impulse is also partially evident. It is not only because of its association with the frightening sado-masochistic fantasies which we noted earlier; more importantly, it is because she feels that her mother disapproves of her sexual desires (and the closely related wish for a baby). This forces a dilemma upon her: on the one hand she wants to express herself freely in defiance of her mother; on the other, she fears the pain which would result from loss of her mother's love and affection; the unpleasant quality of this pain was apparent in her tearful, lonely depression when she was convinced she could not have her kitten.

For an adult, a conflict such as the patient presents seems absurd in the face of reality. It is just this quality of absurdity, however, that leads us to judge it neurotic; the patient is bound and restricted by her fears and fantasies; she has lost her freedom to exploit and enjoy the actually permissible possibilities of the real world. In the light of her childhood experiences, her adult behavior becomes at least intelligible; for we find that her adult neurotic patterns are replicas of childhood models, still alive within her and, though unconscious (before therapy), stamping her with their die. In childhood we find her love for her father and her interest in babies; in childhood we find her running into conflict over this with her mother; and in childhood we find her giving up her love for her father behind the fantasies that even then developed of men as dangerous and attacking creatures. In many little girls (as we have earlier indicated) these are common fears and fantasies in the Oedipal phase of development, but ordinarily the child grows beyond them and can safely allow herself a close, loving heterosexual relationship. It is not clear from what we have learned about our patient exactly *why* she became stuck at this phase of her development; it is clear, however, that her development was arrested at this point, and that her subsequent life was profoundly affected by this developmental disturbance. It is perhaps not entirely accurate to look on this earlier difficulty as a simple *arrest* of progress. Her tendency to give up relationships with men and to turn to her mother for love and support was a return, a *regression,* to earlier, pre-Oedipal phases of development, when the primary focus of a child's life is on his dependent relationship to his mother. Her adult anxiety over loss and separation from her mother as well as her need for her mother stemmed from this earlier time of her life.

Whenever we are confronted with the problem of anxiety, there are two questions that must be asked about it: *What* is the patient anxious about? *Why* is he anxious about it? In Carol E. we can find answers to both of these questions. She is, in the first place, anxious about both her sexual and her aggressive impulses, and their derivative fantasies and feelings. In the second place, she is anxious about them because of the consequences she fears from uncontrolled expression of them. This anxiety of hers has three forms, which reflect the three common types of signal anxiety (which we have earlier distinguished from panic, a replica of the anxiety experienced by the infant who is overwhelmed by uncontrollable and unavoidable stimuli, such as unsatisfied hunger). (1) We find her first of all experiencing guilt (her guilt over the crime of looking at her baby brother, for example), or *superego anxiety,* which dates to the immediate post-Oedipal period of life when parental commands, sanctions, and ideals have been internalized and made an integral part of one's own personality structure as the superego. (2) Secondly, she fears attack and the consequent physical injury to her body. Referable to the genital, Oedipal phase of development, this is called *castration anxiety,* because the fantasies central to it are concerned with genital mutilation. (3) And, finally, she exhibits *separation anxiety*—a fear of desertion by or the loss of the love of an important person, which has its roots in the pre-Oedipal periods when the child's dependency is in the ascendance. She is anxious lest any or all of these fearful situations occur if she does not control her impulses and her wishes. It becomes apparent, then, that anxiety, like the impulses and the ego, has a developmental history; and, like the stages of the other streams of development, the earlier editions of anxiety are found repeated in the adult.

The patient's phobia, as we examine it, proves to be only the final expression of a complex psychological process. The product of specific mechanisms of defense, it stands as the patient's own individual symbol for a conflict that involves many layers of her adult personality structure and many legacies from her childhood phases of development. As a symptom it was not nearly so effective at controlling her anxiety as Francis S.'s conversion hysteria, or at hiding from her consciousness the truth about her impulses as Chester B.'s obsessions and compulsions. But its very inefficiency was the result of an instability in the structure of her neurosis that allowed her with help to get well. Since there was flexibility and fluidity in the functioning of her defenses, she was able to make conscious previously unconscious impulses, fantasies, and feelings; she could benefit from the curative power of self-knowledge.

X

THE PHENOMENOLOGY OF DEPRESSION AND GRIEF

Anxiety, as we have said, is a fearful anticipation of something unpleasant to come; depression, a response to an unpleasant event that has happened. The anticipation of loss, which is central to separation anxiety, derives its power to disquiet the soul from the fact that loss is a painful human experience; it is the occurrence of loss that leads to depression.

We must be clear at the outset about two related, but separate uses of the word "depression." In the first instance, it refers to a group of inner mental events experienced by the individual who feels "depressed." In its second meaning, it is used to designate a clinical syndrome which is defined partly by the subjective feelings of the patient, partly by the character of the patient's observed behavior and partly by the temporal patterns of the symptoms and signs.* Although we shall be using illustrative material from people with clinical depressions, we shall be focusing our attention mainly on depression as an experience, since it is here that we shall find the key to its psychopathology.

Most of us have at some time felt depressed in greater or lesser degree. Since everything changes as time flows, and change entails loss, this is not surprising. "Melancholy,"

* For a full discussion of depressive syndromes the reader is referred to the standard textbooks of psychiatry, e.g. J. R. Ewalt, E. A. Strecker, and F. G. Ebaugh (5), or D. K. Henderson and R. D. Gillespie (6).

comments Amiel,* "is at the bottom of everything, just as at the end of all rivers is the sea ... Can it be otherwise in a world where nothing lasts, where all we have loved or shall love must die? Is death, then, the secret of life? The gloom of an eternal mourning enwraps, more or less closely, every serious and thoughtful soul, as night enwraps the universe."

In the two patients we are about to examine, our task is twofold: (1) on the one hand we must analyze intellectually the phenomena we are to observe; we must isolate, describe and classify the component parts of the state of depression; (2) on the other, we must empathize with the patient. We must attempt, insofar as we are able, to feel within ourselves what he has experienced in order to know immediately and intimately the nature of the phenomena which we are examining. We must allow ourselves to be moved by his account, to look within ourselves for memories of the same feelings in the history of our own lives, to share experiences with him. Such non-rational knowledge cannot be gained by intellectual analysis and conceptualization alone, any more than the beauty of a sunset can be appreciated by observing it through a spectroscope. Each of our tasks requires a separate mental operation.

Both of our patients were the victims of intermittent periods of severe clinical depressions. Reviewing his disorder in retrospect, John C. writes as follows (32):

> The features of the depressive state are precisely the reverse of those of the manic. Instead of a sense of well-being I feel miserable and ill; instead of a heightened sense of reality I seem ...

> ... to move among a world of ghosts
> And feel myself the shadow of a dream.

This feeling is closely linked with a sort of strengthening of the barriers of individuality, a hardening of the shell of the

* Amiel, Henri-Frédéric, *Journal intime,* trans. by Mrs. Humphry Ward, Macmillan and Co., London, 1893.

ego. I seem shut into myself, withdrawn from real contact with the outer world as also from contact with God; the sun does not really shine, the trees and fields are not really green; I am shut in with my thoughts, always of a depressing and melancholy nature.

This sense of isolation, of being cut off from God, one's fellows and the world, seems to me to be the paramount feature underlying the whole state . . .

Moral tension returns in full force. I am haunted by a sense of guilt; my conscience gives me no rest, even when there do not seem to be any particularly grievous sins upon it. Whatever I am doing I feel I ought to be doing something else. I worry perpetually about my past sins and failures; not for a moment can I forget the mess I seem to have made of my life. However I may pray for and think of forgiveness, no forgiveness comes. Eventually the terrors of Hell approach. . . .

As depression progresses . . . instead of the light of ineffable revelation, I seem to be in perpetual fog and darkness. I cannot get my mind to work; instead of associations "clicking into place," everything is an inextricable jumble; instead of seeming to grasp a whole, it seems to remain tied to the actual consciousness of the moment. The whole world of my thought is hopelessly divided into incomprehensible, watertight compartments. I could not feel more ignorant, undecided or inefficient. It is appallingly difficult to concentrate, and writing is pain and grief to me.

As for wickedness, although my mind has not reached the stage of regarding myself as the most wicked person in the world and responsible for all the sin and evil afflicting mankind, I know too well that it can do so. That appalling self-centeredness is the reverse of the delusions of grandeur and power. It leads to the uttermost depths.

In this description we are presented with several common characteristics of depression. Although we must examine them separately they are not necessarily isolated or unrelated to one another. (1) Depression is acutely painful. (2)

There is a feeling of separation from other people and a loss of emotional contact with them accompanied by a sense of aloneness and utter isolation. (3) Secondary to a loss of interest in what is going on around him, the world appears to the patient to be a dull, drab, dead, uninteresting, and unexciting place. These latter two characteristics contribute to (4) the narrowing and lessening of his sense of himself, the constriction and diminution of himself as a person, and his feeling of weakness, smallness, helplessness, and inefficiency, especially as far as his mental powers are concerned. Two further features are manifested in the quality of his thought processes. (5) Everything is an effort, concentration is poor and logical thought difficult. (6) Those thoughts which he does have are gloomy and melancholy. Prominent among these are ideas of being worthless and sinful—the prickings of a stringent conscience.

Let us turn now to a patient trying from the very depths of depression to describe what he felt. This was difficult for him to do, for he was markedly slowed down in speech and movements (a behavior characteristic of some depressive states, known as *retardation*). He spoke in a sad, plaintive, at times tearful and sing-song tone of voice, which was sometimes so low that it was hard to hear him. There were many long pauses between sentences, and what is written took many times longer for the patient to speak than it does to read it. Here, as recorded, is what he said:

> Everything seems to be contradictory. I don't seem to know what else to tell you, but that I am tearful and sad —and no kick out of Christmas. And I used to get such a boot out of it . . . It's an awful feeling . . . I don't get a bit of a kick out of anything. Everything seems to get so sort of full of despair . . . I can't get interested in other people. I only seem to be interested in my own self. Can you offer me any advice in any way? . . .

Sometimes you seem to have a load of friends and yet nobody you really love ... You feel awful lonesome ... You just feel low ... not a laugh nor a kick out of anything ... It's all so sort of vague and hollow—nothing behind it ... I hear and see everybody who comes to work so full of smiles and laughter and happiness. With me it's not like that at all. And why is it that every once in a while I feel it's all going to end in disaster?

I feel so sort of what I call "empty"—nothing in back of you like when you're feeling yourself ... You go to bed and you dread each day when you feel low like that ... And I try to keep saying to myself, like you say, that I haven't been that bad that I should have to punish myself. Yet my thinking doesn't get cheerful. When it doesn't get cheerful it makes you wonder will it all end in suicide sometime ...

I don't seem to have much feeling to want to go places —to concerts like I used to, and back to work. There just doesn't seem to be anything perking. Do you think I've improved at all? ...

I don't know why I don't get some help from praying. I ask God to help me through. I suppose it's my trial— guess I deserted the Lord for a long time ... When you feel low like this it all seems so hopeless. You dread the holiday and the long weekend ... This low feeling is so horrible ...

I cried terribly when the family left Sunday. If only I could be like they are—healthy, be one of them. The old fight seems to be gone ... I can't seem to say that I'm going to get well with any real conviction. It all seems so shallow.

Here once again we observe the painful feeling of isolation from people and things, the sense of a dull, dead world, the slowing down of inner thought processes, the melancholy mood, and the sense of helplessness. Particularly striking is the feeling of diminution and constriction as a person, which he describes as being "hollow," "shallow," "empty—

nothing in back of you like when you're feeling yourself."
It is as if he sensed that he had lost a part of himself; he
appears to feel that he is a different and lesser person from
the self he usually knew. We shall soon see that this is a central feature in the complex phenomenon of depression.

From both of these patients we learn the vocabulary of
depression: loneliness, agony, darkness, gloom, despair,
apathy, aridity, sinfulness, deadness, hopelessness, hell. Here
is a realm where, as another sufferer writes, there is nothing
but:

> A night without a morning,
> A trouble without end,
> A life of bitter scorning
> A world without a friend.*

As we turn now to an examination of the nature of loss,
our understanding will be helped by looking within ourselves to observe our own experience. Our concern is with
the loss of those things to which we are attached, to those
things we like or want, to what, in technical terms, we invest
with *libido,* a word designating that emotional force in all
of us that reaches out to objects in a positive way; liking,
love, wanting, appetite, sexual desire are all aspects of libido. We like what we value—or perhaps more accurately,
we value what we like. We find it painful and depressing to
give up or to lose what is of worth to us; and as an obvious
corollary, we lose without pain or concern only things of no
value.

What we value varies according to the nature of our personality and our past experience. Our own bodies are for
most of us at the center of our system of valuables. Each of

---

* *Poems of John Clare's Madness,* edited with an introduction by
Geoffrey Grigson, Routledge, London, 1949. Clare, a bucolic 19th-cen-
tury English poet, spent the last 25 years of his life in the Northampton
General Lunatic Asylum with a chronic depression, which permeates the
mood and imagery of much of his poetry from that period.

us esteems his physical self and, except under unusual circumstances, does all he can to protect himself from hurting or losing any part of it. Depression is a common companion of illness seriously affecting the body. Patients, for example, who lose a limb by surgery or by accident often pass through a period of reactive depression as they accept the fact of their loss and begin to make plans for a new life dictated by the limitations imposed by their disability.

The depression that ensues in such a patient results not only from the loss of physical function. He is frequently forced by his illness to give up a customary and cherished way of life. A profession, a trade, a favorite sport, an intellectual or artistic talent may all fall victim to the loss of an organ. Hopes and aspirations must be modified; income and security for his family and himself are threatened; his position in the social structure is altered; feelings of helplessness and weakness replace his former sense of strength and competence. All that a man is, the whole network of associations, memories, desires, and attitudes that forms a person's concept of himself is jeopardized by crippling illness. He does not relinquish these without a struggle or without pain.

It is apparent that loss may involve physical objects (whether these are parts of one's body or external valuables) and psychological entities—self-concepts, ideals, social status, etc. We shall later be considering in greater detail the psychological problems created by physical illness. Let us turn our attention now to the most poignant and important of losses—the death of a loved one.

It is a truism that we grow sad and depressed when a person we love dies; it is a truism because grief is universal and normal. In fact, a failure to grieve is evidence of psychological abnormality. Mourning is characteristically a state of mind, but it is accompanied by a host of painful somatic sensations. From a study of the reactions of a group of people to the sudden death of close relatives in a tragic fire, Lindemann (35) makes the following generalizations:

> The picture shown by persons in acute grief is remarkably uniform. Common to all is the following syndrome: sensations of somatic distress occurring in waves lasting from twenty minutes to an hour at a time, a feeling of tightness in the throat, choking with shortness of breath, need for sighing, and an empty feeling in the abdomen, lack of muscular power, and an intense subjective distress described as tension or mental pain. The patient soon learns that these waves of discomfort can be precipitated by visits, by mentioning the deceased, and by receiving sympathy. There is a tendency to avoid the syndrome at any cost, to refuse visits lest they should precipitate the reaction, and to keep deliberately from thought all references to the deceased.
>
> The striking features are (1) the marked tendency to sighing respiration; this respiratory disturbance was most conspicuous when the patient was made to discuss his grief. (2) The complaint about lack of strength and exhaustion is universal and is described as follows: "It is almost impossible to climb up a stairway." "Everything I lift seems so heavy." "The slightest effort makes me feel exhausted." "I can't walk to the corner without feeling exhausted." (3) Digestive symptoms are described as follows: "The food tastes like sand." "I have no appetite at all." "I stuff the food down because I have to eat." "My saliva won't flow." "My abdomen feels hollow." "Everything seems slowed up in my stomach."

The emotional aspect of grief is quite as painful as the somatic. Early students of the psychopathology of clinical depressions were struck by the marked similarity of the mental phenomena of mourning to those of depression. In both there is the same inner anguish, the same loss of interest in a dreary, empty world, the same isolation from other people, the same loneliness and feeling of inner emptiness. Furthermore both mourning and depression are processes having duration in time. Freud described the nature of this process of normal grief in his famous paper *Mourning and Melancholia* (33):

> In what now [he writes] does the work which mourning performs consist? I do not think there is anything far-fetched in presenting it in the following way. Reality-testing has shown that the loved object no longer exists, and it proceeds to demand that all libido shall be withdrawn from its attachment to that object. This demand arouses understandable opposition—it is a matter of general observation that people never willingly abandon a libidinal position, not even, indeed, when a substitute is already beckoning to them. This opposition can be so intense that a turning away from reality takes place and a clinging to the object through the medium of hallucinatory wishful psychosis. Normally, respect for reality gains the day. Nevertheless its orders cannot be obeyed at once. They are carried out bit by bit, at great expense of time and cathectic energy, and in the meantime the existence of the lost object is psychically prolonged. Each single one of the memories and expectations in which the libido is bound to the object is brought up and hypercathected, and detachment of libido is accomplished in respect of it. Why this compromise by which the command of reality is carried out piecemeal should be so extraordinarily painful is not at all easy to explain in terms of economics. It is remarkable that this painful unpleasure is taken as a matter of course by us. The fact is, however, that when the work of mourning is completed the ego becomes free and uninhibited again.

Mourning, as Freud says, is *work;* it requires mental effort and courage extended over a period of time to face the pain of grieving and to combat the tendency of the loving attachment to the lost person to persist. The fabric of memories and associations and feelings that permeate the image of the deceased in the mind of the bereaved survivor does not automatically disappear when the loved person dies. In the process of grieving each of the memories and associations must be revived in the mind's eye; as each is thought of, a fresh wave of grief occurs, which gradually fades. As each separate strand of the fabric of associations is thus worked over, it loses its power to evoke the pain of loss, and the loving attachment to the dead one gradually diminishes until the process is complete and the ghost is laid. The mourner is once again free to live and love in the world of the living.

Grief is a lonely process and it is not often that we can look into the mind of the mourner for an intimate view. Self-revelations such as that which Proust has given us of his reaction to the death of his sweetheart are, therefore, all the more valuable for perfusing our scientific generalizations with life.

> But now [he writes *] these words: "Mademoiselle Albertine has gone!" had expressed themselves in my heart in the form of an anguish so keen that I would not be able to endure it for any length of time ... If all of a sudden I thought of her room, her room in which the bed stood empty, of her piano, her motorcar, I lost all my strength, I shut my eyes, let my head droop upon my shoulder like a person who is about to faint.

The physical and mental pain of Proust's grief is evident. Evident, too, in what follows, is the repeated invocation of the many shades of the dead as the process of mourning progresses.

> I stepped across the room with endless precautions, I took up a position from which I could not see Albertine's

---

* Marcel Proust, *The Sweet Cheat Gone*. Volume 2 of *Remembrance of Things Past*, Random House, New York, 1934. For the purpose of demonstration and for reasons of brevity I have done violence to Proust's order and continuity. The entire book should be read by anyone interested in understanding grief.

chair, the pianola upon the pedals of which she used to press her golden slippers, nor a single one of the things which she had used and all of which, in the secret language which my memory had imparted to them, seemed to be seeking to give me a fresh translation, a different version, to announce to me for a second time the news of her departure . . . At every moment there was one more of these innumerable humble "selves" that compose our personality which was still unaware of Albertine's departure and must be informed of it; I was obliged . . . to describe to all these "selves" who did not yet know of it the calamity that had just occurred, it was necessary that each of them in turn should hear for the first time the words . . . "Albertine has gone." With each of my actions, even the most trivial, since they had all been steeped before in the blissful atmosphere which was Albertine's presence, I was obliged with a fresh expenditure of energy, with the same grief, to begin the apprenticeship of separation . . . to find consolation; it was not one, it was innumerable Albertines that I must first forget. . . .

And here, the grief work done, is the final emergence from gloom, the freedom from the lost love, and the turning to a new life:

Then the competition of other forms of life thrust this latest grief into the background, and, during those days which were the first days of spring, I even found . . . in imagining Venice and beautiful, unknown women, a few moments of pleasing calm . . . This state of which I had just had a foretaste . . . was . . . what would in time to come be my permanent state, a life in which I should no longer be able to suffer on account of Albertine, in which I should no longer be in love with her. Without my being precisely aware of it, it was now this idea of Albertine's death—no longer the present memory of her life—that formed the chief subject of my unconscious musings, with the result that if I interrupted them suddenly to reflect upon myself, what surprised me was not, as in earlier days, that Albertine so living in myself could be no longer upon earth, but that Albertine, who no longer existed upon earth, who was dead, should have remained so living in myself. Built up by the contiguity of the memories that followed one another, the black tunnel, in which my thoughts had been straying so long that they had even ceased to be aware of it, was suddenly broken by an interval of sunlight, allowing me to see in the distance a blue and smiling universe in which Albertine was no more than a memory, unimportant and full of charm . . . The person that I had been so short a time ago, who lived only in the perpetual expectation of the moment when Albertine would come in to bid him good night and to kiss him, in a sort of multiplication of myself made this person appear to me as no longer anything more than a feeble part, already half-detached from myself, and like a fading flower I felt the rejuvenating refreshment of an exfoliation.

Proust's is a normal grief. He speaks for people the world over who even now are slowly working their way through a similar painful, but necessary, process. There are times, however, when grief does not flow so smoothly; it becomes blocked or distorted in ways that have to be considered pathological. From these abnormal forms of mourning we are able to learn even more about the nature of clinical depressions than from uncomplicated, normal grief. For the latter, although it has the similarities we have noted, differs in a major way from depression: in simple grief one does not find the feelings of guilt nor the self-accusatory attitudes that characterize the depressed patient. In pathological grief, on the other hand, these feelings and attitudes are commonly present. Pathological forms of grief occur in people who are made especially vulnerable to losses of all sorts by an organization of character structure which we call narcissistic. We must, therefore, turn our attention now to the problem of narcissism.

XI

Narcissus, so says the old myth, was one of those beautiful Grecian youths who roamed the countryside of antiquity. One day he caught sight of his image reflected in a quiet sylvan pool and, struck with the beauty of what he saw, fell madly in love with himself. Filled with despair because he could not possess what he so deeply desired, he killed himself with a dagger. From a few drops of blood that fell on the ground beside the water grew the flower known ever since as the narcissus.

Such ardent self-love is rare in human experience. There are, however, lesser degrees of loving regard for one's self, or *narcissism,* which are common to all human beings. These concern not only one's physical body (especially in the face of disease and injury), but as well a person's image of himself as an individual and social human being.

All of us, in other words, have varying degrees of self-esteem. In order for a person to look upon himself as having value, he must feel that he is loved by other people, that he has strength and capabilities, and that he is good and loving. The ideal toward which he aspires is to be such a person. A conviction that we are unloved, helpless, or bad leads in all of us to a loss of self-esteem. This loss of an image of our selves which we value, is, like the loss of other valuables, accompanied by depression. As we have seen, a sense of personal helplessness and lowered self-esteem are important elements in the ego-state of people who are depressed; in addition, we may be highly self-critical and self-castigating when we have done something "bad," particularly when the bad action is erotic or aggressive.

In most of us the feeling of lowered self-esteem and depression that results from falling short of our ideals is short-lived. We are easily reassured by expressions of affection and comfort from other people; we "learn from our failures" and determine to do better next time; we reflect that others make mistakes, that no one is perfect, that to err is human; we remind ourselves that though we have failed here, in other areas our achievements are admirable; we are able to be intelligently critical but at the same time mercifully tolerant of ourselves.

Having failed and having lost self-esteem, we are reassured, as we have said, by the continued affection and admiration of others; this has its counterpart in our sense of shame and isolation from people when we are tormented by guilt. We make the assumption that others have the same standards of behavior we hold for ourselves, that they know we have failed, and judge us accordingly. In reality our estimation of ourselves may be quite different from what other people think of us. The feeling of reassurance and the relief from guilt and lowered self-esteem come partly from making this discovery.

It is not surprising that there should be such an intimate connection between our self-evaluation and others' evaluation of us, for in the developing child the former has its origin in the latter. The young child has no inner moral standards or ideals to govern his behavior. He is without conscience; he wants what he wants when he wants it, and any means to get it, fair or foul, are acceptable to him. The child's behavior is controlled by his parents, who impose their own standards on him, partly by force and partly by harsh, angry disapproval of his actions. The child is particularly sensitive to the latter, especially in the early years of his life when his very real helpless dependence on his parents puts him in a position where his self-esteem, his opportunity to grow, his very life depend on the help and love of his mother and father. The loss of these vital supplies is a painful occasion for the child and a strong lever to make him "behave." * His need for his parents' love and his fear of loss of it outweigh the pressure of his own urgent impulses. He learns to control the latter to preserve the former.

Gradually, as he develops, the child makes his parents' standards his own by a complicated process of psychological internalization known as *identification*. These now appear to him to be a part of his own personality; they become his own ideals that are valuable in themselves and guide his behavior whether his parents are there or not. Thus formed, the *superego* now contains in it the praising and criticizing attitudes formerly resident in the parents. The person now judges his own behavior; he praises or criticizes himself in the light of the standards he has made part of himself. But the superego never entirely takes over the task of censor; we never entirely entrust the control of our behavior to this heritage from the early figures of our lives from whom it took its coloring. Self-esteem still depends partly on the favorable regard of other people; most of us are more honorable when our behavior is observable; and all of us still tend to attribute to others the internal attitudes of our superego that historically were once the external attitudes of our parents. The wicked flee when no man pursueth.

Most people arrive at adult life with a reasonable superego; it provides adequate restraints without being overbearing or unduly harsh; it imposes standards and ideals that are within the person's abilities to achieve. It allows the individual to exist for the most part at peace with himself, free of an overburdening sense of guilt and sin. Some are not so

---

* We have already seen one legacy of this early moral suasion in the form of adult separation anxiety.

fortunate; they are born to parents who contribute to an unhealthy distortion of the early developmental process. If the parents set standards for behavior and make demands on the child beyond his capacity to comply, the child develops an exaggerated sense of inadequacy and helplessness. If the parents control behavior by harshness and angry aloofness untempered by sufficient love and tenderness, the child becomes the more dependent on them and the hungrier for the love denied him. As his superego develops, it adopts the parents' unrealistically high standards and ideals, as well as their punitive, critical attitudes, which now internalized, are turned upon the self. As an adult such a person exhibits character traits which have their origin in these childhood experiences. His ideals and goals and his demands on himself for performance are often utterly beyond his capacities to achieve. His failures lead to a dismal sense of inadequacy, of helplessness, and of painfully lowered self-esteem and depression. He is excessively critical of his derelictions. Love, attention, and admiration from other people ("narcissistic supplies") are essential for his self-esteem, and his demands for these supplies are at times insatiable—a manifestation of *oral dependency,* so called because the elements of this dependency and the related disturbances in human relationships are derived from that early period of childhood when oral drives are in the ascendancy and the child is still helplessly dependent on his parents. Adults with these difficulties are described as suffering from a *narcissistic character disorder,* or simply from *narcissism;* it should be recognized that the word narcissism thus used implies *pathological* narcissism, since, as we have seen, all human beings exhibit a certain degree of self-love.

Katherine D. was a young woman with such a narcissistic character disorder. A budding author, she had had several shorter pieces published and was highly regarded in intellectual circles, although the expectation of her friends did not match her own hopes for herself; her ambition was to make as significant a mark on the course of English literature as her beloved idol, Jane Austen. One day she came to a therapeutic hour in the depths of depression and despair. She had a splitting headache, pains in her chest and abdomen, and recurrent episodes of dizziness and light-headedness which convinced her she was about to lose her mind. Her troubles had started the afternoon before when her first novel was returned by the publisher with suggestions for revision. Her hopes crashed; she felt her career was at an end; she could never be the writer she dreamed of being. "I'm a failure," she said. "It's so shameful. I can never show myself to my friends again. I'm nothing. I've never felt so despairing and empty. Last night I lay in bed and sobbed and sobbed. I feel I've never done anything in my life and never will. And now I need help and reassurance from you. I don't get it, and that makes me furious." *

The stigmata of excessive narcissism are apparent in this sketch: the marked loss of self-esteem, the sense of inadequacy and the depression when faced with her failure to achieve an unrealistically high goal; her harsh self-criticism; her shame and need to isolate herself from her friends; her demand for help and reassurance from her doctor. All of us would, of course, be disappointed if we were in the patient's position; but few of us would show the wild intensity of despair that overcame her. In the light of her exacting demands on herself for artistic excellence, the return of the manuscript was a crushing blow; it was proof that she could never be one of the great authors in the tradition of the English novel; the only alternative was total, absolute, abysmal failure. There was for her no intermediate position between unbeatable superiority and unspeakable ignominy.

The same phenomena are apparent in Harold G., a young

* From notes made immediately after the hour.

lawyer with an unusual facility for honest self-observation. He had made an excellent record in law school and was embarked on a promising professional career when he developed acute anxiety and depression which forced him into the hospital. The long history of his character disturbance is evident in what he says of his childhood.

    Pt.   I've always worried about my ability to do things. It has gone on almost all my life. When I was a child I used to try to do things mechanically with my hands. I thought it was the thing to be able to do to show some intelligence. I tried to take one of those dollar watches apart because other boys my age were doing it . . . The mechanism in a watch is fairly complicated, and I decided that I was going to master this to show myself I had the ability to do this, because other people in my family are very mechanically inclined, and I always felt I did not have this ability. So I took the watch apart and cleaned it. I memorized every part in the watch so that I could tell how to put it together again. And I remembered it exactly and put it all back together again. But I did it so that the hands went backwards instead of forwards . . . I couldn't figure out what was wrong with it. I couldn't understand. I had memorized every part. I took it to a watchmaker and the man laughed at me, "Why you've done this thing correctly, but it's all backwards." And this gave me a feeling of insecurity. I have had a feeling of insecurity a long time.

    Dr.   What is this feeling?

    Pt.   That I'm incompetent . . . Also I felt that I wasn't loved. When I was a young boy I was obese—I was very fat . . . The boys used to make fun of me because I was fat —oh, they'd call me "Fat." And they would pick on me and fight with me. But it seems to me these are normal problems that a child has. This is the way life is.

    Dr.   You feel you were more sensitive than you needed to be?

    Pt.   Yes.

    Dr.   Have you any idea why it should have bothered

you, because it's true, there are lots of kids who are fat in this way.

Pt. I don't know. The fear of ridicule by other people has always bothered me. I've always tried to make myself important. This is probably why I've gone to big schools and gone as far as I have, because I like to feel that I'm important ... I've always worried about my inadequacies and fear of failure and what a disgrace it would be in front of my family, because they've always told me I've been a source of pride to them ... They say that people in town respect them because I have all these degrees and that I bring honor to the family. I feel it is my duty to keep bringing honor to the family by doing outstanding deeds instead of just living a normal life and trying to get by in the world. And they've used this as a way of encouraging me to go on and on. I've probably gone way beyond my capabilities. I don't know how I got by ... When I was younger I began studying hard ... I practically memorized the textbooks to get A's in school to please the teachers, I suppose, and to please my parents ... I wanted to be loved so much. I don't know why.

Dr. Can you say anything about it?

Pt. The desire to be wanted and to feel important in someone else's mind. Someone loves you and cares for you and thinks a lot of you.

Among the features that characterize excessive narcissism we see very prominently the patient's intense craving for love and admiration. Much of his behavior appears to have been motivated by this need; he has been able to do very little in his life because *he* wanted to; his actions have been guided by what he thought would please others and make them like him. He is a prisoner of his aspirations, his needs, and his harsh self-criticism. To hold off the pressures of his superego and to maintain his self-esteem he needs a friend ever running at his side to pat him continuously on the back and give him constant reassurance.

The same desperate, almost overwhelming need for love is evident in Anne F., a young woman of eighteen with chronic intrinsic bronchial asthma. In the course of two long, sleepless nights she scribbled the following notes on scraps of paper:

> Woke out of sleep. Saw door closed. Was frightened. Nobody came. Coughing, frightened. Crying hard. Want to talk. Not allowed. Not wheezing much. Just frightened and lonely. Don't want medicine, want company. Crying. Sick to stomach. Not sweating, 12 o'clock (midnight). Not in bed yet. Can think clear now. Getting relaxed now. Miss sister Mary and Donny. Helped me when sick. Need to talk. Crying and lonely. Need company. Hated doctor with medicine (the resident who was in charge of ordering her medication, and who did not give her as much as she wanted or felt she needed). 12:30. Feel cold. Very thirsty. Feel like killing doctor with medicine . . . Sick—sick to stomach. Am very thirsty. Still need company. Lonely. Not wanted . . . Need someone to care. Sick still to stomach. Think I will look at magazine. So sick to stomach. Cold . . . nobody cares if I live or die. Doctor with medicine—hate him . . . Still want company. Think I need a little medicine now. Afraid to ask. Need to see doctor. Sick to stomach . . . Beginning to feel like I'm writing my will or something. Maybe I'll pray. Comfort in that. Still want to talk to someone . . . my father would hold me in his arms. Wish somebody would care about me. Still hate medicine man. Easier to write. Can put anger on paper. What a love letter . . . Still need someone—anybody . . . Miss my father so. Can't stop thinking . . . am still lonely. Going to sit with nurse for a while.

A few hours after her last note, Anne F. died in an acute asthmatic attack. The cause of death was found at autopsy to be the thick plugs of mucous that everywhere filled her bronchioles; she had drowned in her own secretions. She had told no one of the feelings she wrote about, although

her doctor (despite her comment) had given her every opportunity to talk. As the patient indicated, it was apparently "easier to write." Without her notes, no one would
have known that she had suffered such an agony of despair
and loneliness, or how much she had needed love and help
and attention. No one, furthermore, was aware how angry
she was at the "doctor with medicine." During her stay on
the ward, the patient had frequently asked for medication;
the resident in charge had on numerous occasions withheld
this when it seemed medically unwise. He was aware of her
disappointment at these times, but she gave no overt signs
of her reaction of rage to this deprivation.

This response should not come as a surprise to us, for we
have already met it before in Chester B. and Boyd C., both
of whom were roused to anger by the defection of people on
whom they depended. Katherine D. showed the same reaction. "And now," she said, "I need help and reassurance
from you. I don't get it and that makes me furious." The
same phenomenon is apparent in Arthur D., who gives in
his fantasies an indication of the violence and destructiveness of the aggression.

At the age of forty he had been unable to work for two
years because of pain in his back following an injury. He
was chronically depressed and bitter; he felt that he was not
getting adequate help from his doctors, from his lawyer on
whom he depended heavily for advice and support, or from
the insurance company on whom he relied for compensation. Furthermore his wife had not shown him the attention
and concern he wanted from her. As he was discussing with
his doctor the irritability he had felt since his injury, his eyes
suddenly filled with tears, and he burst into racking sobs.
When he could finally talk again, he blurted out that he had
been frightened by a terrible thought: he had imagined himself pounding his wife on the head with a hammer to give

her some idea of how much pain he was suffering. He then
continued.

> I mean, I've had my thoughts—I do a lot of thinking. I
> know there's an easy way out, but God!—I have her and
> my son to think of. I thought of going down to that lawyer
> in Topsfield—I could take a gun and make a mess out of
> that outfit in his office in about five minutes. Another time
> I was coming home, driving the car pretty fast. Another
> car was coming fast. I just wondered what would happen
> if I hit him head on. Well, I didn't because the guy in the
> back seat has got a family. But maybe if I had been alone,
> I might have.

In all of these patients we find an intimate connection between narcissistic needs and anger when the needs are not
satisfied. All of us at times react with disappointment and
anger when we fail to get something we want. The person
with a narcissistic character disorder does the same, but with
a difference that further complicates his already difficult situation. His needs and his demands from others are stronger
and more frequent than in the more mature adult, which in
itself intensifies his feeling of weakness, helplessness, and
inadequacy; there is, therefore, more likelihood of disappointment; he comes to expect, even to look for, defections
in other people, and his sensitivity to slights is heightened.
His angry reactions are profound and violent. They are, furthermore, very frightening to him; they conflict with his
wish to be good, kind, and loving, thereby increasing his already burgeoning sense of inadequacy, helplessness, and
guilt; they threaten to hurt, alienate, and drive away the very
person needed for help and support, thus further increasing
the feeling of insecurity and disappointment. The patient is
thus trapped in a vicious circle where a move in any direction may cause him difficulty. It is a fragile equilibrium of
dependent desire for the necessary person balanced against
rage at his disappointing qualities.

This psychological state of *ambivalence* (or of having an *ambivalent relationship* with an important person) is not a healthy or comfortable one. The shaky equilibrium may persist unchanged when there is little stress upon it, but the narcissistic person is especially vulnerable to the human crises that none of us can avoid. He is particularly liable to have severe emotional difficulties when faced with the death of the individual on whom he depends to supply his narcissistic needs. The ordinary deep pain of losing something valuable is complicated by the added complex of emotions resulting from his ambivalence and his narcissism. The loss may be catastrophic to his equilibrium; at best, it leads to pathological forms of grief. We must therefore turn to an examination of these for the further light that they cast on the problem of clinical depressions.

XII

Margaret P., an attractive 32-year-old woman, came to the clinic ostensibly to discuss her concern over her son, who, she thought, was showing abnormally aggressive behavior. She soon, however, began to talk about herself and complained that for almost three months she had been feeling tired, drowsy, and tense. She said that she felt "dead inside"; she reported that she had lost all interest in her friends and relatives, and no longer cared about the things that formerly gave her pleasure. The onset of this unpleasant set of feelings had coincided with the death of her husband three months before.

In the first meeting with her doctor the patient told her story in a controlled, emotionless way, as if she were describing what had happened to someone else. One could, however, sense an element of tension behind the control, and on one occasion she seemed near tears. Despite this the patient denied any sense of loss or grief over her husband's death, and signs of painful dejection and sadness were absent.

In the course of the early interviews she described the circumstances of her husband's death and her reaction to it. One afternoon, as she was taking a nap, she had a frightening dream: her husband was chasing an unknown man, with the intention of killing him; a policeman was in pursuit of her husband; and she was running after both of them, pleading with her husband not to use violence. She awoke from

this with acute anxiety, fell asleep again and dreamed the
same dream. She was awakened for the second time by the
ringing of the telephone; as she answered she had a presen-
timent that there was something wrong with her husband.
Her fears were confirmed; her mother-in-law was calling to
tell her that her husband had just died from a heart attack.
The patient burst into tears and cried copiously throughout
the rest of the day and night while her family were making
preparations for the funeral.

The next morning her mother-in-law took her aside. She
confessed that in order to break the shock of the news she
had not told her what had really happened. In truth, the
patient's husband had gone to his mother's house and had
hanged himself there from a beam in the cellar. As the patient heard this she suddenly felt all of her emotions of
sorrow and grief dry up and disappear. This concerned her;
she thought it indicated that she did not really care for her
husband.

Then followed a curious further change. It suddenly
seemed to her that her husband was *not* really dead. *Intellectually* she knew that he was, but somehow she felt that
he was alive, but away on a business trip from which he
would return. At his wake and funeral she was calm and
emotionless; she acted as if she were presiding at a tea, and
chatted calmly with friends and relatives about their children and the local gossip.

The feeling that he was alive persisted during the ensuing weeks. In the late afternoon she would behave as if he
were returning from work. At 5:30, the time at which he
usually came home, she would begin looking out the window from time to time, watching for him to drive up to the
house. Rationally she knew all of this was silly, and yet she
found herself frequently cooking enough food to include his
portion, or setting a place at table for him. During this time
she felt no grief; instead she suffered from the symptoms

described earlier. Her main concern was with her boy's behavior, which had been her ostensible reason for coming to
the clinic. It was not only that she thought him too aggressive; she feared that he would grow up to commit suicide
like his father.

It was apparent from her symptoms (her fatigue, inner
deadness, and loss of interest in people and things) that the
patient was suffering from a depression which showed no
signs of resolution or change. It was especially remarkable
that she had no feelings of loss, painful dejection, or unhappiness; not only are these the common emotional state
in depression, but they would have been the appropriate response of grief to her husband's death. Initially she had
started to grieve normally when she had the first news of his
dying, but this had abruptly disappeared when she learned
from her mother-in-law that the cause of his death was suicide, not heart failure. From that time on she maintained
her strange denial of her husband's end. The process of
grieving had been abruptly arrested, there was no painful
but normal step-by-step coming to grips with the fact that
he was gone.

The patient was taken into treatment with the hope of
thawing out the freeze and of learning at the same time more
about what was causing her symptoms. During the fifteen
weekly therapeutic hours that followed, many interesting
changes took place as the patient revealed more about herself. Of particular interest was the nature of her relationship with her husband in the years preceding his death. She
had married ten years previously. The first six years of her
marriage she described in retrospect as "like a honeymoon."
Four years before his death, however, she noted a change in
her husband's behavior following the birth of her second
child, a son. He began to stay out late at night, associated
with friends she did not approve of, and (at least so she
thought) he began to drink heavily; this worried her be-

cause of her long experience with her own father's chronic alcoholism. For some six months she said nothing to him about his change. During this time she was aware of no anger toward him; on the contrary, she felt "hurt," and at the same time blamed herself for what was happening. There must be something she was doing wrong she thought, to make him act so strangely. There was nothing unusual in her reaction; she was never a person, she said, to get angry. When things went wrong, she always blamed herself, and much of her behavior was aimed at pleasing other people and doing things to make them happy; in this way she would herself be loved and appreciated. During these six months the patient first noted transient symptoms of fatigue and attacks of acute anxiety.

At length the patient cautiously raised the subject with her husband of his late hours. She tentatively suggested that perhaps something was wrong—that maybe she could do something to help. Her husband merely laughed and assured her that any "trouble" was all a figment of her imagination. To her surprise, she reacted with a temporary upsurge of rage, lost her temper, and screamed at him to get out of the house. He did so at once and stayed away all night. Immediately the patient felt desperate, and was overcome by a great longing for him. As the long night wore on, she remembered all the nice things he had done for her; she thought of how he would call her daily from the office to make sure she was all right; she recalled the many ways in which she turned to him for help, needed him, and leaned on him for guidance. As the patient described the turbulent emotions of that evening, one caught the first glimpse of an ambivalent quality in her relationship to her husband that became more apparent as one learned more about her.

The following morning her husband came home. Now she begged him to stay. He agreed, providing she would accept stringent conditions for their continued relationship, allowing him to do just as he pleased without objections or comment from her. She accepted these unreservedly; she realized now that she wanted him and needed him badly. From that time on she submitted to the situation without a whisper of complaint. As she said, "I could not be mad at my husband." The arrangement was not easy for her, however; being forbidden to talk to her husband about their problems only increased her sense of distance and isolation from him.

As they emerged, these facts provided important information about the type of relationship with her husband which formed the backdrop to his dramatic death. It was a relationship in which she depended heavily on him for attention, love, and emotional support—narcissistic needs so important for her that she forced herself to put up with a difficult situation without complaint. She was rarely aware of experiencing anger or of feeling resentment toward her husband for the conditions he forced upon her. Indeed, during the first few hours as she talked about his suicide, her only reaction was to blame herself for it. It was her fault, she said. She could have prevented him from destroying himself if only she had been a better wife to him. If she had given more of herself, if she had only been able to persuade him to confide his troubles to her, if she had understood him and his problems better, he would not have been driven to suicide.

Gradually, however, a new note crept into her associations. She first began to express resentment toward her husband for having by his suicide deserted her and the children, leaving them in a financially difficult situation. Then she began to describe how difficult the relationship with him before his death had really been for her. She recalled that at times she had wanted to show anger toward him, but could only run away from him to her room and cry alone. "I loved him and hated him," she said, and then revealed that shortly before his suicide, she had been in such an angry and desperate frame of mind that she would sometimes pray to God that he would die; it seemed to her the only solution to an impossible situation. At times she even had fleeting fantasies of killing him herself. When she heard of his death her immediate, horrified thought was, "My God! My prayers have been answered!" It seemed to her that her prayers and her wishes and her fantasies had been what killed him.

As she began in therapy to express some of her anger, there occurred an interesting change in her behavior: she started to grieve. At first it was only in the therapeutic hours that she could say how much she missed her husband and could recall the good things they had shared. With the memories came the tears and sadness she had not been able to show or experience before. At length, even at home, she began to think about him. She missed him increasingly and would often cry, especially when she remembered nice things they had done together. She would suddenly burst into tears when she saw objects that reminded her of special occasions, such as the silver candlesticks he had given her on their last wedding anniversary. For a time these memories and thoughts filled most of her waking hours to the exclusion of interest in the other things in her life. She was aware of a jumble of mixed feelings—anger at his desertion and his behavior during his life, but also of sadness and love for him as she remembered the nice, lovable things about him.

One night she dreamed that he really was dead. Shortly after this she visited his grave with the *feeling,* as well as the intellectual knowledge, that he was dead and gone forever. It was in the interview after this that she angrily confessed to her prayers that he might die, and to her fantasies of killing him herself.

In the last therapeutic hour, she reported being much better as the result of the changes that had occurred in her feelings and attitudes. She was now quite convinced, emotionally as well as intellectually, that her husband was dead. She had lost the feeling of guilty responsibility for his suicide. Her mood was improved; she was beginning to be cheerful and the sense of missing her husband was less acute and painful. The feeling of being "dead inside" had disappeared, and she found that she had a renewed interest in people as well as in the activities that had formerly given her pleasure. Her friends, in fact, told her that she was a "new person." And finally, she had lost her concern that her young son's aggressive behavior implied that he, like his father, was heading for a suicide's grave.

It was clear by the end of her first diagnostic interview that Margaret P. was suffering from a pathological grief reaction. Her feeling of "deadness inside," her loss of interest in people and things, and her chronic fatigue indicated that she was reacting to her husband's death; it was, however, the surprising absence of grief and the emotional conviction that her husband was alive which led to the diagnosis. When she finally came for psychiatric help, her mild, but unpleasant symptoms had become fixed in a chronic pattern of moderate depression. The initial impression that her difficulty was the result of a blocking of the process of grief was confirmed in the course of therapy; as she became aware of her anger toward her dead husband, she began to experience the pain of losing him. Gradually she worked through her feelings of grief, and emerged at the end of treatment free of symptoms, at peace about her husband's death, and with a renewed interest in living. Therapy had helped to turn a still photograph into a moving picture.

Her husband's suicide was clearly the *precipitating* cause of the patient's difficulty, but it was not the only factor in her illness. Without the events that had occurred before he died it is doubtful whether she would have suffered a pathological grief-reaction. The nature of her character structure and the relationship it led her to make constituted the *predisposing* cause of her emotional disorder.

As she talked about herself and her married life, the narcissism and the ambivalence in her character structure became evident. Her deep need for love and help and protection from her husband was so strong that she was willing to put up with difficult and unpleasant conditions in order to maintain the emotional supplies she needed. For the same reason, the potential anger this distasteful situation aroused in her had to be curbed. For the most part she was unaware of the depth and violence of her feeling, which were apparent in her fantasies of killing him and in her dream just before she learned of his death.

Against this background her husband hanged himself. At first she began to grieve in what appeared to be an appropriate and normal manner. Then, when she learned that his death was not from natural causes but by suicide, the process of mourning abruptly stopped. From her associations in therapy it became apparent that the fact that he had *chosen* to die caused her almost unbearable mental pain. In the first place it meant that he cared so little for her that he was willing to leave her in this cruel way. It felt to her like a desertion and served to increase her feelings of helplessness and inadequacy. Secondly, his behavior raised her fury to new heights of intensity as she felt spurned by him and permanently deprived of the love she needed. At the same time, her augmented rage only increased her sense of guilt and her feeling that she was responsible for his troubles; it seemed to her that in some magical way her fantasies of killing him had brought this to pass. To admit to herself that he was dead and to face the emotions that this fact aroused in her meant subjecting herself to an insupportable burden of grief, anger, helplessness, and guilt. The saving solution was to feel and act as if he were still alive—to *deny* his death; this was the only way she could protect herself against the pain attached to the loss of him. It meant, however, that she could not complete the process of grieving; although her husband was gone, she could not free herself of him. Bound to him, she was dead to the real world of living people. Her *denial* exacted a price.

The patient's maneuver of denial was not a fully conscious, voluntary, thought-out plan of action. It was an ego defense mechanism, and like all defenses it operated for the most part out of the sphere of her conscious awareness. She felt its effect in her conscious conviction that her husband was not dead, and in her lack of feelings of grief, but these did not appear to her to be the result of her own volition; on the contrary, intellectually she was puzzled by her unusual response.

One important fact now becomes evident from our study of Margaret P.'s disorder: ego defense mechanisms are created not only for the purpose of avoiding painful anxiety. They are employed under certain circumstances to combat the pain of loss and depression as well. In Margaret P.'s case, her denial led to an arrest in the normal process of mourning resulting clinically in a chronic depression as the manifestation of a pathological grief-reaction. In the patients we are about to examine, we shall find other defenses against depression that led to even more profound disturbances of personality function.

XIII

The Psychopathology of Depression

Barbara T., a recently married woman of thirty-four, entered the hospital because of crippling attacks of acute anxiety. The palpitations that occurred with these led her to believe that she would at any moment die of a heart attack. Her illness had started at the time of her mother's death two years before. She began her account of her difficulty with these words:

> I lost my mother two years ago—oh, two years and a half, you know. And—well, she had a lot of things wrong with her anyway. And she had a heart attack, and then I figured, well, she's gone, she's gone. I tried to figure, you know—well, it's best for her, you know, the way she was suffering. And then it seemed that whenever I got nervous my heart would start banging. Maybe I've got it in my subconscious mind, you know what I mean?
> *Dr.* Got what?
> *Pt.* A fear of heart trouble, you know. I mean, this sounds crazy to me, but I'm telling you.

In the opening sentences of her history, the patient's associations indicate a connection between her mother's death and her own symptoms: her mother died of a heart attack; the patient became "nervous" and developed somatic sensations involving her heart; she interpreted these to mean that possibly she, like her mother, had heart disease. As the interview continued, she described further her reaction to her mother's death.

Dr. Tell me how you reacted when your mother died.

Pt. I can't cry when anyone dies. I mean, that's the worst part of it. I mean, I felt bad but I just—I'm just not the type that will cry. If I get mad, I don't holler much. I've got a lot of patience, you know . . . I keep it all inside, I just don't like arguing.

Dr. And when your mother died?

Pt. I never cried. I mean I felt bad, but I just couldn't cry. Then I said to myself, "Well, now she's gone, I can't get sick or nothing. I've got to get on my feet," you know —but it just caught up with me somehow. I don't know.

Dr. Tell me what your feelings were when she died.

Pt. Well, I got nervous.

The patient is not entirely clear about the exact nature of her reaction to her mother's death. She could not cry, a fact which indicates some blocking in her ability to express grief. She says that she felt "bad," and at once (seemingly out of context) describes her need to control anger. The only really positive qualification of her state of mind is that she "got nervous."

She elaborated on several factors that contributed to her nervousness. She suffered from a continuous fear that she, like her mother, might suddenly drop dead of heart disease. Associated with this was a fear of being alone lest "something dreadful" happen to her. She could not specify what this "something" was. She was plagued by a fear that she might "explode," "go crazy," lose control of her actions and behave violently. She became preoccupied with thoughts of injury or illness occurring to other people, and was extremely anxious when anyone she knew fell sick. She would develop acute anxiety whenever she heard the wail of an ambulance siren; she was unable to visit sick friends because of the acute panic that overwhelmed her as she approached them. Her abnormal concern with death, disease, and violence suggested that the patient was struggling with a partially disguised aggressive impulse.

Despite her many fears, the patient had managed to carry on with her daily life and household routines until six weeks before coming to the psychiatric ward. At that time she entered another hospital for minor surgery. Because of her fears of sickness and hospitals this was, of course, difficult for her, but by strength of will she managed to force herself to go through with the procedure. She was convalescing uneventfully, when an unfortunate event occurred. An older woman with a severe heart attack was placed in the bed beside hers and shortly died. As the patient said, "I know it was silly, but it just seemed as if they had brought in my mother." In the face of this catastrophe, she was seized with a feeling of panic, ran frantically from the room, and begged to be transferred to another ward. She was discharged home shortly after this, but her fears of dying of heart disease and committing some violent, destructive act became so overwhelming to her that she had to be admitted to the psychiatric ward for further help.

From what the patient said, it was evident that, because of the similarities to her mother's sickness, her fellow patient's sudden death had acted as the precipitant to the acute phase of her own illness. It had intensified the internal psychological conflict that had initially been aroused by her mother's death. Her lifelong relationship with her mother provided the soil in which this conflict grew; it was a relationship characterized by narcissism, dependence, and by ambivalence. On the one hand she had always been very close to her mother; she needed her continual support and love, and depended on her for advice and guidance. She found it hard to leave her mother after she grew up and lived at home until after her thirtieth birthday. To please her mother, she gave up a relationship with one man who wanted to marry her, because she felt she would lose her mother's love if she married. When she did marry in her early thirties, she continued for over a year to live in her mother's home with her new husband.

In addition to her excessive dependence on her mother, Barbara T. had always had difficulty in going counter to her mother's wishes and opinions. Although there were many indications that she resented her mother, the patient had never been able to show these feelings. Her mother had developed grand mal epilepsy while she was carrying the patient. Barbara was convinced that she was responsible for this affliction; no amount of reassurance or medical information to the contrary shook her belief. From early childhood on, she was continually terrified that her mother was dying when she had a spell, despite the fact that her mother invariably recovered from them without serious sequelae. Throughout her life Barbara remained certain that if she failed to obey, if she argued or showed anger toward her mother, she would precipitate a seizure and would cause her mother's death. Her strait jacket of docile obedience and self-control acted to keep her aggressive impulses hidden and to prevent the feared loss of the person on whom she vitally depended.

Such was the long prelude to her mother's death. When the tragedy came, Barbara, like Margaret P., was faced with an acutely painful situation: she had lost the person necessary for her narcissistic needs; at the same time, confronted with her mother's actual death, her guilt over her own underlying aggressive wishes became intensified. Because of her narcissistic, ambivalent relationship with her mother, the loss of the latter aroused intolerable emotions in the patient. Like Margaret P., she was unable to allow herself to experience the painful process of grief. Unlike Margaret P., however, she did not avoid this by denying her mother's death in order by keeping her alive in fantasy to avoid the pain of loss. Instead she employed another ego mechanism called *identification*.

> When my mother died (she said) I—I tried to get a grip on myself. I said, "After all, you can't bring her back, you know." Then all of a sudden I start getting palpitations of the heart. Well, I'm thinking, "Maybe I've got heart trouble." I don't know.

She accepts the fact of her mother's death. She knows that she "can't bring her back"; there is no denial such as we observed in Margaret P. She is aware of no feelings or conviction that her mother is still alive. And yet she does, in a way, "bring her back" by psychologically making a part of her mother a part of herself. The image of her beloved mother at the time of her death was that of a person sick with heart disease. The patient does not relinquish this image nor allow it to die. She keeps it alive, but not as the image of a person external to herself; it becomes internalized and alters her own image of herself. She no longer conceives of herself as a healthy person, able to be active and able to manage her house; rather, she thinks of herself as a person who is sick and in danger of dying of heart disease. She develops symptoms which are for her consistent with this diagnosis, and has to be admitted to the hospital for her illness. The image of herself is the image of her mother, which has entered the fabric of her ego and has radically altered that portion of the ego organization that constitutes her self-image. She has *identified* with her mother; she has made certain behavioral and personality attributes of her mother a part of herself; she has, in this regard, become like her mother, and from then on she behaves accordingly.

In this way she keeps her mother alive. Her attention and mental energies are not directed toward the real fact of her mother's death; she does not experience the pain of this loss.

On the contrary, she concentrates on the image of her mother now living within her; she is preoccupied with her concern over having heart disease. The grief work is blocked, neurotic symptoms replace mourning, and she cannot free herself of her mother.

We do not as yet fully understand the psychological processes involved in the mechanism of identification. Its use as a term to describe certain observable changes in a person's behavior patterns is clear enough: faced with a loss, a person adopts certain behavioral and characterological traits of the lost one; we consider this a change within the ego organization and name it *identification*.* How this modification in the ego is brought about is not yet apparent. Let us approach a clarification by elucidating the concept of *incorporation*, which was implicit in the earlier comment that the patient's image of her mother was "internalized," that it "entered the fabric of her ego." Let us work our way into this new concept with the help of yet another patient.

Clara D. was unmarried at thirty-seven. She had for many years been completely disabled from work by a chronic hysterical paralysis of her right leg, which had eventually led to a marked atrophy of disuse. She lived alone, supported by public welfare, had no real friends and almost no contact with human beings except for her doctor in the Psychiatric Clinic, who had helped her over a long period of time with friendly and kindly support. She exhibited toward him the strong ambivalence and dependence characteristic of the narcissistic personality organization with which she was cursed.

Unfortunately her doctor had to move permanently to another city, and his sudden decision to do so gave him

---

* To simplify the discussion, identification is considered here only in its relation to loss. For a more complete exposition of this common mechanism, the reader is referred to Brenner (7), Glover (10), or Hendrick (12). See note at end of this chapter.

little time to warn or prepare the patient for this event. She reacted violently to the loss of the relationship.

> Suddenly when I got the news around April that he was leaving, I received an awful shock to my whole system ... somehow or other I couldn't seem to face it without Dr. Jones ... I felt safe and secure with him ... When I heard it, it was like a nightmare to me ... He represented real life to me ... I never felt so alone—in the whole city there was no help for me.
>
> I'm scared what is going to happen to me—what I'm going to do ... I cried, "I've got to go to him. I've got to go to him ... I've got to be where he is!" ... He helps me fix my life and now I feel like something inside is gone ... I felt safe with him ... and so I've just got to have him. I know I sound like a child, but this is what I'm experiencing. And when I have these panic spells, I've just got to have him, that's all—do or die, I've got to have him. Then I know intellectually that he's really gone, and I know I'm here. But it's all these emotional feelings and—oh—I feel as though he was so much help, but it's time that I stand on my own two feet. So help me God, this is the only thing I want from anybody—so I can go to work and be independent. But here I am, and I hate myself for it.

The intense pain caused her by the loss is evident as she movingly describes her loneliness, her desperation, her panic, and her feeling of helplessness without her doctor. The overwhelming intensity of these feelings vividly delineates the nature of abnormal narcissistic needs, especially when one recognizes that this is the cry of a 37-year-old woman—not an infant. The patient is herself aware of the inappropriate quality of her needs. Her behavior conflicts with her ideals for herself, and this only increases her painful inner state as she suffers from lowered self-esteem; as she says, she "hates herself."

The patient makes a further interesting remark. In the

context of talking about the absence of an external object (her doctor) she says, "I feel like something is gone inside." She elaborated on this a short while later:

> I feel as though part of me has gone with Dr. Jones, and I just feel half here . . . Jane is the big part of me, the part that he's helping, and that's gone. And I feel I've lost this, so I'm trying to bring these parts together—in other words I just feel separated. So I'm trying to pull two parts together—I've got to get that other part of me . . . When I'm trying to bring Dr. Jones back, I'm trying to bring this part back to me that belongs to me—that's the way I feel . . . I just feel so—so separated like—it's so hard to explain. I think this is the point that's given me all this pain—as though I've got to go to him or he's got to come back or I've got to bring that part back to me . . . I wrote to him and pleaded with him to put me together in one piece again . . . I feel as though something's gone inside of me.

In the patient's experience there are three images: she, herself, who has been left behind; Jane, the part of her the doctor has been helping; and Dr. Jones. Each of these has the vividness and reality for her of real entities. Logically and rationally she *knows* that this is "silly," but from an emotional and perceptual point of view this is the actuality for her. And yet each of these three is not a completely separate and autonomous being; each is intimately associated with the other as part of a greater whole. When Dr. Jones leaves, Jane disappears with him, leaving the patient feeling that "something is gone inside." Nor are Dr. Jones and Jane unrelated; there is a close intermingling in her mind of the images of the two of them so that when she is "trying to bring Dr. Jones back, I'm trying to bring this part back to me that belongs to me (i.e. Jane)." The fusion of Dr. Jones and herself is apparent as she talks about having him "right inside me":

Sometimes I start crying. I call for Dr. Jones and then I feel as though he's real near to me . . . close to me . . . beside me . . . almost as though he's right inside me. This is what I feel . . . It's as though when I call him, I get ahold of him and that he won't run away from me again . . . I get closer to him and I really cry it out and I feel as if I've got him so close—right inside. (To demonstrate, the patient grabbed at an imaginary object in front of her and pulled it toward her, pressing her clenched fists vigorously against her sternum.) These are the thoughts that are really coming to me as we talk, because I don't know how to feel or express it . . . But it's like I've finally caught him again . . . as if I'd brought him back to me.

It is difficult for most of us to share Clara D.'s experience with her; it is difficult to know the state of her awareness as these events occurred. For most of us the image of an absent person remains a pale simulacrum of the original; it is clearly an *image* that we evoke within us, fashioned of faintly imagined representations of the original which we recall from memory. There is no confusion between this image and the image provoked by the real sensations (auditory, visual, tactile) the person arouses when he is actually before us. Occasionally, at times of great emotional turmoil (the death of a loved one, for example), one has a "sense of the real presence" of the absent person; the "presence" is more than the faint image pictured in one's mind's eye; it feels as if it were "really there" external to oneself. There were elements of this phenomenon in Margaret P.'s emotional conviction that her husband was about to come home from work each night. It is vividly described by Clara D.

There is yet another aspect to Clara's experience that makes it alien to the ken of most of us. Her sense of her own identity as a person, her feeling of oneness and unity is disturbed. Dr. Jones, Jane, and herself are real separate entities, yet at the same time parts of her fragmented self scattered about the country. We may liken her condition to a triangle: composed of three connected lines it has the unity and quality of being a triangle. Torn apart at the apices, the triangle disappears, but the lines retain their identity and their capacity to form part of a triangle once more when they are rejoined. To an external observer (like the part of Clara D. who observes and describes what she experiences), who has seen the triangle before it was sundered, the single lines are separate objects but at the same time they are felt to be a part of the destroyed triangle which they originally formed.

A mere analogy can give us only a faint idea of the condition of Clara D.'s state of mental awareness. It is impossible really to know what she has felt unless we too have experienced within ourselves the same phenomenon. It is difficult, therefore, to know exactly what she means when she talks of "getting ahold" of Dr. Jones and having him "right inside" her. She is apparently not talking entirely in metaphors. She really feels that she is a divided person, that "Jane" is gone, that she has got to be put together again, that she has to take them inside her.

As in the other patients, her loss occasions an almost unbearable pain, an important element of which is her feeling that a part of her has been physically torn from her. Relief from her grief comes from taking the lost part back inside of her body—*incorporating* it. The term *incorporation* does not, of course, refer to the real act of taking an external object into one's body; it refers to the patient's subjective, but vivid feeling that this is occurring.

In considering these mechanisms by which individuals attempt to avoid the painful feeling of depression that results from loss, we must keep in mind the fact that, as in the problem of anxiety, the defensive maneuvers are not usually completely successful. In the depressive *illness* (i.e. the clinical syndrome), depressive affect (i.e. depression as an experienced feeling) is a central manifestation among the varied symptoms, despite attempts to avoid it. In fact, as we shall shortly discover, the defensive operations complicate the problem and themselves produce symptoms characteristic of the depressive illness. Before examining these phenomena, however, we must first turn our attention to some of the genetic precursors of the mechanisms we have been observing.

The tangible, vivid reality of her images makes Clara D.'s experience seem alien to us, whose mental images are pale beside the sensations that come from the stimuli of the real, external world. And yet all of us have probably experienced something comparable in the unremembered past of our infancy. One cannot, of course, learn directly from the infant what he experiences; he has not the language to tell us even if he would like to. One can, however, construct a model of the nature of the infant's experience from the observations one makes of the development of the normal child, and from the observations of pathological growth which cast some aspects of development into bold relief. From these facts one infers that early in a person's life he is not aware of the difference between himself and the outside world. Initially the different experiences of putting his own fingers, a pacifier, and his mother's breast in his mouth are the same; he does not distinguish between what is a part of himself and what is not. His impulse life is at this period of his life dominated by the biological primacy of his mouth and the sensations arising from it. One has only to watch an infant to note this—to observe how he puts everything in his mouth, explores with his mouth, enjoys not only nursing but sucking itself. His mouth is useful and at the same time is a source of pleasure. What exists he makes his own by actually physically putting it in his mouth and when possible incorporating it. It is only through repeated experience day in and day out that he learns that sucking his thumb gives

sensation in his mouth *and* in his thumb; that sucking a
pacifier gives sensation in his mouth alone; that sucking his
mother's nipple provides milk to satisfy his hunger, whereas
the pacifier is not so generous; that he can control the presence of his thumb, whereas his mother's nipple is not so reliable. It is often not there when he wants it, and he has to
yell to make it appear to assuage the pain of his emptiness.
Thus slowly he begins to learn that some objects differ from
others; he begins to develop a notion of his own physical
body as distinct from alien objects. The earliest rudiments
of an ego vis-à-vis the world make their appearance. The
earliest rudiments of critical judgment and logical evaluation of the world are seen when the infant realizes that it is
the nipple, not the thumb, which gives milk; that the bustling movements of his mother preparatory to nursing him
mean that food is coming, so that, hearing these, he stops
his yelling as he *anticipates* what is shortly to follow.

There are interesting similarities between the phenomena
which Clara D. describes and the model of the process of
an infant's growth and development. Particularly striking is
the way in which she confuses herself with another person
and fails to differentiate between inside and outside. Furthermore, she makes something her own by taking it inside
—by incorporating it. She sees the world in a manner that
characterizes the infant's experience of it. She has reverted
to earlier modes of psychological functioning which once
dominated her mental life in the past history of her infancy.
She has become cognizant of earlier states of awareness
which in most of us remain unconscious. The present distortions of her mental processes are understandable in the
light of her past.

If we now compare Barbara T. and Clara D. we find similarities and differences. Both have a narcissistic character
structure and both form ambivalent relationships with other
people. Each of them responds to the loss of an important

person with unsupportable grief, and each attempts to avoid the pain by making at least a portion of the important person a part of herself. The difference appears to lie in the method which each uses to accomplish this internalization. In Clara D. it has the quality of being real; she feels that she is in actuality incorporating physical objects into the substance of her body. In Barbara T. the process involves less substantial entities; a mental image, a memory of her mother becomes synonymous with her image of herself, and she behaves accordingly. The image that she originally referred to her mother she now refers to herself. A change of reference and an internalization of the qualities of an image have taken place.

If we turn again to the process of growth and development of the child, we find precursors of these differences in our two adult patients. The child does not long remain in the amorphous state of confused intermingling with the world around him. By six to eight months of age he has developed an awareness that he is a distinct entity in a world of people and objects. He recognizes that as a separate being he ends with his skin and that other objects begin. As the months elapse, this position solidifies, and he gives up his attempts physically to incorporate the world. But this primitive biological orientation leaves as a legacy the disposition to identify with the people and objects around him. *Identification* is normally a major element in the relationships which the young child forms with the people in his environment. He adopts their modes of behavior, their customs, their character traits by internalizing his image of these and making them his own. This is now a psychological, not a physical process. It stands halfway between the feeling of the infant that "all is me," or all is to be physically "taken into me," and the awareness of the mature adult that other people are separate entities, that they have characteristics of their own different from oneself. In one's mature, adult relationship with others one can like or dislike their qualities without having to change oneself in their image—to identify with them. One can remain securely oneself in a varied world.

Barbara T. was not, like Clara D., aware of a process of internalization leading to her similarities to her mother. She knew only that she feared dropping dead of the same disease that killed her mother. Her identification was not a consciously carried out mental act. She was aware only of the end product of the process in the form of her likeness to her mother. We infer that the process of internalization occurred unconsciously, and had its roots in the more primitive, physical process of incorporation. As we thus conceive of it, identification and incorporation are aspects of a larger process. Incorporation refers to the impulse, the need to take in which sets the process in motion; identification refers to the changes observable in the ego as a result of the internalization.

It should furthermore be noted that in these early phases of his life, the child is initially in a highly dependent relationship to his parents, especially his mother, at a time when his oral impulses and dependent needs are in the ascendancy. He is particularly sensitive to loss, which produces in him marked feelings of helplessness. At the same time he is beginning to react with diffuse rage to the frustrations of his needs and to the parental curbs placed on his behavior as he develops a will to act and wishes of his own. Ambivalence, therefore, also normally characterizes the relationship of the young child to his parents. In the normal process of growth and development, the child outgrows these earlier modes of behavior, and as he passes through the Oedipal phase to the latency period (from approximately seven years of age to puberty), he develops his ability to see other people as individuals quite separate from himself, and to love them in a giving, unselfish manner. He relinquishes much of his earlier egotistical, demanding dependence. Too great frustrations in the early phases of childhood may produce distortions and arrests in development which later appear in the adult as the narcissism, dependence, and ambivalence characteristic of the patients we have been examining. They result, as we have seen, in a sensitivity to loss and in the employment of developmentally primitive defensive maneuvers, which produce a feature of clinical depressions that has not as yet been elucidated. We must therefore now turn to a consideration of the violent self-criticism, self-injury, and suicidal impulses that characterize the severe depressive illness.

A certain degree of self-criticism is understandable as a consequence of the failure to live up to the ideals set for one's behavior (which, as we have seen, is felt as a lowering of self-esteem), but the violence of the attack on oneself often goes far beyond what seems warranted by the nature of the crime. For example, a woman of forty-one said to her doctor, "You're going to kill me, aren't you, Doctor? That's all I deserve for my sins. Just put me in a box and dump me in the river." A man of forty-seven declared, "I masturbated when I was sixteen—that's caused all the misery in the world." A man of thirty-two ripped open his belly with a knife. A sixty-year-old woman slashed her neck with a razor and had to be constantly restrained from throttling herself when her wound failed to kill her. A woman in her fifties lowered her head and charged into the wall across the room; the impact broke her neck and she remained quadriplegic until she died.

The quality common to all of these patients is the violent aggression directed against themselves. It comes as no surprise to us that people who are depressed are filled with strong aggressive impulses, but most of the patients whom we have examined directed it away from themselves. We may recall that in his disturbed state on the day after Christ-

mas Boyd C., for example, was urged by an inner impulse
to throw pitchers, rip sheets, "take a swing at someone."
There was, however, another object for his aggression—
himself.

> If [he said] you should tell me right now, "Boyd, we're
> going to take you over tomorrow to cut those legs off," I'd
> be happy . . . God! I've burned my legs. I've stuck needles
> into them. I've really abused them in the hopes that there's
> something I'll do. Oh, I'd just like to get right ahold of
> them and tear the damn things apart. Just get right in—
> right with my hands and just—just tear 'em up! Just to get
> some feeling—something in there. I actually would—I'd
> like to take that whole thing and just have enough strength
> in my hands where I could rip 'em to shreds . . . You don't
> know how tempting it is at times to want to take a knife or
> fork or anything and jab just as hard as I can into them . . .
> You feel like you want to jump out a window or hang your-
> self . . . Sometimes I think I would be better off dead. I
> do! If it wasn't for the wife and kids—I've told my wife
> lots of times, "Oh, I'm so damn fed up with this type of
> thing I might just as well go out and put a bullet in my
> head as to sit around in this damn wheel chair and get fat."
> . . . I'm worried at times if I get one of these damn crazy
> notions to take a knife to my legs and cut 'em off or some-
> thing. God! that scares me more than any other feeling
> that I have. Because it is something I would be doing to
> myself and I wouldn't be hurting anyone else but myself . . .

The patient's last sentence indicates a partial awareness
that the rage directed toward himself is partly his rage at
other people. In either case it is murderously destructive.
The same turning of anger upon himself was evident in
Arthur D. As a preface to describing his frightening impulses to shoot up his lawyer's office, he talks of suicide: "I
know there's an easy way out—but God! I have her and my
son to think of." His fantasy of smashing head-on into a car
coming toward him nicely combines murder with self-de-

struction. It is this tendency to suicide that makes the severe clinical depression as potentially lethal as any fatal physical illness.

The aggression thus directed against the self is the same aggression characteristic of people with narcissistic character structures and ambivalent relationships. There are at least three ways in which it becomes turned inward rather than outward toward other objects. In the first place the tendency toward self-criticism for failure to achieve one's ideals forms a ready channel along which aggression may flow. The more exacting and demanding the super-ego organization, the greater the amount of aggression that is directed selfward. Secondly, the ego defense of *turning in of affect* brings about a change in the direction of aggression from objects toward the self as a means of controlling the impulse. Finally, the mechanism of identification leads to a redirection of aggression as a result of the internalization of the image of the lost person.

A patient observed by Karl Abraham, for example, was filled with bitter, but untrue self-accusations. "A female patient," he writes (29), "was brought to the asylum on account of a melancholic depression. She repeatedly accused herself of being a thief. In reality she had never stolen anything. But her father, with whom she lived, and to whom she clung with all an unmarried daughter's love, had been arrested a short while before for theft."

The precipitant of the patient's depression (melancholia) is the loss of her father. In response to the loss, she identifies with a part of the image of her father; his role as a thief is internalized and so alters her image of herself that she accuses herself of crimes which were in reality those which her father had committed. The aggression originally directed at her father for his misbehavior and desertion of her follows his image as it becomes internalized; now, as the patient upbraids the internalized image, she appears to be upbraiding herself. The aggression is directed inward.

As we reflect on this patient's process of identification, we find that the mechanism has in a sense misfired. In her attempts to internalize her father's image in the face of losing him, she has (for reasons not entirely clear) identified with his unpleasant characteristics—i.e. his being a thief. It is this part of his image that shapes and colors her own image of herself. She now judges *herself* as bad; it appears that all the anger originally aimed at the deserting father is now employed by her superego in *self*-castigation as she suffers from a conscience that belabors her for her father's now internalized faults. Here we must recall that in discussing the nature of obsessions and compulsions we mentioned the difference between those phenomena and depression that lay in the relation of the superego to the ego: in obsessions and compulsions, the ego does not entirely accept the judgment of the superego, but attempts to ward off the guilty anxiety by further defenses; in depression, on the other hand, the ego, altered by identifications and its helplessness in the face of loss, experiences the full force of the castigations of the superego; it surrenders completely to a sense of its own evilness, ignominy, and worthlessness—at times executing the sentence of its judge in suicide.

In our introductory comments on the problem of depression we distinguished between depression as a feeling (an affect) and depression as a clinical syndrome. We are now in a better position to understand the two meanings of the word as we review in summary what we have learned. Depression as an affect is a universal and normal experience. Almost all human beings at some time in their lives feel depressed as a result of lowered self-esteem or the loss of something of value which may along with the pain of the loss (grief) induce a lowering of self-esteem. In order to free oneself from one's attachment to the lost object and to be able to turn to new interests and people, one must experience grief, a process requiring time, effort, and the capacity to face the pain of loss. Disturbances in this capacity may lead to depression as a clinical syndrome, which does not have the same wide frequency of occurrence as depression, the affect. It is an illness which afflicts a more limited number of people made susceptible to it by their narcissistic character structure and the ambivalent nature of the human relationships they establish. In them, as in their more normal fellows, lowered self-esteem and loss produce a feeling of depression, but because of their narcissism and their strong dependent needs, the feeling of depression they suffer is particularly painful. They are especially sensitive to loss which so lowers their self-esteem and increases their psychic pain that it may become intolerable. Because of their abnormal sensitivity, the stimulus that produces such an affect in a narcissistic person may be relatively slight; a mild rebuff or the minor defection of a person they rely on, which in more normal people would cause little or no disturbance, may precipitate as severe a feeling of depression as the loss by death of someone important to them. The pain is further heightened to an unbearable intensity by the anger that stems from their ambivalence. To protect themselves from this pain, they employ abnormal mechanisms of defense (the heritage of early and immature phases of development); denial of the loss leads to a blocking of the process of grief; identification (and its companion, incorporation) leads to an internalization of at least a part of the image of the lost object, resulting in a variety of somatic complaints, violent self-castigation, and suicide. In most patients, the defensive operations are not entirely effective, and one finds a mixture of the painful affect resulting from loss and the effects of the partly successful defense mechanisms. In other words, in the predisposed individual, the *affect* of depression, which is a normal response to loss and lowered self-esteem, is complicated by additional psychological factors which conspire to produce the *illness*, depression.

It should now be evident that depression (both as affect and as illness) is a highly complicated human experience. The psychopathology of the clinical syndrome of depression is complex; a full understanding of it requires an understanding of the multiple causal factors that contribute to it: precipitating environmental events (loss); predisposing causes that rest in the nature of the patient's character structure (narcissism, dependence, and ambivalence); psychogenetic factors that have produced the vulnerable adult character structure (distortions of development during the early period of a child's life when he is normally narcissistic, dependent, and ambivalent); and dynamic processes occurring in the adult's psychological equilibrium as it is effected by the impact of the loss (pain, lowered self-esteem, anger, ego mechanisms of defense). The rich variety of individual manifestations of the depressive states can be understood psychologically only by taking into account all these many variables.

A Note on Incorporation, Introjection, and Identification

These three terms are used in the psychiatric literature in a confusing and inconsistent manner. Some authors employ them as if they were synonymous; others attempt to differentiate among their meanings. In order to simplify a complex subject, a consideration of *introjection* as possibly distinct from *incorporation* and *identification* has been omitted from our discussion of depression. The latter two terms have been used to refer to two different aspects of a larger psychological process, the *internalization* of external objects. *Incorporation* is here understood to mean a psychological mechanism, the precursors of which are found in the earliest phase of the child's development; it is intimately linked to the processes of taking objects into the body connected with the oral impulses of that phase. *Identification* stems from a later phase of the child's development; although the term implies an internalization of *images* of external objects, it is more closely related than incorporation to the changes in the structure of the ego that result from the identification. In other words, in *incorporation*, the emphasis is on Id functions; in *identification*, on Ego functions, although both systems are probably to some degree involved in each process.

XIV

SOME MAJOR DISTORTIONS IN EGO FUNCTIONING

The patients we have just been examining have for the most part struck a responsive note in the majority of us. Their disturbances in mood, whether slight or severe, have been comprehensible to us, just because, as we have seen, depression is a universal experience. We have perhaps not been able entirely to understand *why* a patient should respond to a minor event with a major depression, but *what* he feels we can know directly from having ourselves felt the same; we are able to empathize with him. The patients we are about to observe are in a different category. Because of the character of their mental disturbance, few of us have shared their experiences, and few of us can *really* know the nature of the mental states they describe. Much of what they say and think and do seems bizarre and alien to us. We are, therefore, about to enter a realm where the landscape is unstable, the inhabitants unreliable, and events unpredictable. A voyager who returned from the borderlands of that country recounts his experience as follows:

I was in the library of a school of theology with two or three strangers. We sat in the corner of a room lined with books, and I saw through a window a pleasing countryside of rolling open fields and copse. I know that I looked over the books with interest, but cannot remember any of the titles; I was also aware, without having been there, that the room above was similarly full of books.

Suddenly the room was changed; the books were gone, and against one wall was a large, comfortable double bed. Beside it stood a toilet and washbowl. As I was about to use the toilet, I noticed for the first time a window directly behind it from which I could see and hear many people sitting around the tables of an out-door terrace restaurant. To my embarrassment two people directly against the window on the opposite side of the wall looked in just as I began to void. I hastily closed a shutter that covered the lower half of the window, and rather uneasily continued to urinate. Then I climbed into bed, and was about to doze off when it dawned on me that a woman visitor was due to visit the seminary. I remembered somehow having been told that she was a famous lady preacher and that her visit was an honor and privilege for those of us in the seminary. Thought instantaneously became reality and she was in the room with me. I was out of bed and fully clothed, and she was apparently getting ready to climb into the bed I had just left. I was struck by the fact that she looked fortyish, had long, graying hair pulled severely back from her forehead and tied in a knot in the back. She was a complete stranger to me. Suddenly, however, as I looked at her again, she changed into a woman I had met casually some ten years before. I had a vaguely uncomfortable sense that she disapproved of me, although she seemed friendly enough on the surface. When she climbed into the bed, I remember thinking to myself, "That bed hasn't been made over clean for her," and feeling that this was wrong. I decided it was time for me to leave the room. On my way out I noticed a pile of jewelry on a small table. On closer inspection I found a number of brooches made from old Roman coins. I was enchanted with the details of the delicately wrought chariots and warriors and scenes of animal sacrifice that covered the faces of the coins, and thought to myself "I should take some of these home with me as presents for my family." At that instant, I noticed that each brooch had a large metal "M" attached in relief to its surface, and I realized then that the whole treasure belonged

to a fellow student and that it was too late for me to get
presents for my family. Without my being aware of leaving
the room, I suddenly found myself in the main entrance
hall of the building. A pad had been thrown on the floor of
a corner for me to sleep on, and I lay down to rest. At that
point I noticed that there was an information desk set into
the wall to the left of me. It seemed to me that I was
standing in a position where I could see both the man behind the desk and myself lying on the floor. As I looked,
the night-watchman came walking down a long corridor,
approached the clerk behind the desk and asked for a cup
of coffee. As the clerk handed it to him I could see through
the opaque sides of the paper cup that the powdered coffee
was not completely dissolved in the water. This made me
extremely uneasy and I decided it was time to leave. Abruptly, I was outdoors walking down a country path, accompanied by an unknown girl. All at once a large bird
hovered on wings over my head as it pounced on a large
moth. I reached up and grabbed the bird from the air. It
jabbed at my hand with its beak and dug its talons into my
skin. I remembered that I expected to be hurt, but was
pleased when the pain was minimal and felt quite proud of
myself for my bravery. I turned to the woman and said
"This is a sparrow hawk," thinking to myself that I had
known at first sight what sort of creature this was since, I
said to myself, the sparrow hawk is the only bird of prey
that hovers suspended in air on its fluttering wings. As I
spoke, the bird answered me, agreeing that he was indeed
a sparrow hawk. It seemed quite natural for a bird to talk,
and we had a long conversation before he finally flew
away. Unfortunately, I cannot remember what was said.

The voyager is, of course, a dreamer and his travel diary
a dream. As psychologists, our concern with dreams is focused on the nature of the mental processes that occupy that
third of our life we spend asleep. As psychopathologists,
our interest in the dream is twofold: on the one hand, it
often provides valuable clues to the elements in an individ-

ual patient's psychological conflict; on the other, it supplies us with analogues of mental processes exhibited by patients with severe mental illness.* Let us, therefore, examine the character and structure of our sample dream.

First and foremost is the fact that the dreamer hallucinates. Although the images of his dream are the product of his own sleeping imagination, he sees, hears and feels them as if they were real objects and people external to him. While asleep, he has no more doubt about their reality than he does when awake about the objects in the universe which he perceives through his senses. It is only after he wakes that he is able to see that he has been dreaming; then he is able to distinguish between his fantasy (the dream images) and actual reality; asleep he lacks the capacity for thus testing the reality of his experience.

Secondly, we find evidence of a disturbance in the dreamer's image of himself. His self-image does not have the unity and integrity common to the waking experience of most of us. At one and the same time, for example, he is lying in his dream on a pad in the corner and standing where he can observe both himself and the clerk behind the information desk. A further distortion of perception is apparent in the dreamer's knowledge that the coffee powder is not thoroughly mixed with the water, despite the fact that this is hidden from his vision by the opaque paper cup. He knows it by a sort of "sixth sense," by a direct awareness not derived through the usual channels of sensation; there is a direct line of communication between him and the coffee without the interposition of sensation. In short, the boundary lines of his image of himself are not sharp and stable: he can break into two, and he appears to learn the secrets of inanimate objects without benefit of information derived

---

* Our concern here is only with the latter. For the special problems of dream analysis, the reader should consult Freud's systematic works on the subject (9, 25).

through his senses; for most of us sensation lies at the boundary between ourselves and the external world.

Finally we must note about the dream a quality of bizarreness which is composed of several elements. Scenes shift abruptly and discontinuously. People change their identity; the furniture of a room is unpredictably altered. Unusual things happen; birds talk, toilets are placed against windows opening into restaurants, sleeping pads are spread on the floor of public corridors, one is dispossessed of one's bed. And yet none of this seems remarkable to the dreamer; he goes from one adventure to the next quite unconcerned at the inconsistencies and logical absurdities of what is happening.

The dream introduces us to a world of thought radically different from that of waking life. In the latter, objects are ordered in space and time, and changes occur in systematic patterns which can be expressed in logical, conceptual terms. The human being in the real world of waking usually has no confusion as to his own personal unity and identity. What he learns of the world around him he learns from the information about it provided by his senses, and by the logical, conceptual operations of his mind. His sensation is interposed between himself and the world, and ordinarily a man has no direct knowledge of the people and things around him except as it comes through his senses. The boundary lines between himself and the world are intact and firm.

Waking thought, furthermore, is guided and determined by the demands and exigencies of the external world. It conforms to reality. The thought of the dream state, on the other hand, is determined by the dreamer, without regard for the demands of his environment. It is his wishes, his feelings, and his impulses that determine the form his images take. He creates his own world around him capriciously, as the spirit moves him.

That these two modes of thought are called *primary proc-*

ess thinking (i.e. that of the dream) and *secondary process thinking* (i.e. that concerned with reality), implies a hypothesis as to their origins. Primary process thought is likened to the state of mentation of the infant who has not yet developed an image of himself as separate from the world; neither has he learned to think in rational concepts; his images are determined by his needs and impulses, and he does not as yet distinguish between his inner fantasy and external reality. As he grows, his ego develops in complexity and strength; he becomes more aware of the demands of reality, he learns to understand reality and to manipulate it to provide his needs; he secondarily develops the capacity for logical thought and motor skills, as well as the ability to test the consonance of his own thoughts with the state of reality. In this way he adapts himself to survival in the world. In other words, as the human being develops, this latter secondary process thinking tends more and more to supersede the more primitive primary process thinking. The latter does not entirely disappear, however, as the secondary mode grows stronger. In adult life there is always a potential for both, and the proportions of each fluctuate. When the symbolic logician is solving his formulae he is almost entirely under the sway of secondary process thought; when he dreams, the balance tips the other way. Most waking fantasy is somewhere in between. We shall return to these concepts after a consideration of some of the manifestations of major mental illness, for dream and fantasy are not the only abodes of primary process thinking. Of particular importance for the student of psychopathology is the fact that in the major mental disorders one finds defects in some of the basic functions of the ego. As a result major distortion of thought and perception take place which follow more closely the modes of primary rather than secondary process thinking.

It is time, therefore, for us to turn our attention to these phenomena, although they are not entirely unfamiliar to us.

Joan A. in her ecstatic vision and paranoid ideas, and
Schreber with his somatic hallucinations both showed us
such disturbances in a marked degree, and more recently we
have examined the splitting of her self-image experienced by
Clara D. Clara on the one hand appeared actually to feel
that she was thus divided into two parts, and confused with
the image of Dr. Jones; on the other hand, she knew this
was "silly"—that is, that in reality such things do not occur.
In Walter F., a young man of nineteen, we may observe a
similar breaking down of the boundaries of himself. He
found it extremely difficult to communicate to his doctor
what he was describing, as if there really were no adequate
words to convey his meaning.

> Here's my impression [he said]. When you speak to me,
> or when I speak to you, it doesn't seem right. That is, you
> know what I'm saying, and in turn, if you say something
> to me, I know what you say, but it sounds as though—
> when I talk now—it sounds as though I'm talking to me.

A moment later, again with obvious trouble in finding the
right words, he said,

> Well, I'm afraid that what I'm saying to you right now
> is—is—I know what I'm saying, but I don't know. That is,
> I can hear my own voice, but I'm not sure that you can
> hear it in the same way—that I express it. I know what I
> was saying, but it doesn't seem as though I'm saying it to
> you; it seems as if I'm saying it to myself. I don't know if
> my thought is going in the right direction.

The patient appears to be experiencing a confusion between his perception of himself and his perception of his
doctor. He perceives talking to his doctor as talking to himself. He is not quite sure who he is and who his doctor is,
where he ends and where his doctor begins. There is a confusion of identities; he is not certain about their discreteness
or the boundaries between them. His concept of himself as

an independent unit separate from others is disordered; in other words his ego boundaries (the boundaries of his self-image) are no longer intact.

There were other indications of a disturbance in the integrity and unity of his identity. He felt that if he wanted to do something he would not be able to translate the mental wish into bodily performance. The two (impulse and action) were wrenched apart; he could not bridge the gap. He was, furthermore, afraid of "losing his senses," as he put it; he was afraid of slipping into a state of being (or non-being) where he would be nobody, disintegrated into nothing, dissolved into the universe. Furthermore, he had a peculiar sense of time. He felt that his own time-sequence was running backward as compared with that of other people—that when everyone else had arrived in the 1970's he would have lived backward into the 1940's. This was for him a directly perceived and very frightening awareness of the movement of time.

Again, as with Clara D., Walter F. appears to recognize that the perceptions he has of himself do not accord with what can really happen; although his perceptions caused him near panic that he would dissolve into nothingness, he still speaks of his experiences as being "as if I'm saying it to myself"; there is still a provisional quality about them. In the account that Gérard de Nerval * has left us of his madness (which led eventually to his suicide by hanging), the distortions in his perceptions have the quality of utter certainty for him.

> When I reached the Place de la Concorde [he writes] I thought of killing myself. Several times I started toward the Seine, but something stopped me from completing my plan. The stars shone in the sky. Suddenly it seemed to me

* *Selected Writings of Gérard de Nerval* trans. and with an introduction by Geoffrey Wagner, Grove Press, New York, 1957.

that they were all extinguished like the candles I had seen
in church. I thought that the hour had arrived and that we
had come to the end of the world predicted in the Apoca-
lypse of Saint John. I thought I saw a black sun in an empty
sky and a red ball of blood above the Tuileries. I said to
myself, "The eternal night is beginning, and it will be
terrible. What will happen when men find that there is no
more sun?"

I returned by the Rue Saint-Honoré and pitied the be-
lated country folk whom I met. When I came to the Louvre
I walked as far as the square and there a strange sight
greeted me. I saw several moons moving swiftly across the
clouds, driven rapidly by the wind. I thought that the earth
had left its orbit and was wandering through the firmament
like a ship that had lost its masts, approaching or receding
from the stars which grew alternately larger and smaller.
I contemplated this chaos for two or three hours and then
set out for Les Halles.

A short while later Nerval was hospitalized.

At first I imagined that all the people collected in this
garden [other patients in the hospital] had some influence
over the stars and that the man who was walking in an incessant circle was regulating the movement of the sun . . .
To myself I attributed an influence over the moon's
course . . . I gave a mystic significance to the conversations
of the attendants and to those of my comrades. It seemed
to me that these people were the representatives of every
race in the world and that together we had to reorganize
the courses of the stars and further develop the sidereal
system . . . My own role seemed to be to re-establish universal harmony by means of Cabalistic arts and to seek a
solution in summoning the occult powers of the various
religions . . .

That thought led me to think that there was a vast con-
spiracy between every living creature to re-establish the
world in its original harmony, that communication took

place by means of the magnetism of the stars, that an un-
broken chain around the earth linked the various intelligences devoted to this general communion, and that songs,
dances, looks, magnetized from one to another, betrayed
the same aspiration.

From that moment on, when I felt sure that I was being
subjected to the tests of a secret initiation, an invincible
strength entered my soul. I imagined myself a hero living
under the gaze of the gods; everything in nature took on a
new aspect, and secret voices, warning and exhorting me,
came from plants, trees, animals, and the most lowly in-
sects. The speech of my companions took mysterious turns,
whose sense alone I could understand, and formless, inanimate objects lent themselves to the calculations of my
mind; from combinations of pebbles, from shapes in cor-
ners, chinks or openings, from the outlines of leaves, colors,
sounds, and smells, emanated for me hitherto unknown
harmonies.

Nerval's perceptions are radically distorted in two direc-
tions. He has in the first place lost his sense of himself as
a distinct being in a world of other distinct beings. Instead
he is in mysterious direct communication with objects and
"intelligences"; knowledge comes directly to him without
the intercession of the sensations that most of us rely upon
to give us information about the world. Furthermore he can
directly influence external objects (the moon, for instance)
without bothering to use his musculoskeletal apparatus
which is interposed for most of us between our wishes and
accomplishing them.

Secondly, Nerval's perceptions of the world around him
have created a universe that radically differs from the standard cosmology. Black suns, multiple moons, celestial balls
of blood, the earth broken loose from its orbit—these products of Nerval's own mental activity have become utterly
real for him; they color his perception of his environment,

and he does not question the veracity of his hallucinations. When he sets them against external reality, the latter loses. The world is made over in his image of it. His failure to recognize the subjective, phantasmal nature of his hallucinations indicates in him a disturbance in an important function of the ego—that of *reality testing*. Let us examine this further by observing the function as it returned in a man who had temporarily lost it.

Gerald T., aged thirty-four, was brought to the hospital in delirium tremens. It was quickly apparent that he had no idea where he was: he insisted that his hospital room was a rooming house "a few doors down from McGintey's Bar and Grill." When questioned he usually missed the actual date by three or four weeks. Despite his marked disorientation he was alert and feverishly busy day and night. It was soon apparent that he was hallucinating; he would stare intently at blank walls, evidently entranced by what he saw. He would listen acutely to an invisible "companion" and reply in staccato sentences, carrying on long conversations in this manner. A great part of his bustling activity was devoted to pushing, grunting, bracing his feet, tugging, and seeming to guide a heavy object now this way, now that; occasionally he would yell out "Hey, watch it, Joe!" He was generally quite oblivious of the people who were standing around watching him; his whole attention was focused on his job. Rarely, by persistently tapping him on the shoulder one could momentarily distract him; he would then give the intruder a quick, annoyed glance and mutter curtly and condescendingly, "Get away, boy! Get away, boy!—I'm busy!"

After many hours of this incessant activity, the patient finally fell asleep. He was seen again by his doctor immediately upon awakening. Now he was alert, quiet, responsive, and in complete contact with the doctor. He talked and answered questions relevantly, and was no longer busy with private activities, or with private sights and sounds and sensations; he was no longer disoriented nor hallucinating. He described what had been going on during the previous few hours as follows:

> I had to go some place and I rode there on an electric train . . . a little toy electric train. And I rode so fast I couldn't slow down . . . When I'd come to an intersection I'd fly over the thing and then land back down on the tracks again . . . I was supposed to have helped a man down the hill with a great big ladder, and I was going down through the square with this big ladder, and I was tugging and tugging and tugging, and the only way I could steer this thing, which was a great huge thing in the air, was through sheer force—to pull it and to try to drag my feet. It was like a big ladder, but it had a base on it to render it portable. It had wheels, and the man who ran the thing— oh, it had no motor; it would coast—and I wondered how the man could handle the thing. And he used to look out through a little peep hole . . . There was a little cab and a seat in there, and then this big ladder up in the air. And I helped him, like I say, down through the square, and I was trying to hold the thing. And down in there somewhere we took a turn to the left, and I hit some old fellow, and I dragged him in front of me and I finally got the thing stopped, but only after a great deal of struggle physically.

It soon became apparent that the patient was describing and remembering his recent hallucinations as if they were events that had really happened to him. He did not initially question the actual occurrence of these bizarre experiences. Gradually, as he continued to talk, he began to look somewhat puzzled; then suddenly he paused, and said, "You know, I think it's all just a great, big, wild dream, because none of it makes even one quarter of one percent of sense." A few moments later, as he was talking about guiding the

ladder through the square, he began examining his hands.
Asked why he did so, he replied:

> I looked at my hands to see if that actually happened.
> If it had, my hands would be all beat up . . . I guess it must
> have been a dream, because otherwise you'd have fourteen
> cops after you. And secondly, you would never be allowed
> to push a great big ladder down the street. And certainly,
> if you had a ladder to transport, you'd transport it by truck.
> I mean, if you take the thing apart, either I have just come
> out of a great big dream, or I have had some wild dreams
> in the last few days.

From this it was clear that as the patient recalled his recent hallucinatory experiences, he began to compare them
with other experiences that came to him from external reality through his senses—his noticing, for example, that his
hands were not battered and blistered and bruised. He began
to compare the events of his hallucinatory period with his
knowledge of the nature of the world as he knew it from
previous experience. As he did so, he realized that there was
a discrepancy between the two sets of data. He now accepted the sensations from the external world as real and
valid; these took precedence over the hallucinatory images
of his toxic psychosis; on this basis, he judged as unreal, as
"dream," the inner-derived hallucinatory experiences which
he had previously accepted as reality. Such is *reality testing*
—the ability to distinguish between experience of inner
events and experience of outer events, between fantasy and
reality (of both the physical and social environment), between hallucination and sensation derived from the outside
world. It is a function so basic to our normal adult waking
mental life that we are hardly aware of its existence. Disturbances in the function lead to behavior that is usually
clearly recognizable as abnormal.

The same loss of the ability to test reality was evident in

Sandra M., aged thirty- six, who also manifested a further disturbance in ego functioning resulting in a gross disorganization of her thought processes. As she was listening one evening to a popular male radio singer of the day, she began to feel sexually aroused. Soon she began to experience all the physical sensations, vaginal and elsewhere, of having sexual intercourse. This puzzled her until at the end of his song the singer exclaimed "Wow!" Then she suddenly realized that it was he who was having intercourse with her from a distance.

She could not at first understand how this was possible, but then the explanation dawned on her: Two engineers at a local radio station had been at work for some time in a secret subterranean vault beneath the station facilities. Here they had perfected a small machine which a man could strap to the inside of his thigh; this, when turned on, would enable the wearer to have sexual intercourse with her from afar. The two engineers were delighted with their invention because, as she said, "they felt it had great commercial possibilities in the taverns in the South End." By the time she came to the hospital the machine was apparently in full use; she complained that she had hardly a moment free of the sensations of intercourse, and she had long grown sick of it.

As with Gerald T. we find her suffering from hallucinations, predominately the tactile sensations of sexual intercourse, which are as real to her as if she were in reality participating in the act. Again, like Gerald T. during the acute phase of his illness, she is unable to see that her sensations are derived from inner processes, and are not from the stimuli of external reality. More than that, she devises a system of ideas to explain the cause of her hallucinations. Here, too, her reality testing function fails; she does not see the absurdity of the ideas in comparison with the real structure and nature of the external world. Her image of the world is distorted not only by the private sensations she imposes on it, but as well by the system of private and fallacious concepts she employs to explain her world—that is, by her *delusions*. Let us examine these further.

Obviously, her explanation that someone is having sexual intercourse with her from a distance is absurd. The sexual desire and the erotic sensations that she experiences arise within her; they are not produced by the external stimulations of male partners. Despite this, the patient attributes them to the agency of others; she makes other people responsible for producing the sexual sensations that are in reality her own. She *projects* sexual desire and lasciviousness onto others and looks upon herself as the passive, unwilling victim of their machinations.

Her *projection* is an ego mechanism of defense. Rather than being a loss of a specific ego function, it constitutes an active operation of the ego by means of which she can keep from her own consciousness the awareness of her own sexuality. By ascribing its source to others, she avoids the responsibility for having such feelings and desires; they arise through no doing of her own. Projection is not a new concept for us. It was evident in Chester B.'s phobic concerns with the dangers of the world that surrounded him—with elevators, sewers, and streetcars. However, Chester B.'s reality testing was intact; he knew that his fears were "silly," that the world was not as his fantasy painted it. For Sandra M., on the contrary, her fantasy is the world. The actuality of external reality fails to temper the strength of the projected images of her fantasy, which then take on the nature of delusions.

We must now examine two further patients who will show us in a negative sense a disturbance in the ego's capacity for conceptualization and at the same time the positive emergence of elements characteristic of primary process thought. George R. was a man in his fifties who for many years had been a patient in a large state hospital. One of the

jobs assigned to him in the ward where he lived was to help
the ward attendant every morning to make the fifty-odd beds
in the huge dormitory where all the patients slept. This he
did quite docilely and co-operatively despite the fact that he
called himself with great pomp and pride "George Amory
Rooney, President of the United States." He insisted that he
had been legally and duly elected to this office, but had been
done out of his job by sinister politicians who had taken
over the reins of government. He was suspicious of everyone, Democrat and Republican alike, and was constantly
on the watch against a plot to take his life. Every night he
would insist that for his own safety he be locked in one of
the private rooms at the back of the spacious dormitory.
This had to be crossed to reach his room, and invariably
when he came to the middle of the dormitory on his way
to bed he would drop to the floor and yell to the attendant
who was accompanying him, "Get down, you dumb son-
of-a-bitch, they're shooting at us." The latter would have to
fall to his hands and knees and the march to bed would be
continued in that fashion. Furthermore, he believed that as
President of the United States he owned the hospital. Once
a week he dispatched a long letter to the superintendent who
was, he thought, subject to his orders; therein he stated of
any of the staff who had displeased him in the preceding few
days, "Dr. X is a dumb son-of-a-bitch and is to be fired immediately." The weekly communiqué invariably contained
a long list of such aggrieved commands. Despite his conviction that he was President, that he was all-powerful, that
he owned the hospital and could fire whom he liked, that
the superintendent was his lackey, George R. never seemed
perturbed that the doctors he had dismissed remained in
service, he never complained at being kept as a mental patient on a locked ward, he never objected to being ordered
about by lowly attendants in the hospital routine, and with
equanimity he made hundreds of beds. The two logically

incompatible sets of ideas rested side by side in his mind
without apparent conflict. He never seemed to consider that
one attitude precluded the other. He appeared to have lost
the ability to harmonize, to unify, and to integrate separate
ideas into a logical whole. If two concepts were logically
mutually exclusive, he did not discard one as being inconsistent with reality. His consciousness could encompass both
concepts without intellectual embarrassment or recognition
of a logical dilemma. The synthetic function of his ego was
impaired and at the same time there emerged a type of mentation in which mutually contradictory ideas could exist har-
moniously side by side—a characteristic of primary process
thinking.

Harold P. at twenty-nine showed an even more radical
disorganization of his conceptual thought processes, which
invaded the structure of his language. This can best be seen
in a passage from an interview with him during his hospitalization:

> Well, the solution with that—the two points about the
> naked women is that—the two points with naked women
> is—is the misuse of—of that design in—and also the—
> the temptation to misuse. They used these two functions
> to wishful thinking and put out a disoperability. In fact,
> they actually (I believe from background) had 14 girls
> which they used in—in their services—and—and both
> male and female. And it—it is essentially a crime and—
> and a disorder. And—and it—it is—they—well, even in-
> filtrate the church and they even infiltrate the schools and
> things like that. That is quite correct. The—the problem—
> it—it may be at the highest level. There—the general man-
> ager himself (I—I have not had contact with him person-
> ally) but the supposition is that way. The—McCord—the
> gambling head is sufficient power that he over-rules the boss
> a bit. I thought—I thought it was by him being a partner
> and—and the—the impression was he reversed himself on
> things and they louse each other up. They do it them-

selves personally and everybody else. And—and the problem—well, with McCord—I hear that he's a relative of Mr. Winston, the—the boss who is there. I—I suspect Mr. Winston was in the service and—and they use the service as background facility arrangement. But the trouble with that—that is for warfare, and they force, you know, the tapping with the stick or the impression of irritation, you know, in—in there. Gives the effect you're going batty and stuff like that. And—and they actually have associated with the church. They're—they're angry against priests and against the church—the association they did not want it in. So to some extent they—they—contacts have been established whereby they can enter more quietly, you know, where they will not be attacked and will not call attention to and the—the church will not be attacked specifically that it is present. Because they're both protecting the church and being the benefit—both—both cases it is— such is the case. And also the young—I—personally have studied so much and—and helped—kept track of things because although unfortunately my mother has been ill and I've watched over her and taken care of her, it has given— granted me an ability which is most interesting insofar as I am not only—well, I am a good son actually. It—she— in her sickness she has been perverted, it sort of seems by her illness and by—and also by people's reactions to her illness if they do not understand to some—some extent. And Watson talked to somebody by the name of Ordway and he—he told him something about my mother. I have an idea that they changed her mind to attacking my mind, but I was my mother's mind and balance and guide, see. And since that being the case it—it was of a destructive nature—fighting against her own balance and her own mind, you know.

At first sight this appears utterly chaotic and senseless. Gradually, however, as one reflects on the patient's communication, one begins to get a vague, general notion of what he is talking about: there is some sort of widespread

plot abroad to bring mischief to himself and his mother and
the church and schools, using the armed forces and the crim-
inal services of lewd men and women, and employing the
tactic of creating minor annoyances like "tapping with the
stick" to "give the effect you're going batty."

If one tried to be more specific about what is happening
than this; if one wonders what is the relation between the
fourteen girls and the church and the patient's mother; if
one tries to determine exactly who is doing what and how
and to whom, one is trying to force more information from
the patient's language than it contains. By ordinary standards his sentence structure is delapidated and his syntax
atrocious. He breaks off in the middle of thoughts and introduces ideas that seem to have no logical connection with
what has gone before. He makes seeming *non sequiturs* such
as "I personally have studied so much and—and helped—
kept track of things because although unfortunately my
mother has been ill, etc." He says things loosely and approximately, as, for example, ". . . they're both protecting
the church and being the benefit—both—both cases it is—
such is the case." He uses new, coined words like "disoperability" and elaborate clusters of words that sound as if they
should mean something, but don't, such as "background
facility arrangement."

In short the patient appears to be utterly illogical. In ordinary usage, language is an attempt to communicate about
the world. Words stand for things and the temporal and
spatial relationships among them. Although it is rarely
reached, the aim of language is to communicate clearly: as
objects are distinguished from one another, so should the
words that denote them be clearly defined. The terms that
express relationships should accurately mirror and convey
the relations that exist among objects. The logic of language
should reflect the logic of the observed universe.

The patient does not abide by these rules. His terms are

poorly defined, their referents unclear, and his syntax conveys little idea of the normal observable relationships of objects to one another. But it is not that he is being *il*logical —that is, that he is trying to abide by the usual rules of logic and syntax and is doing a bad job of it. Rather he appears to be *a*logical, or perhaps better, *para*logical—he is operating in accordance with principles other than those of ordinary logic.

What seems to link together the various people and institutions which he mentions is not their external spatio-temporal relationships. Rather it is the significance with which he endows them as being somehow involved in the diabolical plot of perversion and destruction which he senses about him. He can jump in his confused, alogical abrupt way from the fourteen girls to McCord to the church to his mother, not because they have an actual external connection with one another, but because they all have a place as subject or object of the plot. And the plot is not for him a sharp intellectual concept, but a vague, poorly defined, and delimited feeling of all-pervading evil. He is, in other words, talking about his own private inner world of reality; it obeys its own inner laws of behavior, like dreams; it does not conform to the usual more logical operations of the external sensory world that is common to most of us. His thinking and experience is *autistic*, and his language reflects the nature of this private world, even to the point of containing neologisms like "disoperability" when it is necessary to create them in his attempts to communicate. It is clear, however, that his being in the grip of this inner world radically distorts the patient's perception of the outer world and his ability to deal with it in a rational fashion. His ego functions are inoperative if not irretrievably impaired; reality testing, the capacity for conceptual thinking and logical synthesis, his self-image are all severely disorganized. His ability to perceive the external world as a logical, self-consistent set of events is disturbed, nor can he order his thoughts and words into a language structure paralleling the structure of external reality. Like the dreamer he is under the sway of primary process thinking. Unlike the dreamer this is not for him a temporary condition to be dispelled by awaking; it is the chronic mental state of a chronic mental disorder.

From what we have seen it is evident that there are major incompatibilities between primary and secondary process thinking. This, as we have said earlier, should not be construed to mean that the former is abnormal, the latter normal, or that the latter normally entirely supersedes the former. It is closer to the truth to understand that every human being retains the capacity in greater or lesser degree for both types of thought processes. Primary thought is psychogenetically more primitive; as the ego develops, secondary thought processes become increasingly operative. Most of us as adults live in a world where we perceive external events with reasonable clarity, and see them as being ordered in place and time in such a way that information about them can be logically structured, scientifically manipulated, and communicated accurately to others. We live by and rationally adapt ourselves as well as we can to what we, perhaps uncritically, call reality.

But each man retains the tendency to revert to the earlier mode of thought when he dreams, when he creates, and when he is mentally ill. It is particularly in this latter group that one finds perceptions of the world that are distorted, or at least different. Those with major mental illness seem less bound to and less bound by the conventions of the real world around them. Instead, inner forces and fantasies spring up in them to color and drastically distort their perceptions and beliefs about themselves and the external world. Their logic, if it is a logic, is one of a region where time is meaningless, where objects and people do not have sharp distinctions from one another, where polar opposites live in harmony, and where rational concepts are super-fluous.

The regression in illness to developmentally more primitive patterns of mentation is, however, never complete. It is not accurate to say that the adult when he suffers a major mental illness exactly reproduces the state of awareness of the infant, or conversely that the nature of the infant's thought processes indicates that he is mentally ill. This is to ignore the universe of experiences the adult has traversed in his lifetime, which make for the richness and uniqueness of his personality even when its structure is crumbling. Even with his disordered psyche, the sick adult is a thing apart from the infant with his relatively simple mental apparatus. The manifestations of the adult's illness result from the fact that specific regressions in his mental functioning to more primitive modes of thought lead to a serious distortion of his entire personality. A study of the factors leading to such a regression of thought processes is central to the complex problem of the etiology of the major mental disorders. We must, therefore, now turn our attention to a consideration of some of the difficulties that face the investigator in this area.

XV

Major Distortions in Ego Functioning—
Some Questions of Etiology

In our examination of Gerald T. our interest was focused primarily on the changes in his function of reality testing. We did not comment on the fact that he was disoriented both with regard to time and to place. Disorientation is a disturbance of one of a group of intellectual functions which include (as well as the capacity to determine accurately one's location in space and time) memory, attention, and comprehension. In certain types of mental disorders any or all of these functions may be affected.

Samuel G., for example, was an eighty-two-year-old retired lobster fisherman who was brought to the hospital suffering from a mild bronchopneumonia. He soon recovered from his infection, but during his stay on the ward it became rapidly apparent that his mental status was markedly abnormal. This was not evident to the casual observer; Sam was always polite, docile, and friendly. But a few moments of conversation with him disclosed major difficulties. In the first place he insisted that he was in his rooming-house, not in the hospital. Furthermore, he was convinced that the Majestic Burlesque was "three doors down and over," and he frequently stood at the ward window, staring at the morgue across the street, in the hopes of catching a glimpse of some of the dancing girls on their way to work. For him the date fluctuated somewhere within the limits of the first decade of the twentieth century; Taft was President; and although the snow might be falling heavily outside his window he was as liable to say it was July as January. He seemed to remember many of the events of his youth, and indeed would at times talk garrulously about these to anyone who would listen. But any memory of the more recent thirty or forty years of his life was quite gone. He could not remember what he had had for breakfast that morning, never knew his doctor's name, and constantly forgot where the bathroom or his bed was. He liked to wander and frequently left the ward unobserved to explore the hospital; invariably he would be unable to find his way back, to the consternation of the nurses who would have to hunt for him. This difficulty was solved only by affixing a large piece of three-inch adhesive tape to the back of his bathrobe inscribed "Please return me to Ward 2." During his stay in the hospital, Sam showed no improvement in his mental functions, and since he could no longer adequately care for himself, it was finally necessary to transfer him to a state mental hospital for chronic care.

It came as no surprise to the ward staff that Sam did not improve, for during his stay it had been determined that he was suffering from chronic, progressive disease of the brain, the result of damage to brain cells secondary to widespread cerebral arteriosclerosis. In fact, the diagnosis had been established in part from the characteristic pattern of his mental functioning which we have just observed. Indeed, whenever changes in intellectual functions of this sort are found, they are almost invariably produced by gross dysfunction of the brain, the result either of an acute toxic state (the delirium of fever, alcoholic delirium tremens, etc.) which is usually reversible, or of anatomical changes in brain tissue (injury, chronic toxicity, vascular disease, degenerative diseases, paresis, etc.) which are usually chronic and progressive.*

On the other hand, although many *disorders of ego function* (e.g. disturbed reality testing, hallucinations, disorders of the ability to conceptualize, delusion formation, disturbances in the boundaries of the self-image) are referable to gross acute or chronic disturbances of brain function, this is by no means invariably the case. On the contrary, there is as yet little known about the neuroanatomical, neurophysiological, or biochemical basis for most of the major mental disorders that afflict younger human beings. By any physiological measurement presently available, the function of their brains is not appreciably different from that of the brains of mentally well people. The question of the cause of the serious disturbances of mental function is clearly a complex one. In fact, it is inaccurate to speak of *the* cause since, as we have seen, each mental dysfunction may be associated with more than one apparently causal factor. In order to gain a more intimate experience with the complexity of the problem of etiology, let us single out the hallucination and pass in review a variety of conditions, both natural and experimental, which have led to the production of this phenomenon.

Among the early attempts to explore hallucinations experimentally, the use of hypnosis provided a tool of varying efficacy. In addition to his study of posthypnotic suggestion, Bernheim (20) described a number of experiments dealing with the production of hallucinations. He writes, for example:

* The reverse is not necessarily true—that is, brain damage does not always produce detectable changes in intellectual functions. For a discussion of other mental functions (e.g. judgment and mood) affected by brain disorders as well as for a description of the various clinical syndromes produced by brain disease, the reader should consult a standard textbook of psychiatry (e.g. J. R. Ewalt, E. A. Strecker, and F. G. Ebaugh (5), or D. K. Henderson and R. D. Gillespie (6)).

In Mme. G——, . . . an intelligent, impressionable, but not at all hysterical woman, I induced the most complex post-hypnotic hallucinations, in which all the senses took part. I made her hear military music in the courtyard of the hospital. The soldiers came upstairs and into the room. She saw a drum-major making *pirouettes* before her bed. A musician came up and spoke to her. He was intoxicated, and made unbecoming proposals to her. He wished to embrace her. She slapped him in the face twice, and called the sister and nurse, who ran up and put the drunken man out. This entire scene, suggested during sleep, developed itself before her, both spectator and actress, as vividly as reality. She had not been able to experience similar hallucinations before. She could not get rid of this one. She looked around and asked the other patients if they had not seen and heard what was going on. She could not distinguish between the illusion and reality. When it was all over I said to her, "It was only a vision I gave to you." She understood perfectly that it was a vision, but insisted that it was more than a dream and that it was as vivid as reality.

The content and action of Mme. G.'s hallucinations were determined for her by the experimenter's suggestions. In the account that the American psychiatrist and novelist, Weir Mitchell, has left of his experiences after taking mescaline, his images are his own, activated or released by the drug. In recent years the experimental investigation of hallucinations has been furthered by the use of a variety of hallucinogenic drugs, in particular mescaline, an extract of the cactus, peyote button, and d-lysergic acid, a derivative of ergot. But empirical knowledge of such agents has apparently always been man's. The local Indian tribes of the Southwest have long used the peyote button to produce religious ecstasy. And the date of Mitchell's article (1896) (44) indicates a scientific curiosity long before the current attempts at systematic study.

I had [writes Mitchell] a certain sense of the things about me as having a more positive existence than usual. It is not easy to define what I mean, and at the time I searched my vocabulary for a phrase or word which could fitly state my feeling. It was in vain . . . The display which for an enchanted two hours followed was such as I find it hopeless to describe in language which shall convey to others the beauty and splendour of what I saw. I shall limit myself to a statement of a certain number of the more definite visions thus projected on the screen of consciousness.

During these two hours I was generally wide awake . . . Time passed for me with little sense for me of its passage. I was critically attentive, watchful, interested and curious, making all the time mental notes for future use . . .

A white spear of grey stone grew to huge height, and became a tall, richly finished Gothic tower of very elaborate and definite design, with many rather worn statues standing in the doorways or on stone brackets. As I gazed, every projecting angle, cornice, and even the face of the stones at their joinings were by degrees covered or hung with clusters of what seemed to be huge precious stones, but uncut, some being more like masses of transparent fruit. All seemed to possess an interior light, and to give the faintest idea of the perfectly satisfying intensity and purity of these gorgeous colour-fruits is quite beyond my power. All the colours I have ever beheld are dull as compared to these . . .

After an endless display of less beautiful marvels I saw that which deeply impressed me. An edge of a huge cliff seemed to project over a gulf of unseen depth. My viewless enchanter set on the brink a huge bird claw of stone. Above, from the stem or leg, hung a fragment of some stuff. This began to unroll and float out to a distance which seemed to me to represent Time as well as immensity of Space. Here were miles of rippled purples, half transparent and of ineffable beauty. Now and then soft golden clouds floated from these folds, or a great shimmer went over the whole of the rolling purples, and things, like green

birds, fell from it, fluttering down into the gulf below . . .
A long while after I saw what seemed a shop with apothe-
caries' bottles, but of such splendour, green, red, purple,
as not outside of the pharmacies of fairy land.

On the left wall was pinned by the tail a brown worm of
perhaps a hundred feet long. It was slowly rotating, like
a catherine wheel, nor did it seem loathly. As it turned,
long green and red tentacles fell this way and that. On a
bench nearby two little dwarfs, made, it seemed, of leather,
were blowing through long glass pipes of green tint, which
seemed to me to be alive, so intensely, vitally green were
they . . .

I was at last conscious of the fact that at moments I was
almost asleep, and then wide awake. In one of these magic
moments I saw my last vision and the strangest. I heard
what appeared to be approaching rhythmical sounds, and
then saw a beach, which I knew to be that of Newport. On
this, with a great noise, which lasted but a moment, rolled
in out of darkness wave on wave. These as they came were
liquid splendours huge and threatening, of wonderfully
pure green, or red or deep purple, once only deep orange,
and with no trace of foam. These water hills of colour
broke on the beach with myriads of lights of the same tint
as the wave. This lasted some time, and while it did so, I
got back to more distinct consciousness, and wished the
beautiful terror of these huge mounds of colour would
continue.

A knock at my door caused me to open my eyes, and I
lost whatever wonder might have come after.

Although Mitchell's visions are perhaps richer than those
produced in the laboratory, they have the same characteristics of the hallucinations that usually follow the administration of both mescaline and lysergic acid. *Visual*
hallucinations are prominent and color is often described as
having an unearthly intensity and beauty. The visual imagery is frequently of vivid, abstract geometrical patterns

(which Mitchell described as a prelude to his later visions), and the hallucination of formed objects so striking in Mitchell's account is a less frequent occurrence. The quasi-mystical "sense of the things about me as having a more positive existence than usual" often accompanies the sensory phenomena. But before the aspiring mystic reaches for his draught, he should know that as often as these substances deify, they produce in their victims terrifying visions and dread premonitions of ineffable evil; the active principle is Manichean.

Compare Mitchell's experience with those of the poet Æ (36), for whom such airy and colorful visions were not uncommon.

> Instead of a dingy office [writes Æ] there would be a sky of rarest amethyst; a snow-cold bloom of cloud; high up in the divine wilderness, solitary, a star; all rapt, breathless and still; . . . Once, suddenly, I found myself on some remote plain or steppe, and heard unearthly chimes pealing passionately from I know not what far steeples. The earthbreath streamed from the furrows to the glowing heavens. Overhead the birds flew round and round crying their incomprehensible cries, as if they were maddened, and knew not where to nestle, and had dreams of some more enraptured nest in a diviner home. I could see a ploughman lifting himself from his obscure toil and stand with lit eyes as if he too has been fire-smitten and was caught into heaven as I was, and knew for the moment he was a god . . .
>
> There was a hall vaster than any cathedral, with pillars that seemed built out of living and trembling opal, or from some starry substance which shone with every colour, the colours of eve and dawn. A golden air glowed in this place and high between the pillars were thrones which faded, glow by glow, to the end of the vast hall. On them sat the Divine Kings. They were fire-crested. I saw the crest of the Dragon on one, and there was another plumed with bril-

liant fires that jetted forth like feathers of flame. They sat shining and starlike, mute as statues, more colossal than Egyptian images of their gods, and at the end of the hall was a higher throne on which sat one greater than the rest. A light like the sun glowed behind him.

There is a striking similarity in these visions to Mitchell's mescaline hallucinations. One finds the same majestic imagery, the same emphasis on color, and the same magical quality of mystical rapture. These were, however, visions induced not by drugs, but by meditation. Meditation is a psychological process; it is an ability acquired only by long practice and heroic self-discipline. The man who can meditate has the capacity to control the focus of his attention and awareness. He can at will exclude thoughts and sensations from his consciousness; he can voluntarily fix his attention on a single thought or object and hold it there steadily without interruption by the multitude of other thoughts and sensations that tend continuously to crowd into conscious awareness. This is not easily done, as anyone can attest who has tried to hold his attention for even a few seconds on *one* idea without the incursion of *any* other thoughts or images. The psychology of meditation is not well understood. Apparently the emptying of consciousness of its usual content of thought opens it to new states of awareness, which at times take on the garb of visions. In this it appears to be related to the somnambulic state of the hypnotic trance.

Possibly also related to meditation is the phenomenon of sensory deprivation. In this experimental procedure, the subject is deprived of sensations emanating from his environment by removing in so far as possible the source of the stimuli, or making them monotonously constant. His ears are plugged, his eyes blindfolded, and tactile and kinesthetic sensations are reduced by the application of splints and cotton padding about his body. After lying for hours in such isolation, subjects studied by Bexton (37) reported waking hallucinations of "integrated scenes." A man, for example, saw a "procession of squirrels with racks over their shoulders marching purposefully across a snowy field." Another saw "prehistoric monsters walking about in a jungle," or again "a miniature rocket ship discharging pellets and felt them hit his arm." Disease, as well as the experimenter, may provide the conditions of sensory deprivation. Patients in tank respirators for paralytic bulbar poliomyelitis, for example, may experience hallucinations as a result of the monotony and diminution of visual, tactile, and kinesthetic sensations. One such patient, immobile in his tank, believed that he had been driving through the Connecticut countryside in a blue convertible with the top down (38).

Bodily disease may also lead to hallucinations through other mechanisms not adequately understood. These appear to be related to changes in brain function associated with fever, exogenous and endogenous toxins, and less clearly defined factors related to stress as, for example, in post-operative deliria. A man in his forties, who in the course of four weeks had had several operations for a severe and complicated vascular condition, had a number of vivid and terrifying hallucinations during a protracted period of delirium. Two of them he described as follows:

> The most frightening experience I had [he writes] occurred just after my last operation. My first recollection was one of great difficulty in breathing and very confused, opaque surroundings. Finally, things came into focus and I found myself completely under water in a steel chamber with a dozen or so other people. All were holding on to handles fastened securely to the wall and were flutter-kicking their feet slowly as one would do in a swimming pool holding onto the edge. My private male nurse was on one side of me and my wife was on the other, each holding on with one hand and kicking their feet very, very

slowly. With the other hand they were holding me down. Every now and then someone would swim away from his hold but would then immediately swim back and resume the horizontal position. I complained bitterly that I could not hold my breath any longer and while I realized that it was probably necessary for me to remain under water, stated in no uncertain terms that I would like to come up for a breath of air and then promised that I would come right down again. They smiled and laughed and said no, that I must stay where I was. While academically I realized that I was probably in no danger, I became terrified of drowning, feeling that probably because of my condition I was not able to stay under water as long as they, so started to fight my way to the surface. As they both continued to hold me down, I suddenly got the thought that they were trying to drown me. . . .

In a very tiny room just off my room . . . there lived a person whom I never saw. This room must have been very thin because it was concealed in the wall between my room and the adjoining room which, I believe, was the nurses' sitting room. At night this person would open up an almost invisible slot in the wall between his room and mine from which tiny tentacles of wire would begin to appear.

Usually he would start out with just one seeking tentacle which would work its way very, very slowly out the slot and down one of the nearby walls, generally near the intersection with the ceiling. The manner in which these wires were moved was very ingenious. It was something like snaking a rope to make it go from one place to another while lying flat on the floor. This manipulator, by the faintest motion, could move a wire at a snail's pace. After the wire had reached possibly three or four feet, a second wire would follow along next to it holding, at its end, a very tiny device which he would use to support the first wire at the point where possibly gravity might have pulled it down off its precarious position on the wall.

I used to lie in bed fascinated watching this procedure going on because it was done so very slowly, carefully and deliberately that never did one of the wires fall off. If the manipulator wanted one of his wires to descend, he would only have to wait until gravity dropped the seeking end and it would then form a right angle with the primary line and begin to snake down the wall toward the floor.

The manipulator used these wires (sometimes he had as many as 50 or 100 of them out at one time) mainly as an amusement to himself. Frequently he would go all the way around the room to a catch which would hold one of my doors open and, very carefully, snap it in the opposite position from that which it normally held. He would occasionally try the route across the ceiling and, since he had gravity working very hard against him all this time, would put out endless bearings until the whole network became very complex.

I had a flashlight by my bed and when the night light would not illuminate the room well enough to see exactly what he was doing, I would follow the seeking end of the wires with my flashlight. I think he almost appreciated this assistance as I imagined that I sometimes heard a sort of chuckling noise from behind the partition. Lights, in fact, didn't bother him a bit as I could turn on the big light by my bed illuminating the room quite satisfactorily and get a very clear view of his whole setup.

Several times my wife came into the room while he had one of his networks in operation and although I pointed them out to her, and could see them very clearly myself, she was unable to make them out (45).

Although some of this patient's visions may have been initiated by the many stimuli of hospital life (surgery, nursing care, etc.), they were by no means entirely illusions— that is misinterpretations of real stimuli from the external world. The patient in his delirious fancy elaborated on whatever may have been the source of his experiences; he furnished his world with the products of his vivid fantasy, made real for him in the form of hallucinations.

Finally, let us examine a patient for whom the precipitating factors were more complex than those we have already observed and in whom the hallucinations formed only a part of a much larger psychological disorganization. John S., a boy of fourteen, was brought to the hospital following a tragic accident. He had made a miniature bomb by stuffing the heads of kitchen matches into a small metal container. Without warning this exploded as he held it, severely mutilating his right hand. In the hospital his hand was cleaned, debrided, and bandaged; during these emergency measures, he seemed calm, and all during his first week on the pediatric ward he appeared untroubled and comfortable.

One morning with little prior warning he was taken to the operating room to make the first change of bandages. The patient became suddenly very fearful, and asked that he be given ether while the doctors worked on his hand. He was assured that the procedure would not hurt and was offered a blindfold to prevent him from catching sight of his wound. The patient refused, and when the bandages had been removed completely exposing the hand to view, he took a quick look. The injured hand was not a pleasant sight: the middle finger was completely gone, as was most of the ring finger, and the terminal phalanges of the others. The palm was totally denuded of skin, and the whole was drawn together into a grotesque shape amid a jungle of wires holding fractures in place. Swollen to twice its natural size, and an angry red, it looked, as an observer said, like "the claw of a monster."

After a rapid glance, the patient suddenly cried out, "My God, what have I done! What a horrible hand!" At once he began to plead with the doctor, "Cover it up! I don't ever want to see it—cover it up! Cover it up!" In spite of the patient's terrified pleas, it was not possible to cover the hand until a senior surgeon had come to advise on further procedures; the hand remained exposed and in full view for over three-quarters of an hour.

After his initial outburst, as he lay there on the operating table, the patient grew quieter. He stopped begging to have his hand covered, but began repetitively singing in a low tone to himself a blues song with his own words: "My hand is gone—I ain't got no hand." At last the procedure was finished, and with his hand rebandaged, the patient was returned to his room, where his mother was waiting for him. At the sight of her, he burst into tears, cried intermittently for an hour, and then fell off to sleep.

When he awoke some four or five hours later, the nurses on the ward noted that his behavior had changed. He seemed quieter than usual, less responsive to them, preoccupied, and withdrawn into himself. From his movements and facial expressions, it appeared that he was hallucinating, though initially the patient said nothing to confirm this impression. Over the next couple of days the patient began to talk and it became clear that he was profoundly disturbed. He spoke openly about seeing and hearing "a bunch of men" on the ledges outside of his window, who were going to "beat his head off." When he was visited by the psychiatrist he would point a toy gun at him, and in deadly earnest say, "What will happen to you when I pull the trigger? This is a real gun." He repeatedly expressed great concern about his body: he feared that he was rapidly losing weight, and was convinced, despite evidence and reassurance to the contrary, that his calves were wasting away to nothing. He was observed to be constantly touching and fingering his penis, though he made no comment about this. What was particularly disturbing to the ward personnel was that he made sexual advances toward all the nurses, and began to masturbate openly and shamelessly. This resulted in his being transferred to the psychiatric ward, where all of his difficulties persisted. He continued to hallucinate, to suffer from delusions, to masturbate openly, and to remain withdrawn from and indifferent to people around him, except on those occasions when he would impulsively and inappropriately make sudden advances to a nurse.

John S.'s disturbance was clearly not limited to the fact that he was hallucinating. He was withdrawn from the people around him; his behavior was inappropriate and showed a lack of concern for social demands; he was preoccupied with his body; he entertained delusions; in short he was suffering from a major disorganization of personality which led to the diagnosis of acute schizophrenia.*

From our brief review of hallucinations, it is evident that many factors may lead to the appearance of them. These factors, as we have seen, may be understood in either neurochemical or neurophysiological terms (experimental drugs, physical illness, sensory deprivation), or in psychological terms (hypnosis, meditation, emotional trauma). And the etiological relationships are complicated. Delirium tremens, for example, is regularly associated with the prolonged heavy intake of alcohol. But the relationship between the two is not so simple as it at first sight appears; it is not yet clear, for instance, whether the hallucinations are the result of the direct toxic effect of alcohol on brain tissue, of the response of the latter to the abrupt withdrawal of alcohol, or of the avitaminosis secondary to making alcohol the staple of the diet. Again, in sufficient doses, lysergic acid produces vivid hallucinations, especially of repetitive geometrical patterns, and it seems reasonable to ascribe the distortions in perception to the effect of the drug. There still remain, however, many as yet undiscovered intermediary steps between the administration of the chemical and the appearance of the hallucinations; the exact nature of the biochemical

* For a description of the various forms and symptoms of schizophrenia, cf. J. R. Ewalt, E. A. Strecker, and F. G. Ebaugh (5), or D. K. Henderson and R. D. Gillespie (6).

changes effected by the drug in brain metabolism is not known.

So far we have considered only the question of the *form* of the experience—that is, whether the idea was manifest as a thought or as a hallucination; we have said nothing about the etiology of the *content* of the thought in any of the forms it may take. It would be inaccurate to say that the administration of a drug causes the content of a thought. The mescaline swallowed by Weir Mitchell did not create in him the hallucination of the beach at Newport; it may have determined the fact that it came to him in the form of a hallucination, but it did not determine the shape and appearance of the image that represented Newport beach. If Mitchell had not already been familiar with Newport, it could not have appeared in his imagery. The drug may have *released* the memory of it; it did not create it out of nothing. It acts as a *precipitating* cause. To understand the etiology of the content of hallucinations it is necessary as well to take into account the *predisposing* causes in the past experience of the person who hallucinates—that is, to approach the problem of etiology within a psychological frame of reference.

When we turn to hallucinations which arise in connection with severe psychological stress our attempts to single out causal factors are even more difficult. That stress may precipitate a profound disorganization of psychological functioning became clear during the Second World War, when many men were seen to develop an acute schizophrenic reaction rapidly "cured" by removing them from the stressful situation. The nature of the "stress" could not be so well defined; anything from induction into the service to several weeks in combat might lead to the psychological disturbance. The sensitivity of the individual to stress, the sort of person he was, the type of character structure he brought to the stressful situation—these became important causal factors in determining the nature of his reaction.*

Such questions become of central importance in studying the profound mental illness, schizophrenia. These are no mere academic questions. Over half of *all* hospital beds (medical, surgical, psychiatric, etc.) in the United States are occupied by patients with schizophrenia. As a chronic, at present incurable, illness it brings untold emotional and financial hardship to many families. It is a major concern for those interested in problems of public health.

The etiology of schizophrenia is not a simple matter. Developmental, hereditary, neurochemical, neurophysiological, psychological, and sociological factors all have a part in producing the clinical syndrome. Which of these factors will ultimately prove to be of central importance is not as yet clear. Each of the scientific disciplines has observations and theories of relevance; and each of the disciplines has a language and theoretical concepts better adapted than its sisters' for dealing with *some,* not all, of the observations. Few investigators can work comfortably or effectively in more than one field at a time; each has to choose what interests him most. He must, however, respect the endeavors of his fellows to elucidate the area they have chosen to study. It is naïve and scientifically irresponsible, forsaking all others, to proclaim the truth for one path through the jungle.

* This, of course, ignores the complicated problem of determining and defining the chain of psychological, physiological, and neurochemical steps leading from stress to reaction.

Part IV

Emotions, Illness, and the

Therapeutic Relationship

XVI

DEFENSES AS CHARACTER TRAITS

Our attention has thus far been focused on patients with clinical disorders manifested by symptoms usually considered psychogenic. Our task in the final chapters is threefold: 1) to discuss the role of psychological conflict in the production of character structure; 2) to examine some of the complex interrelations between psychological and physiological dysfunction—the human reaction to injury and illness, and the contribution of character structure and emotions to bodily disease; 3) and lastly, to consider the nature of the relationship between the doctor and his patient, and its therapeutic value.

Before turning to the first of these considerations, we should do well to pause for a moment to review what we have learned about the production of the varied symptoms of emotional disorders. It is evident now that these are not all cut from the same cloth. Some of them, such as anxiety and depression, are fundamental reactions in and of the ego organization to both inner and outer stimuli. Others represent the emergence through major distortions and defects in ego structure either of primitive modes of mentation ordinarily not conscious in the waking adult, or of primitive id impulses little modified by the activities of the ego. The latter is found in people with sexual aberrations or impulsive behavior such as Charles L., who raped and killed a passing woman; the former is seen in those patients with severe mental illness in whom primary process thought predominates. Finally there is that wide spectrum of symptoms which results from the action of the ego defensive operations on the impulses and feelings striving for expression. Isolation, undoing, projection, displacement, conversion and others impose modifications on the underlying impulses resulting in the clinical manifestations of hysteria, phobic reactions, obsessive-compulsive neurosis, and other clinical syndromes.

Our focus has so far been primarily on symptoms—that is, on those manifestations of psychological functioning which appear either to the person suffering them or to an observer as abnormal, which are often painful or undesirable, which commonly arise as a reaction to a precipitant and persist in the form of mental illness as a disabling alteration in the person's previous functioning. Symptoms are usually differentiated from character traits, although it is not always easy on the basis of the differentiating criteria to distinguish one from the other.

Character traits as opposed to symptoms are habitual patterns of behavior that form an integral part of the individual's psychological structure. They make their appearance early in his life and persist as more or less stable organizations; they give him his individual stamp, and are usually accepted by the person as integral and desirable aspects of himself. They are the manifestations of innate skills, talents, and intelligence; of the direction and strength of drives; of the force and potency of the ego ideals and conscience; and of ego defenses. It is to this last category that we must now turn our attention, and to the implication that character traits as well as symptoms may be born of psychological conflict.

Not all character traits that are defenses are to be considered abnormal because they arise from conflict. On the contrary, many of them are stable and valuable bricks in the complete psychological structure. There may, however, be certain characterological organizations that function well under ordinary circumstances but predispose their owners to psychological difficulty when they are faced with specific types of stress. Let us, therefore, turn to a consideration of some of the character traits related to dependency needs. This will provide us with an example of defenses as character traits; it will show us something of the complex problem of predisposition; and it will permit us to examine a type of character organization which plays an important part in the production and complications of physical illness. As such it is a human psychological phenomenon with which all doctors must be conversant in order to understand their patients and to treat them effectively.

Let us approach these problems by returning to Boyd C. When we observed him before (Chapter III), we found him in the midst of an acute emotional turmoil related to his having spent Christmas day in the hospital away from his family. At that time his psychological equilibrium was under the stress imposed by anger welling up within him, apparently as a response to the fact that his wife had not telephoned him. He attempted to alleviate the acute anxiety related to his anger by employing a variety of ego defense mechanisms to control his impulses—especially negation, displacement, and avoidance. These were emergency defensive measures, so to speak; they were employed ad hoc to meet the specific problem created by his situation on the ward. Once his impulse to aggression subsided, there would no longer be a need for the temporary defenses called up by his anxiety to provide protection. The behavioral manifestations of his negation, displacement, and avoidance would disappear as the acute conflict abated.

Boyd C. showed other defenses, however, which had developed early in his life, that served in a more permanent and continuous manner to protect him against underlying dependency needs. These had become part of the fabric of his ego structure and contributed to the characteristics that distinguished him as the sort of person he was. Before we examine these phenomena in some detail, let us first review briefly the history of the patient's difficulty.

Some four months before the patient came to the psychiatric ward he was severely injured while at work. His job involved a particularly hazardous and arduous set of operations at a foundry. He had applied for the position when he learned that five men before him had quit at the end of a week because the work was beyond their capacities. The patient looked upon this as a challenge and felt it to be an opportunity to prove himself a better man than most. Through strength, grit, and determination he succeeded. Unfortunately, one day, after he had been working for three months, he stumbled, fell and struck his lower back a violent blow against a sharp piece of metal. At once he noticed numbness and paralysis from his waist down, and was taken immediately to the hospital.

Following a laminectomy he rapidly improved. At the end of two months there remained of his initial complete paralysis only a moderate weakness in his left lower leg. He managed to get around easily with crutches, and was transferred to another hospital for a course of rehabilitation to help speed up the process of a return of function. One day, while shaving, his legs suddenly gave way beneath him and he collapsed to the floor. Once again he was completely paralyzed from the waist down, but this time it was determined in extensive examination that his paraplegia was hysterical; there was no evidence of a lesion in his spinal cord as a cause for his paralysis. Because the emotional factors in this new development were not clear, he was transferred, now confined to a wheel chair, to the psychiatric ward for further evaluation and an attempt at treatment.

During a series of psychiatric interviews a great deal was

learned not only about his injury and his symptoms, but about the history of his life and the sort of man he was—his likes and dislikes, his hopes and fears, his attitudes, his opinions and prejudices. Of particular importance for our concern with the emotional aspects of illness was the nature of his problems with his dependency needs. During one of the interviews he described his lifelong difficulty in permitting himself to rely on other people.

> I don't have any really close friends, anyway. I've been more or less on my own, you know. In fact, when you get right down to it, I don't think I have a really close friend because I always kept my troubles to myself. All the scrapes I got into, I kept them to myself. I wasn't one to cry on somebody's shoulder. I always figured that when I left home I had to make my own way one way or another . . . I want to make my own way. I like people; I get along good with people; I like to be around people and to be associated with them. But I want to be here and I want the other guy to be there . . . I want to stand on my own two feet, and if anybody has got to have anybody to lean on, I want him to lean on me, not me lean on him. You understand what I mean?

The attitudes and ways of relating to people which the patient describes are habitual with him. He accepts them as a part of himself, both as he actually is and as the sort of person he wants to be. He places a particular importance and emphasis on independence and self-sufficiency. This was an attitude in marked contrast to the actual facts of his life as a patient. His paralysis confined him to a wheelchair, and forced him as a cripple into the position of being highly dependent on other people. His psychologically induced symptoms placed him in just the situation which he wished consciously to avoid. Despite this paradox, he gave a number of reasons for wishing to avoid a position of dependency which became apparent as the interview continued:

I detest having people doing things for me. I don't want them to start doing things because there might come a time when I'd build up that confidence in them to a point where I'll expect that little boost over the curb or the help off the chair or something, so that I get half-way up, and I'll slip back and they'll let me go—boom! I wish I could explain this. When I come to a curb, I want to go over it myself rather than accept help. When I go to that curb and just set in a chair to wait for someone to come and lift me over it, the need is built up. I've got so I expect it. I've built that need where that I won't try for myself to do it, and one day, I'm at that curb, I need the help to get over it, and people are going to keep walking by; they're not going to stop.

It is evident that the patient is afraid to allow himself to depend on other people lest they disappoint him. There is, of course, always a risk of disappointment when one relies on others, but this does not deter most of us from looking occasionally to family and friends for help. The patient's fear of dependency and his anticipation of frustration both appear unduly strong. He gave as one reason for his attitude an unpleasant experience that had occurred when he was sixteen. He spent the summer of that year away from home working on a temporary job. Regularly he sent money back to his mother so that she might put it in his savings account toward his future education. When he returned home early in the fall he discovered that his mother had spent most of his savings for herself. Of his fear of dependency he said:

... Maybe it goes back to a point where I wanted to depend on my mother. I hate to keep saying my mother all the time because it makes me think it's all her fault. Thinking that if this is a psychosomatic thing I can shove all the blame on her and there's nothing wrong with me. I don't want to do that—but, anyway, I did depend on her; I had faith in her that she would come through in this particular situation with the money and everything, and, Jesus, it was just—there was nothing there. And maybe in an unconscious way I just don't want to put my confidence or depending on anyone to do a certain thing for me because when there is a desperate need for it I will have this big let-down.

Dr. The situation in Florida was painful.

Pt. For a period of six to eight weeks I felt pretty bad about it.

Dr. How did you feel?

Pt. Well, it's so long ago that I can't tell you exactly —when I first heard about it I was mad. I was teed-off, and if it had been anyone else but my mother I probably could have cussed them out in good shape, I was that mad . . . I could have attempted to knock hell out of them . . . Then when I was told "Until you're 21 I can do whatever I want with your money," it was just a feeling of disgust, and then after the disgust left there was no feeling. I had no more feeling about it than I would with a total stranger . . .

Dr. She really hurt you a lot.

Pt. She did, yes, and it was deep hurt. It wasn't anything I could go and bawl about for a few days, or if I happened to think about it go and bawl. I don't cry now when I think about it, but you have that emotion of anger; you have that feeling of disgust that almost makes you sick . . . like you just got your shoes shined on a Saturday and you're going some place special and you're walking down the street and a dog has messed in the street and you go and step in it. The smell would make you kind of sick from stepping into it and you're disgusted because you stepped into it and think "Why the hell didn't I watch where I was going?" The combination of being mad and disgusted and everything kind of boils up inside and kind of makes you sick . . . If there's any possible way I can avoid talking about this I don't talk about it. I haven't even told my wife about it . . .

Dr. I think being hurt by your mother like this makes

you expect it from everyone else. Perhaps this is why you don't want to get into a situation where you might get hurt again.

Pt.   Yeah, I'll go along with that. I won't say I expect it from everyone, but I'm not going to let myself get into a situation where if it does happen again, I'll be hurt again. In other words if anyone is going to be hurt, I'm going to do the hurting. It's going to be the other guy.

Dr.   You're not going to take any chances.

Pt.   No, sir, that's definite. I suppose you could say that I just don't trust anyone . . . I'm just not going to get into a situation where I have to. That's the whole thing.

The patient gives as a reason for his lack of faith in others' dependability the fact of having been so bitterly disappointed by his mother. His explanation is an oversimplification; it takes more than one such experience to produce the disillusionment and defensive independence that formed so strong a part of his adult character structure. His mother had always been an unstable person, addicted to alcohol, and frequently away from the home involved in ephemeral affairs. His exposure to her inconstancy and untrustworthiness had begun in his earliest childhood. The episode he recalled from his adolescence was a particularly dramatic symbol of a long series of disappointments at her hands.

There was yet another reason for his fear of depending on others—the strength and magnitude of his needs. This first becomes apparent in his definition of a friend:

I have a lot of acquaintances and I know a lot of people, but to me, if you and I were friends—my interpretation of a friend is if you came over to me and said, "Gee, Boyd, I got a heck of a cut on my hand here—or leg. Something's happened to me and I can't use my leg; there's an operation that's never been performed and they need a nerve out of your back or they need a piece of bone, or maybe the leg itself. A friend to me is the kind of guy where I'd say, "All right, I'll give you the bone; I'll give you the nerve; I'll give you my leg." That to me is a friend.

Although he attributes the need for "a nerve . . . a piece of bone, or maybe the leg itself" to someone else, this is his own fantasy of the magnitude of a claim one friend may make on the generosity of another. The insistent strength of his needs was evident in his relationship with his wife. Despite his experience with his mother and his general isolationist attitude, he made an exception in the case of his wife, who was, as he said, "the only person in the world I have any faith in." There were times when a job required him to be away from home for long periods of time. He would often be overwhelmed by feelings of longing for his wife, which were sometimes so strong that he would be forced to quit his job to go home to her. He describes the longing as follows.

The longing makes me feel helpless because I throw away everything that I've gained. I've got security on a job and I might be making good money, or I might be well established in any particular situation. Then I get that damn longing and that lonesomeness, and I just throw everything aside. That's why I say I'm helpless; when that feeling gets the best of me, that's it . . . When I feel this lonesomeness coming on, if I'm away from home, I work harder at physical work; then I can throw that feeling off. Whereas if I don't work harder, well, then I get that deep, deep lonesome feeling. It seems to me there's a need, almost a physical need, just the same as an alcoholic needs a drink. I get that deep down craving for the family, and I just—well, I'm like an alcoholic; I throw everything aside to get that drink or the family. . . . Say I've let my feelings go to a point that I'm actually depending on a person, just the same as a plant or anything is depending on the water to grow or the air to breathe. Well, suddenly when that thing is shut off you're just going to wither up and blow away.

The nature of his needs makes them a problem for the patient. Few of us would seriously demand or expect from another the gift of a leg. And few of us find ourselves as driven by our needs as Boyd C., who likens his longing for his wife to the alcoholic's craving for drink or a plant's need for water; it becomes a matter of life and death for him. If the patient's wants are so strong and of such magnitude, he is right in expecting that other people will not gratify them. They could not possibly be expected to give him as much as he wants. He is aware that his needs, if unleashed, would be endless, insatiable, and unreasonable; that his voraciousness could alienate the very people he turned to for help. Coupled with his distrust of others' reliability, the very strength of his needs leads to his anticipation of disappointment. To avoid this, he must avoid any reliance on others; to allow himself to depend at all on other people would be to be overwhelmed by the strength of his wants and to suffer inevitable frustration. His solution is to lean over backward to be completely self-sufficient and independent; * he combats his dependent needs with the defense of *reaction formation* (his exaggerated independence) under the impetus of his anxious anticipation of disappointment. A reasonably stable psychological equilibrium is thus created between the

---

* The one exception to this rule in the patient's life was his relationship to his wife. He was able intermittently to indulge his dependency in this relationship, but not without conflict, which was most evident in his adult work patterns: He would find employment in his home town and work satisfactorily for several months; gradually he would grow increasingly restless, anxious, and uneasy at the closeness of his tie to his wife. When this finally mounted to an unbearable degree, he would throw up his work, and get a job as a traveling salesman that kept him away from home for months at a time. On the road he would hardly think of his wife for long stretches of time until suddenly the longing, which he likened to the alcoholic's craving for drink, would erupt into his consciousness. Helpless in its grip, he would drop whatever he was doing and rush home. This alternating cycle repeated itself over and over again. In his relationship with others he kept his dependency under strict control; with his wife he swung between the two extremes of clinging closeness and utter distance.

underlying needs striving for conscious expression and the defense vigilantly keeping them out of awareness. The latter is evident in the character trait of marked independence. The dependency needs are hidden from view and from expression; they are nonetheless there, ready to break through should the equilibrium be altered. We shall soon see how, under certain circumstances, this may occur.

There was yet another factor that made the position of dependency frightening to Boyd C.; he was concerned over the aggressiveness of his demands:

> It's a feeling [he said] that I will get to the point of accepting and accepting and accepting; that I'm going to— gradually that acceptance is going to turn into a demanding thing . . . Like a baby—a baby cries in the crib. You go in. The baby is helpless; he absolutely cannot help himself. The only way he can make his wants known is through his crying. So after a while the thought gets through to him that whenever he wants attention he can cry. He's helpless, so you go in and pick him up; you rock him; you walk the floor—most anything apparently will do. And after a while you satisfy his feelings of helplessness. You soothe him, pacify him, whatever you want to call it, and he's contented and goes to sleep. But as he grows older that feeling of helplessness changes to a thing of demanding nature. In other words, he's crying not because he's helpless (he's helpless in a way), but his cries are demanding for you to come in and pick him up.
>
> If it came to the point where that I would accept this help and kept continuing to the point where I'd more or less demand it, I'd be a regular damn gripe every minute of the day, and night whenever I was awake. Over at the other hospital . . . I wasn't satisfied. I was overbearing and demanding. I made an ass of myself—that's the plainest way to put it.

Once again the patient paints a vivid fantasy picture of the magnitude of his demands in his imagery of the howling baby. If he allowed his needs full expression, they would be excessive. At the same time he is aware of the amount of aggression associated with his needs—partly as an element in his active striving for satisfaction, partly as an almost inevitable response to the frustration resulting from the failure of others to gratify his wishes and dependency. We have already observed the nature of Boyd C.'s aggressiveness. We saw it turned against himself when he talked of ripping open his legs and of killing himself (Chapter XII). We saw the acute anxiety it caused him (Chapter III) when he first felt that he was losing control of his urge to violence. If, then, he allowed himself to depend on others, his needs would be frustrated; this would unleash in its train a violent reactive aggressiveness, provocative of intense anxiety. The act of open dependency would expose the psychological structure to a double jeopardy—to the pain of disappointment and to the torment of rage. To avoid these dangers, it is essential to remain utterly independent.

When we first considered (in Chapter III) the nature of Boyd C.'s anxiety over aggression, we were dealing with only a fragment of his total conflict; we can see his aggressiveness now as part of a larger constellation that includes his strong underlying dependency needs as well. And our earlier inference that he was angry at his wife for not calling him on Christmas day takes on increased plausibility in the light of what he reveals about his desperate longing for her.

The same combination of fear of dependency, reaction-formation, and aggressiveness is evident in Thomas W., who at twenty-nine was severely disabled by rheumatoid arthritis:

> At night in my sleep tears would be rolling down from my eyes; that's how much pain I was in. I would feel blue and everything else. It got so that I couldn't even reach my mouth. (Because of stiffness in his shoulders the patient

had been for a period unable to feed himself.) I think the idea that I've always been independent more or less, so to speak—I always never had anyone do anything for me. The fact that people had to do things for me probably disturbed me quite a bit.

Dr. Did it really?

Pt. Yeah, I mean, like today, when I go to put my jacket on a lot of people want to go to help me. I won't let them. I won't let them for two reasons. One is I don't like anyone to help me anyway. And second, if you start letting people do too much for you, the first thing you know, you're not doing those things. Or you get so darn lazy. You don't do anything, and you're not using your body, and I'll wind up the same way I did the last time (a period when he was immobilized by his arthritis for a number of weeks in bed).

Dr. So the problem was that you couldn't do things for yourself. Other people had to help you.

Pt. That's right. That bothered me quite a bit.

Dr. How?

Pt. My disposition was no good at all. Like if my wife would do something for me and it wasn't quite like it was supposed to be, well I'd get angry, you know . . . I didn't like the idea of me having to be angry towards my wife. That always bothered me. And the idea that people had to do things for me, I never liked that.

Dr. I wonder what bothered you about it.

Pt. The fact, as I said before, I had always been so active during my life. I had always done everything for myself. I'd been so active that the fact that someone else had to do it for me, and that I couldn't do it—I don't know how I would describe it. It just bothered me. It always bothered me to have someone else do it for me, that I couldn't do it myself. Because, like I say, I always have been so independent. Well, I worked even before I got out of high school; I was working, helping out the family. Responsibilities came to me early, in other words—earlier than with a lot of kids.

It is clear that the patient dislikes having to depend on others, that he leans over backward to be independent, and that he is afraid of the aggression that wells up inside him when he is in a position of having to take help from other people. His ideal for himself and his image of himself is that of being a self-reliant person. This has always been characteristic of his personality and of his relationships.

The degree of strength which the aggression may reach is especially apparent in what William J. says of himself. Like the others we have been examining, he had been a similarly hard-working, self-reliant man throughout his life until a severe back injury at the age of forty-five forced him into a position of almost complete helplessness. He found his dependent state so intolerable and so much in conflict with his ideal of strength and self-sufficiency that he became deeply anxious and depressed, and filled with ideas of committing suicide.

Some of this trouble [he said of his anxiety and depression] may be from home. I don't like to say that, but it probably does upset my nerves . . . When the children get me nervous at home, maybe that's what starts this thing off. That's why I said to the doctors if this thing was going to continue this way, why—that is before anything happens at home—I'm not one that wants to do bodily harm or anything like that, you know; what I mean, kill anybody, like that, when you come down to it. But I thought before anything did happen, that my nerves were going to crack up or something . . . and I thought if I was coming down with that, why, I thought I would rather go into some veterans' home and have constant care and somebody to take care of me, to tell you the truth.

Dr.   You've been rather scared of yourself, then?

Pt.   I'm not really scared of myself. I know I could walk down the street and nobody would ever fear any harm from me. I would never do any bodily harm to anybody, or anything like that.

The depth and violence of William J.'s aggression stand out through his negation as he describes his fantasies of the harm and murder he would not commit. In all of these patients the aggression goes hand in hand with the dependency; and in each of them both the aggression and dependency create an inner psychological conflict. The threat of each underlying impulse to emerge arouses anxiety, and the patient attempts to control it with an ego defensive maneuver. We have seen that reaction-formation, manifested as a character trait, is a major defense employed to contain the dependency. The aggression is handled in the same way. Consistently these patients describe themselves as "easy going," "good-natured," "even-tempered." They "never get mad," "never have arguments," and "get nervous and walk away from an argument" if they are near one. If they do admit to occasional feelings of anger, they emphasize the fact that "they hold it in," "never show it," and "just go off alone till the feeling disappears." Others who know them independently corroborate the descriptions the patients give of themselves; they confirm from their observations the even, calm, unruffled behavior that characterizes this group of people. Conscious suppression and unconscious repression of anger are prominent defenses in addition to their reaction-formation against aggressiveness, manifested as an excessive compliance, agreeableness and co-operativeness in situations where self-assertiveness and aggressiveness might be more appropriate.

In summary, people with this type of character structure appear to be self-reliant, self-controlled, even-tempered, and independent to a striking degree. Behind this characterological exterior are excessively strong dependency needs and aggressive impulses, which are ordinarily kept unconscious and inoperative through the defensive function of these ego character traits. Whenever the underlying needs and impulses tend to emerge into consciousness, they come into conflict with the person's ideal image of himself as strong and self-reliant, and produce an anxious expectation of disappointment that further reinforces the countering defenses.

Several of these phenomena are already familiar to us. Dependency needs, aggressive demands, and anger at frustration all formed, as we have seen (Chapter X) an integral part of the psychological organization of the type of person described as having a narcissistic character disorder. Both types of people, those with a narcissistic character disorder and those whom we have been considering here, exhibit the same quality and intensity in their dependency needs and their reactive anger. Where they differ is in the expression of their impulses. The person with a narcissistic character disorder quite openly makes dependent and demanding relationships to people around him, and such behavior does not appear to run counter to his ideals for himself; he openly tolerates these needs. This, of course, is just what does not occur in those we have been examining here. On the contrary, they lean over backwards to hide equally strong, but generally unconscious dependency needs. One openly expresses his needs; the other has defenses against it. In both cases the needs appear to be unusually strong and demanding. There is less difference between the two groups in their handling of aggression; as we have seen, the aggressive impulse creates anxiety in both, which leads to defenses against it.

It appears, then, that although one group differs from the other with regard to external behavior, in both groups the underlying needs and impulses are the same. Both have a basically narcissistic orientation; both are strongly driven to depend on others. One group accepts this in themselves; the other is afraid of it, and erects defenses against it. It is the defenses that make for the differences between the two. Both types of patients are seen to have character problems categorized as narcissistic. Within this larger category, each forms a distinct sub-group determined by the nature of their ego structure.

In describing the patients we have just been examining we have judged their tendency toward independence to be overdone, and have labeled it a defense, *reaction-formation*. This should not be taken to mean that a drive toward self-sufficiency is in itself abnormal. On the contrary, the development of independence and the growth away from dependence is essential to the maturation of all human beings. What we see in both groups of people with narcissistic character problems are extremes of otherwise normal human traits— of too great dependence that puts them at the mercy of other people, or of too great independence that deprives them of the joy of an intimacy with others based on mutual trust and love.

We should be cautious in seeing only the pathological aspect of these character defenses. The over-independent person may, in fact, find his defense an asset. Despite the fact that it is an exaggeration of normal self-reliance, it enables him to take responsibility, to accomplish herculean tasks, to be a pillar of society as a hard-working, reliable, and effective individual. The problem lies in the fact that he is vulnerable to psychological difficulties when faced with situations that place stress on his particular personality organization. When he develops a chronic physical illness or suffers a disabling injury he is liable to severe emotional reactions that may seriously disrupt treatment and rehabilitation. We must, therefore, turn our attention to the psychological processes that lead to such difficulties.

XVII

Psychological Complications of Physical Illness

To understand how a psychologically vulnerable person encounters difficulties in his struggles with an illness, we must keep in mind the fact of the psychological equilibrium that results from the conflict between the underlying needs and impulses on the one hand, and on the other the ego defenses restraining them. In some patients it is the defenses that contribute to the psychological complications of illness; in others, it is the needs and impulses. Let us consider the former first.

A striking feature of the patients whom we examined in the last chapter was the extent to which they exercised control over their feelings and behavior. They could tolerate neither dependency nor aggression; the emergence into consciousness of either of these aroused anxiety that mobilized and strengthened the countering defenses. The ideal on which they tried to model their behavior was that of a strong, silent, self-reliant, rugged individual carrying on alone, courageous and uncomplaining in the face of adversity.

To a great degree many people of this sort are able to achieve their goal. To an observer, they appear carved from granite; stoical, serious, determined, and undaunted by trouble, they stick conscientiously to their duties no matter how difficult the way. At the same time, they maintain an aloofness, an emotional reserve, a soberness and lack of spontaneity that often make real communication with them difficult. They do not readily talk about themselves, their feelings, their thoughts, hopes and fantasies, their troubles and anxieties. It is not only anger and dependency that is controlled within them; it is also the expression, and usually the awareness, of any feeling—especially feelings that would indicate a crack in the armor, a touch of human weakness. They cannot ordinarily permit themselves to be anxious, or sad, or angry, or to feel longing; their emotions are controlled until they mount to an intensity where they can no longer be contained. Then they erupt so violently upon the person's awareness that he feels completely overwhelmed and helpless in the face of them. The point of explosion is rarely reached, but when it is, there may result a severe disorganization of psychological structure. There is no middle ground between rigid control and violent feeling.

Such self-control characterized James M. At forty-seven he was dying of a carcinoma which, originating in a tonsil, had invaded much of his nasopharynx despite prolonged X-ray treatment. The dying was slow and uncomfortable. His lesion was painful and foul-smelling; he found it hard to eat and drink; his tongue was swollen to twice its normal size. Despite this he never complained or appeared discouraged, frightened, or depressed. Asked how he felt about his illness, he replied,

> I don't know exactly what I've got here. They never told me exactly what I have except a tumor. But it hurts so much. Is that part of the tumor? I don't know. If I knew, maybe I could take a guess.
>
> *Dr.*   You're still puzzled?
> *Pt.*   Still puzzled what it is. Maybe a tumor or an abscess or even a cancer. I don't know. They haven't told me.
> *Dr.*   Have you asked what it is?
> *Pt.*   I've asked everyone of them what it is. They haven't said anything. It's only a growth.

Dr.　Are you worried about it?

Pt.　No. That's a funny thing, but I never worry about anything, because worrying don't pay. All through my family trouble (the patient had finally been divorced after years of marital difficulties) I never worried about it. I just walked out of that house and forgot about it. Outside of home and my own folks, nobody knew I had any trouble. I was in the office everyday and everyone thought I had the best family ever. So when I left they all said, "What's the matter with you leaving such a good wife?" I never told them I had a good wife.

Dr.　They assumed it?

Pt.　They assumed it. She wasn't the wife she was supposed to be. So I've been laughing and smiling all my life.

James M.'s acceptance of his tragic situation is heroic. It reflects an attitude that, as he tells us, has characterized his response to trouble throughout his life. It should not detract from our admiration of his courage to recognize that his attitude results from the defensive ego maneuvers against dependency, aggression and fears of weakness we have recently been examining. It should also be clear that as a defense his attitude serves the useful purpose of protecting him from the anguish that could result if he allowed himself to be aware of all the implications of his illness. His defense is a merciful anodyne.

There are situations, however, where this sort of attitude may interfere with medical treatment to the point of jeopardizing a patient's life. Marion D., for example, who at fifty-six was operated on for carcinoma of the breast which had metastasized to the axillary lymph nodes, was doomed to an early death that might have been avoided if she had consulted her doctor sooner. She gave the history of her illness as follows:

Dr.　What was it you came in here for?

Pt.　For pain in my back and vomiting. And when

they gave me the thorough examination that they do, I knew they were going to find this breast condition. Nobody knew it except myself, but I knew that if I ever got into the hospital again I'd never get away home without it being taken care of.

Dr. You knew about it?

Pt. Oh, yes, because you could see it. It was definitely to be seen.

Dr. You had that for how long?

Pt. I've had it for over a year, Doctor. It had been kind of bad I'd say for about a year.

Dr. You noticed it before that?

Pt. Yes, you see, I was in the hospital two years ago, and at that particular time it must have been setting in because I noticed it myself then, and I said to myself, "Well here I am in the hospital and if there's anything to this they'll surely notice it with all the nurses." I was in a private hospital, the nurses bathing me, and I did have to have special nurses there because I was so ill. So I did say to one nurse that that one breast looked funny. "Oh," she says, "that's nothing more or less than an inverted nipple." Well, when anyone in the profession, a private nurse, makes light of anything, well, naturally you don't think it's bad. If she had said, "Well, you must have that taken care of," and impressed it upon me that I should—well—

Dr. You didn't talk to your doctor about it?

Pt. No, because the nurse spoke that way to me. Then this past year I have been so sick with the other that every time I had the doctor I'd say, "Well, this time he'll probably give me an examination and he'll see it." I had been waiting for him to see it. Then up to the night that I came here for the operation my own doctor still didn't know it. But I did tell him before I came in.

Dr. You did?

Pt. I did, because I thought it was only fair. These doctors in here I knew would find it. Because all they had to do was undress me and they could see it. You see, he never examined me, only below my waistline, abdomen and bowels. So I didn't think I was doing the right thing by coming in and not letting him know that they were going to find something else that he didn't know anything about. And it was my fault that he didn't know about it. (The patient suffered from chronic pyelonephritis for which she regularly saw her family physician. Upon admission to the hospital for an exacerbation of her kidney disease, the carcinoma of the breast was discovered on physical examination.)

Dr. Why?

Pt. Because I should have told him. That's how I really feel. You see the breast didn't bother me. This poor thing didn't bother me at all. It probably would have soon because it looked badly.

Dr. It did?

Pt. Yes, it did. It did look bad to me, and I didn't know too much about it, and I think the first night on emergency they said that it was sort of an ulcerated lesion. Is there such a thing?

Dr. Yes.

Pt. Well, that's what it looked like because it got to be like a little tiny sore and then it had gotten hard. It never drained, though. There was never any drainage from it. There was never anything on my clothing, and I was very careful not to injure it in any way. I never wore a too tight bra. I have read about every single operation that has ever been performed on cancer. I take all the current magazines. I have read every single one of those, because I had every idea that I had something that was leading up to that particular thing. Years ago I bought an old doctor's book for ten cents, I think, and it showed all sorts of different pictures and if you have this you should do such and such for it, and it showed a picture of a woman's breast that looked something like mine was starting to look. "Well," I thought, "so you've got this or that. If you have a bad heart, you have to live with it. If you have bad kidneys you also have to live with them and have them treated. If you have a cancer you have to live with that

and have something done about that. What's the difference what it is?"

Like James M., Marion D. faces her serious illness stoically and courageously. Unfortunately for her she took the
same attitude toward her difficulty when she first noticed the
signs of a cancer that was at that time in all likelihood surgically curable. Her behavior was not the result of ignorance. On the contrary she possessed considerable factual
knowledge about cancer from having read about it in popular magazines. She had been fully exposed to the vigorous
public health campaigns to alert the laity to the nature, danger, and treatment of malignant disease. She had also consulted an antiquated, but more technical "doctor's book,"
where she found a picture of carcinoma of the breast that
matched her own lesion. She had, moreover, observed and
followed the progression of her own malignant growth. She
was clearly not in want of information about cancer in general, or about her own disease in particular.

Despite this she had done nothing for two years. Initially,
she asked a *nurse*, not her *doctor*, about her breast and was
so readily reassured by the nurse's misguided statements that
she did nothing further as her cancer developed before her
eyes. She *passively* hoped her doctor might one day examine
her above the umbilicus and stumble on her difficulty, but
she did nothing *actively* to call it to his attention. She behaved as if the cancer had nothing to do with her; as if its
progression meant nothing; as if the repeated exhortation
in popular articles to watch for the "danger signs" and
"catch cancer early" to improve chances of cure had no
bearing on her own problem. She appeared to be *denying*,
not the fact of her cancer, but the significance and implications of it, her concern about it, and the need to take action
concerning it. It was the psychological mechanism of denial
which resulted in her coming to surgery with a lesion for

which there was little hope of cure; it led her to dissipate her chances for recovery, which had been optimal when she first noticed the signs in her breast. Her psychological functioning had provided a major and fatal complication to a physical illness.

We have seen the mechanism of denial before in our examination of pathological grief. Margaret P. (Chapter XI) denied with partial success the fact of her husband's death in order to avoid the pain consequent on losing him. In Marion D., and James W., the denial is aimed not so much at the fact of having a malignant disease, as at the meaning, the seriousness, the implications, and the consequences of a cancerous growth. They are thus spared the anxiety inevitably attached to recognizing the full import of their illness. It takes little imagination to understand what is frightening about the idea of cancer. It is a disease that means possible death, disfigurement, pain, and prolonged weakness and disability. Treatment, whether surgical or radiological, is prolonged, expensive, uncomfortable, and often (as in Marion D.'s loss of a breast) involves physical mutilation. Marion D.'s denial permitted her to avoid these many anxieties at the expense of her life.

Cancer is, of course, only one of a host of painful and debilitating diseases that afflict mankind. Any serious illness causes a disruption in a man's life and imposes a stress on his psychological organization; the more serious the illness, the more severe the stress. A person, for example, confined to a hospital bed with multiple fractures is beset by many troublesome changes. He is prevented from engaging in his usual work and familiar daily activities. He is often deprived of income at the same time that he is burdened with large hospital bills and doctors' fees. He is separated from the comfortable familiarity of his home and family, and is dumped into the strange, frequently frightening environment of the hospital. Perhaps the hardest deprivation of all is the loss of his independence and autonomy in almost every aspect of his private life. His meals are brought to him in bed and he may even have to be fed; he must be provided with a bed-pan or urinal; he is unable to bathe himself. For almost anything he wants, he has to ring for the nurse, on whom he is forced to rely for his needs. His injuries have deprived him of his ability to do anything for himself; he is in many ways in the position of the infant who has not yet developed the capacities that injury has wrested from the adult.

Most people are able to tolerate the conditions imposed on them by illness. They recognize that a return to health requires a temporary surrender of autonomy and strength. They can permit themselves to depend on other people, to expect and ask for help, and even to a certain extent to enjoy the dependency and freedom from responsibilities that sickness brings. This is a *healthy reaction to temporary disability;* it is a rational response on the part of the sick person, who taking all factors into account, voluntarily surrenders a part of his independence in order to create the best climate for his recovery. It is, of course, easier to make such a healthy response when an injury or illness imposes only temporary disability. Even though the illness entails discomfort and psychological stress, one can reconcile oneself to it in anticipation of a complete recovery of health and capacities.

When an illness is chronic or imposes a permanent disability, the adjustment to it is harder to make. In considering the problem of depression, we noted in passing that grief is a necessary part of the emotional reaction to the loss of a limb. Any illness that results in the loss of a part of one's body, or in a loss of function causes a painful distortion in one's body image. The experience of loss goes beyond one's image of oneself as a physical being; it involves as well changes in one's image of oneself as a social being, as one is forced to give up one's occupation, hobbies, and customary activities that form a part of one's cherished ideals; in particular one is faced with surrendering much of one's autonomy, self-sufficiency, and independence.

It is small wonder then that a severe disabling illness evokes a response of depression; it is a normal response to such misfortune. A failure to be emotionally upset over the loss resulting from disability reflects in most cases a failure really to have come to terms with the disability, really to have accepted the loss, or to have faced the implications of it. One must, so to speak, grieve for the lost part, the lost function, or the lost self-image. And just as in the pathological grief reaction a failure to grieve over the loss of a loved one may be the result of a denial of the loss, so in illness a similar sort of denial may, as with Marion D., protect one from the painful affects associated with the loss imposed by disability. But Marion D.'s denial also prevented her from having adequate medical treatment; in Herman P. denial interfered with successful rehabilitation.

Herman was a hypertensive man of thirty-nine, the father of three children, who was referred to a rehabilitation clinic following a right-sided hemiplegia which had resulted from a left cerebral vascular thrombosis. His initial aphasia had rapidly cleared, but he was left with a weakness in his right arm and leg, and a loss of fine movements in his right hand. It was the latter that was particularly tragic for the patient. He was one of a handful of artisans in his community who had the skill to perform a difficult but vital industrial process that required a high degree of dexterity with his hands. His ability enabled him to make over two hundred dollars a week. Following his stroke his income ceased, and he was forced to live on the small sum provided by disability assistance. In the face of the hardships this caused him and his family, he became understandably depressed. At times he even thought of suicide, and began to sleep with a loaded revolver under his pillow, in the hope that he might wake up in the middle of the night and have the courage to shoot himself.

In this condition he was referred to the rehabilitation clinic for physiotherapy and vocational guidance. During his first few days he noted an increase in strength in his shoulder muscles, although there was no change in the function of his fingers, which was permanently lost as a result of the damage to his brain tissue. The patient was, however, tremendously encouraged by this improvement. Although no one had given him any reason to believe it, he developed the idea that he would soon be entirely recovered and able to return to his old work. His depression disappeared, and he became cheerful and optimistic, but his fallacious belief presented a major obstacle to his management. It was a medical fact that his hand would never recover the skilled function necessary for him to return to his old job; in order to proceed with vocational rehabilitation, he would have to be helped to find other less skilled work, with an inevitable drop in his weekly wage. The patient resisted all attempts to get him to consider other types of employment. He refused to think about them. He denied the possibility of a permanent residual impairment in his hand, and insisted that he would soon be entirely well and back at his old job. His attitude completely blocked any reasonable and possible vocational plans that might be made for him.

Throughout all of this period, the staff of the rehabilitation clinic had refrained from telling him directly that his hopes of recovery were false; they had hoped that he would come to this realization himself as a result of the vocational goals the clinic was setting for him. The patient's idea was too fixed, however, to yield to this indirection, and it was finally felt necessary for the success of rehabilitation to confront him gently but firmly with the truth about his hand. When one of the doctors took him into his office to discuss this with him, the patient was at first cheerful and friendly. He talked with seeming equanimity about his previous depression and despair, and then commented on how rapidly he was improving, expressing a confident expectation that he soon would be returning to his two-hundred-dollar-a-week job. When the doctor gently indicated that his hand would be permanently disabled necessitating a change in employment, the change in the patient was sudden and dramatic. His cheerfulness and confidence dissolved before the doctor's eyes. He became agitated, tremulous, depressed, and tearful, and at once began to talk about having no choice but to go home and shoot himself. The doctor, alarmed at this response, retreated as gracefully as he could, and shortly thereafter ended the interview with a few noncommittal words of encouragement. When the patient returned to the clinic the following day, he behaved as if nothing had happened. He was again composed and cheerful, and again was convinced that he would soon be completely well and back at his old job. His behavior forced the staff of the rehabilitation clinic to sail between Scylla and Charybdis—between a suicidal depression on the one hand and on the other a completely unrealistic denial of the fact of his permanent disability. The dilemma thus created was an impassable barrier in his journey toward a feasible vocational goal.

In Ralph N., aged thirty-eight, the problem raised by his attitude toward illness not only initially interfered with his consulting a doctor, but it prevented him from following a medical treatment plan that was prescribed to forestall an extension of his disease process. His job as a truckdriver entailed long hours and heavy lifting; the patient especially prided himself on his physical strength, the amount he could lift single-handed, and the long hours he worked without resting. One day while he was struggling to raise a heavy crate alone into his truck, he was seized by a severe substernal pain—so severe that to his chagrin, after managing to put the crate where he wanted it, he was forced to go home. Even then he tried to make light of his symptoms, and it was only on the insistence of his wife that he saw his family doctor the following day, who recognized that he was suffering from a myocardial infarction and insisted on his entering the hospital. There he found the complete bed rest required of him almost intolerable, and was constantly discovered by the nurses sneaking out of bed to smoke the cigarettes that had been forbidden him. After his discharge he was unable to follow the doctors' urgent advice to work at an easier job. He considered anything other than hard outdoor labor to be "sissy's work," and refused to explore the possibility of a less strenuous occupation. He felt that he could not be a man, free and independent, unless he continued to drive his truck. He, therefore, returned to his long hours and heavy lifting, and before too many months were ended, he was readmitted to the hospital with a second myocardial infarction.

In each of these three patients their behavior was motivated by a variety of anxieties. Some of these were realistic —the fear, for example, of the pain of surgery, or the insecurity resulting from a serious drop in wages. But a major element in their anxiety was their concern over being weak or helpless or dependent as a result of being sick. The idea of this so conflicted with their ideals that they were forced to deny the implications or possible seriousness of their symptoms. They could not tolerate even the amount of weakness and dependency required temporarily of a patient to ensure his return to health; the idea of a permanent diminution in their powers was unthinkable. Their denial was an ego defense mechanism which led to psychological complications of their physical illnesses.

In the group of patients we are now to consider, it is not primarily the functions of the ego, but rather the pressures of the underlying needs and impulses that result in complications. Instead of minimizing a major illness (as in the patients we have been observing), they tend to exaggerate a minor one. Bradford T., for example, a man of thirty-seven, suffered a minor back strain as a result of twisting his trunk too suddenly. He gave his history as follows:

They gave me baths, real steam baths, and then they gave me tub baths. X-rays they gave me, injected vitamin B, I think it was, into my veins intravenously, and Friday he kept saying that I seemed to be getting better. I mean, "I think we'll let you home by Friday." He said, "Have you got your belts with you?" I said, "Yes." He said, "I'm going to strap you up." So they shaved my back. Now I'm no medical man, but it didn't seem right to me to be strapped up with adhesive tape for the nerves, so I figured maybe they weren't telling me the true story. Maybe it was a bone, and they were just telling me nerves to keep me from worrying about it too much. Then they strapped me. I got home, Friday it was all right—no, it wasn't Friday; I don't know, I had so many restrictions I can't remember. Well anyway, I just went out of my mind Saturday, I think it was. I jumped into the bathtub, but I pulled the strapping right off because I could feel it pulling the nerve. A friend of mine who is going to be a doctor said, "Have you got a strapping on that?" I said, "Yeah." He says, "You better call a doctor and ask him if you can take it off." Well anyways, he took it off without the doctor's advice, and after I had taken it off, we—my wife was trying to get the doctor. In the interim she didn't know what to do with me the pain was so severe. I jumped into the bathtub, filled it up with hot water, jumped out, lay down, bent down on my knees, stood on my buttocks, just to get the heat. Then I would take hot turkish towels and wrap them around me; then I put my belt on, threw my belt off; then I would pull my pajamas on. I ripped my clothes—my clothes were ripped to shreds from pain. Finally I couldn't stand it any more; I was going out of my mind and we called Dr. G. He told me, "Well," he said,

"It's strictly nerves, so let's make an appointment again with Dr. C." which was yesterday, and we made it with Dr. C. Got over here all right; came over in my brother-in-law's car. I was propped up in front; I had plenty of room for my feet, and I sat on an angle. I had a pillow in back of my head, and I lay down most of the way; it wasn't bad at all.

Got in here and the girl said, "We're going to put you in a wheelchair." All right, I got in the wheelchair, and they wheeled me to the Bunker Building. Then she wheeled me to Dr. C.'s office over those cobblestones (actually tiled flooring). Everytime she hit one of those cobblestones I almost jumped out of my skin. Finally she got me upstairs, and I went in to see Dr. C.'s secretary, and she says, "You'll have to sit in the waiting room out there." And the pains were coming and coming and coming. Well, I'm not a baby, but I started crying like I've never cried in my life. I just couldn't stand it.

I don't know if you were there, but some doctor came along, and he got me into another room where there was a big table with a board on it I presume was an examining room. He kept me there until Dr. C. came. In the meantime Dr. C., he took my left foot like this, and he took it like that, and he bent it back like that. When he brought it back it was all right. Then I says, "I want a prescription for codeine. I think something is going to happen."

As soon as we got riding in that cab, and where he had pulled my leg—I still got it now. It's still there now pulling up. Instead of one muscle like a charlie-horse, everything is all bunched up in groups. By the time they got me home I was all undressed. I was in the cab naked—stark naked in the cab. Fortunately the cab-driver happened to be a medic in the army, and he calmed me down quite a bit. At home I called my doctor. Nobody home. I called the nurse; I got two nurses, both registered nurses next door, and my doctor has given them instructions that they could give me a needle any time I needed it. They weren't home. Finally I got hold of a doctor, and he gave me a needle. Put me out for about three hours. It was so bad this morning that my wife was crying, and that's the way it's been the past two weeks.

The patient accompanied his remarks with grimaces and groans and contortions that emphasized the ferment and tumult of his florid exaggerations. He does not use language to communicate the facts of his illness; he does not describe the nature of his pain—its location, quality, duration, and radiation. He says nothing of how his trouble started, how it progressed and unfolded. Instead, he concentrates on the emotions he has experienced and the effect his difficulty has had on himself and others. In word and deed he tells his audience of the magnitude of his suffering, despair, and need for help. As James M. minimizes a mountain, Bradford T. magnifies a molehill. This is not history but drama.

Bradford T. is a not uncommon figure in the field of medicine. One is frequently faced with the patient whose symptoms and incapacity far exceed the extent and severity of the physical lesion that underlies them. They complain constantly and insistently of pain and often demand medication, especially narcotics, for relief. They are quite incapacitated by their symptoms and call frequently and unnecessarily on the nurse for little services. They insist on special privileges, call their doctor day and night, and usually have their families hovering anxiously around, full of solicitude and concern. They freely take and little give, and are quick to anger when their demands are not met. They criticize the doctor for his lack of attendance, complain of the nurses' slowness in answering their calls, and accuse their families of indifference. Their illness is lost in a fog of behavior aimed at demonstrating their helplessness and neediness; their incapacitation controls those in attendance on them. In their weakness lies their strength.

If we observed such overtly dependent and angrily demanding behavior in a person not physically ill, we should have no hesitation in categorizing him as having a narcissistic character disorder. The fact that he is ill, however, must caution us against treating his behavior when sick as characteristic of his behavior when well. In truth, patients like Bradford T. have often, *before* they became ill, been a totally different sort of person. Strong, independent, self-sufficient, and self-controlled, they have seemed impervious to difficulties. Illness or injury causes a revolution in their behavior; they become as dependent as they had before been independent, as helpless as they had been self-sufficient, as emotional and mercurial as they had been self-controlled and stoical. They have gone from one extreme to the other.

There is yet another contrast that borders on the paradoxical. Despite the fact of their almost total incapacitation, despite their appearance of helpless passivity and demanding dependency, these patients stoutly proclaim, like Boyd C., their strength and self-sufficiency. They attribute their present behavior to their symptoms. "I'd go back to work tomorrow, Doc, if it weren't for this pain" characterizes their attitude. And yet their pain, their other symptoms, their incapacities are far greater than what is warranted by the nature of the underlying physical lesion.

A partial resolution of the paradox is to be found in the psychological equilibrium we have examined that results from the conflict over dependency needs and aggression. The ego defenses of reaction formation and denial underlie the self-sufficient, stoical pattern of his behavior before his illness, as well as the image of himself as being strong and independent which he still maintains despite the utter incapacitation resulting from his sickness. The striking helplessness and demanding dependency that characterize his behavior when sick result from the emergence of his underlying strong dependent needs and aggression that have long been held in check by his defenses. It is the chance occurrence of an illness or injury that alters the patient's equilibrium and permits the appearance of the underlying impulses and needs. The symptoms are the channel through which the underlying forces come to the surface. At the same time, it is the symptoms which allow the patient, though totally helpless, to maintain his image of himself as strong and independent. Illness is an accident; the patient need assume no responsibility for it; he is the victim of unfortunate circumstances. It is not his fault if he is helpless and weak and dependent; sickness beyond his control has caused his condition. The patient is still not aware of his own underlying dependency needs and wishes to be taken care of; the symptoms, by carrying the full load of responsibility, protect him against the painful awareness of these underlying forces; at the same time, the illness permits their expression and gratification. ("*I* didn't quit my job," said a husky, but helplessly incapacitated man. "My *legs* did.") A new psychological equilibrium is created in which the symptoms play a central role; first produced by a physical lesion, they are now intensified and prolonged, without the patient's conscious awareness that this is happening, by his emotional needs and character structure.

This should *not* be interpreted to mean that the patient finds pleasure in his symptoms or *consciously* magnifies his incapacitation. On the contrary, he is usually deeply troubled by his invalidism and is often genuinely depressed because he can no longer be the active, independent person that still constitutes his ideal for himself. Even though his symptoms are largely neurotic (i.e. the result of emotional factors), they appear to him as imposed from without by the agency of a cruel fate. He remains unaware of his own strong underlying needs and impulses that supply the motivating force toward his symptoms, whose psychological function it is to express these needs at the same time keeping them hidden from the patient's consciousness. We are familiar with this psychological phenomenon from our earlier examination of symptom formation resulting in phobias, obsessive-compulsive neurosis, and hysteria. In the patients we are considering here, complaints originally produced by a physical lesion act as a nucleus for the formation of extensive emotionally induced symptoms, which in their turn lead to chronic invalidism. Without these added emotional factors, the patient would not be incapacitated by the symptoms arising from the physical lesion alone. The course of his injury or illness has been significantly affected by psychological complications.

We begin now to see why the type of character structure we have been examining renders a person with this psychological organization particularly vulnerable to illness or injury. It is important to realize, however, that the shift in equilibrium is not accomplished in an instant. On the contrary, the process is usually a lengthy one before the end point of invalidism is reached. Initially, many patients show the denial and refusal to accept any limitations of their activity which we have examined earlier; it is only gradually, under the influence of a variety of external forces, that the underlying needs and impulses alter the patient's psychological structure and behavior.

The external forces are of two sorts: (1) there are those that conspire to make the patient's habitual defenses inoperative, and (2) there are those that encourage the underlying needs and impulses into more open expression.

If the patient's illness or injury is a severe one, and especially if it forces him into inacivity (as, for example, in the case of fractures or acute arthritis), he is during this time deprived of his habitual defensive behavior of activity and self-sufficiency. When surgery is required, further inactivity is unavoidably imposed on the patient. Furthermore, the people around him may discourage the patient's attempts to maintain his autonomy and activity; his doctor, perhaps over-cautious, discourages his wish to return to work; his family urges him to "take it easy"; his lawyer, if the patient is involved in litigation over compensation, advises him not to do anything until the case is favorably settled; the delays in beginning court procedures and industrial accident hearings protract the patient's period of enforced inactivity. By the time it is finally possible for him to return to activity and self-sufficiency, he may find an alteration in his family structure that makes a resumption of his former role difficult. His wife, for example, who has gone to work during his illness, may be loath to give up her new job even though her husband is now ready once again to become the provider for the family; he thus finds another obstacle in the way of his return to activity. Any or all of these factors, by interfering with his ability to be independent, active, and self-sufficient, weaken his defenses against the strong underlying dependent needs.

At the same time that external forces are diminishing the effectiveness of his defense, other influences encourage the expression of the underlying needs and impulses. Sickness brings with it the sympathy, solicitude, and attention of family and friends; they cater to the invalid's wants and relieve him of his responsibilities. If the patient is hospitalized, nurses and attendants wait on him, and his doctor shares with him his concern for and interest in himself. If the patient is entitled to sick benefits or compensation, he is given money during the time of his incapacity, which may become in effect being paid for being sick. It is felt both by the patient and those caring for him that he is entitled to these ministrations when he is sick; there is no loss of face in accepting help when one is afflicted by an illness or injury over which one has had no control.

As we have seen earlier, the average person can be subjected to these forces without serious psychological consequences. He can permit himself the *regression* to the more helpless, passive, infantile modes of behavior forced on him by sickness; at the same time he can give up this behavior when he is physically well. His regression has been for him a means of providing the best surroundings and opportunity for recovery. His psychological organization has a healthy flexibility and adaptability.

It is just this flexibility and adaptability that is missing in the patients we have been examining here. Initially they strongly resist the role of being an invalid because it forces them into a position of dependency which they have totally repudiated in all their adult relationships. If finally the long-unsatisfied underlying dependency needs do break through and find gratification through the symptoms of illness, it is hard for the patient to give these up when he is physically well. The regression that should be a temporary response to illness provides a new solution to his old psychological conflicts; the helpless invalidism becomes fixed as a new pattern of behavior as inflexible as the patient's previous unbending self-sufficiency and independence.

The importance of these psychological phenomena cannot be gainsaid; they are prominent among the common causes of chronic invalidism following injury or illness. Once the pattern of chronic invalidism has made its appearance, it is frequently impossible to reverse the deleterious result because of the inflexibility of the new psychological equilibrium that produces it. The pattern must be prevented from occurring in the first place. Prevention requires on the part of the doctor (1) knowledge of the type of psychological organization that sensitizes people to these disastrous complications of physical disease; (2) knowledge as to whether the individual patient he is treating falls within this category of vulnerable people; (3) action aimed at minimizing the external influences that set in motion and push to the disastrous end the changes in psychological equilibrium which result in chronic psychological invalidism.

XVIII

THE CONCEPT OF
PSYCHOSOMATIC MEDICINE

Before we turn to a discussion of some of the basic principles underlying the management of patients with emotional problems, let us pursue our consideration of the relationship between psychological conflict and physical disease. We have so far been concerned with patients in whom physical illness, by imposing stress on their psychological organization, produced an emotional disturbance secondary to the initial disease process, which in turn led to complications in the original disorder. Our interest now lies in those patients in whom emotional conflict contributes to the production of physical disease. In a number of chronic, remitting, at times fatal, illnesses (notably duodenal ulcer, ulcerative colitis, rheumatoid arthritis, asthma, certain skin disorders, thyrotoxicosis, hypertension, and migraine headaches) emotional factors may play a prominent part in producing the onset or exacerbation of symptoms. We cannot here systematically examine the evidence bearing on this problem or review the theories devised to account for the observations.* Our concern is, rather, with a basic concept of psychopathology that emotional conflict is a causal factor in the physiological as well as psychological dysfunction of the human being. To demonstrate that concept, let us examine some fragments of the life history of Gordon C., who at thirty-seven was inca-

* The reader who wishes to explore this topic further should consult F. Alexander (48) or E. Weiss and O. S. English (60).

pacitated by chronic rheumatoid arthritis symmetrically involving his jaw, wrists, shoulders, knees, ankles, and toes.

The patient was the youngest of four children, and ten years younger than the next oldest sibling, his sister Mary. Both by his own and by Mary's account he had been a sickly and pampered child. Always a poor eater, he had been subject to frequent vomiting spells which were particularly liable to occur in the morning before he went to school. For the first several years of his life he was "a pretty child with long curls." As the baby in the family, he was "spoiled" by the rest; a "mama's boy," he "cried a lot to get his own way."

Gordon never liked school and had finished only six grades when he began working, at the age of sixteen. As he grew he appeared to develop no purpose or interests. He worked aimlessly and sporadically, went out casually with girls without apparently forming any strong ties, and was socially most attached to the "fellows," who were his contemporaries. As he entered his twenties, he still remained very much attached to his home and his mother. She continued to indulge him as she had all of his life; he paid no rent, and had no responsibilities even at home, where his mother kept his room clean for him, picked up his clothes, and otherwise waited on him. Her sudden death when he was twenty-three was a severe blow to him; he sobbed and screamed and "had to be held down by three men." As he said in explaining his grief, "I was her pet—I was still at home after all the others left." After her funeral, the patient went to live with his sister who "had been a second mother to me."

A year later (during World War II) the patient entered the Coast Guard. For the first eight months he was stationed only a few miles from home. For the first time in his life, now aged twenty-four, he was away from his family and his familiar group of male friends. He was often able to get home on week-end pass, but during the week he "felt lonesome and missed home." In this setting he first developed mild epigastric pains, the early symptoms of a duodenal ulcer. He said of this period:

> I missed going out with the boys at home and stuff like that. Missed dancing; missed the whole crowd, you know— certain places we'd go to visit. Start thinking of them things and then you'd get down. That's what brought it [the ulcer] on, I guess. I guess that's the only thing that can bring it on—when you think.
> *Dr.*   When you think?
> *Pt.*   Sure. When you got something to occupy your mind you don't think as much. So it used to be when I used to lay in bed, and stuff like that. When you didn't have nothing to do, you'd start thinking . . . I used to get lonely once in a while.
> *Dr.*   What was the lonely feeling like?
> *Pt.*   Well, I just wanted to be home—just wanted to be home, be with the fellows, you know. I don't remember anything else. (Pause.) That's natural for anybody.
> *Dr.*   Sure, but I was wondering particularly in your case how it affected you.
> *Pt.*   I don't remember how it affected me. I guess I was lonesome.

The patient's gastrointestinal symptoms were a chronic annoyance to him, but even when they persisted month in, month out, he did not consult a doctor. Initially, as we saw, he blamed his trouble on "thinking." After his transfer to a new base he attributed his continued pains to the irregular eating imposed by his duties. The strangeness of his new location did not bother the patient greatly, because he had made a friend in basic training who was transferred with him. Eventually, when their duty required them to find quarters off the base, the two of them rented an apartment together. The friend was an active, friendly, outgoing person, who appeared to treat the patient like a younger brother. He took him home to visit his family in the South, introduced him to his friends, and arranged dates for him; he allowed the patient to look to him for help and support. One day the friend, craving more action than his land-based job provided, volunteered for sea-duty. Within a few days he was gone, leaving the patient behind alone in the apartment they had shared. A week later the patient suddenly felt dizzy and faint, vomited up a large amount of blood, and was hurriedly taken to the hospital where he was found to have a bleeding duodenal ulcer. Of his friend the patient said:

> We worked together; we went through basic training together. He was the closest friend I had. To tell you the truth, he was the only one.
> *Dr.* How did you feel when he left?
> *Pt.* I was sorry to see him go. He was a good friend.
> *Dr.* You were pretty sorry to see him go.
> *Pt.* Oh yeah, we were good friends.
> *Dr.* It must have been quite different after he left.
> *Pt.* Well, I missed him. It's natural. You live with a person eight months—know him for over a year and a half, two years, well, you get to know him. But he was the only one I was real close to. A good friend.

In the hospital his bleeding rapidly subsided, and in addition the pains that had plagued him for so many months entirely disappeared. At the end of six weeks he was discharged from the hospital and from the service because of his medical disability. Two weeks before the episode of bleeding the patient had met a woman eight years older than himself. She visited him frequently during his hospitalization, and after a courtship lasting fifty days they were married immediately upon his discharge.

At once the patient and his bride returned to his sister's home, and lived with her and her family for four and a half years before he and his wife could "find a place of their own." During these years and after they had moved into their new apartment, the patient was frequently out of work. Fortunately his wife had steady employment, and through her efforts they were able to live in moderately comfortable circumstances. When they set up their own household, they furnished their apartment out of savings from her earnings. Throughout this time, although he paid no attention to his diet, the patient had no further pain nor other symptoms of ulcer.

A year after they had moved out on their own, the patient found work in a ladies' glove factory that proved to be a steady job. When he worked, he did so quietly, conscientiously and assiduously. A temperate, soft-spoken man, he antagonized no one, and was generally liked by those with whom he was associated. Not long after he had gone to the glove factory, the employees were unionized and the patient was elected the first president of the local shop. His new duties proved to be time-consuming and arduous, and were furthermore in addition to, not in place of, his regular work in the factory. Although he was paid a small honorarium for his administrative functions in the union, he still had to rely on the competitive race of piece-work to make an adequate income. His life was far from peaceful; he described it as follows:

> *Dr.*   What was it like being president of the union?
> *Pt.*   Oh, it was all right. Lot of headaches to it. Complaints and all that, and I used to have to go and straighten out the grievances with the boss, but it never bothered me.
> *Dr.*   How do you mean "bothered" you?
> *Pt.*   Well—I never let it get me, if I had an argument with the boss over something.
> *Dr.*   What would happen?
> *Pt.*   Sometimes he'd holler his head off.
> *Dr.*   He would?

Pt. He'd blow his top.

Dr. Yes, what would happen?

Pt. I'd just straighten it out.

Dr. How would you feel?

Pt. Well, I just did it because I had to. I'd have to go and argue for the people. If they had a complaint, I'd have to go in and straighten it out with him. It was nothing to me.

Dr. I see.

Pt. I'd argue—I'd talk with him and see if we could straighten it out.

Dr. It sounds strenuous, being president.

Pt. Well, everyday you had somebody complaining: they weren't getting their bonus right and I'd have to go straighten that out. Or they wanted a window closed, and another wanted the window open. They'd come and squawk to me to go and see the boss. Little things like that. Of course sometimes the boss would get wise and cut down on the bonus and the union contractor wouldn't allow it. Well, then I'd have a big squawk. I used to get some awful complaints.

Dr. Did you really?

Pt. You're working with a bunch of girls and you get more complaints. Fellows, see, they're all right. It's always the women. They're always arguing. One makes a dollar more than another, they want to know why . . . But I just straighten it out myself with them instead of going to the big boss. (Here the patient was silent for a number of seconds.) But over all it wasn't bad. It wasn't too strenuous. It was all right. (The patient yawned audibly)—Get tired lying down there on the ward.

These comments about his situation were the first mention the patient made of his union presidency. They occurred in the middle of the third hour-long interview between the patient and his doctor. They came as a surprise to the doctor; in initially giving his history the patient had mentioned that while he was employed in the glove factory he had first noted pain, redness, and swelling in his wrists—the early manifestations of rheumatoid arthritis. He denied being under any unusual stress at this time. For example, his doctor asked him with reference to the onset of his arthritic symptoms:

Dr. What were you doing at that time? What was happening? What was going on? How were you feeling?

Pt. Oh, I was feeling all right. As far as my general health was concerned, I was feeling all right. It was just as I said—the wrists. It just seemed to come on. What caused it, I don't know. I've been trying to figure it out. Maybe I got run down. That's the only way I can figure it.

Dr. Maybe you got run down?

Pt. That's what I figured. Maybe I got run down—tired, and got so that my resistance got so low that the arthritis came on.

Dr. What could have got you run down?

Pt. Maybe working too hard.

Dr. You were working hard?

Pt. I was working hard, yeah—rushing. Maybe that's what did it. And then over-action of the wrists, moving them too much could have caused it. Or the legs, because I had to kick a foot press; so maybe that could have aggravated it too. But I tried to figure if anything happened that could have caused it and I can't think.

Dr. How were you working hard?

Pt. Well, on the job.

Dr. You mentioned that you were working fast—getting as much done as you could.

Pt. The more you did, the more your salary was, because you're on the bonus system. If you turned out more work, you got more money.

Dr. Were you doing anything else at that time? Did you have any other duties?

Pt. No. No—I didn't work nowheres else; no part-time work. No. Just did that and then I'd go home. (The patient paused.) Something brought it on, but what? . . .

Dr. Do you remember any particular strain you were under apart from working so hard at that time? Was there anything you were doing or involved in?

Pt. No—just home life. Just ordinary. Nothing that I remember.

It was shortly after this protestation of normalcy that the patient casually mentioned the fact of his presidency of the union. When his doctor expressed surprise that he had not spoken of this before, the patient blandly replied that he "had forgotten it." We have seen from the account quoted earlier how his position placed him between the fire of his complaining fellow employees and his angry employer. At the same time he not very convincingly asserted that it "was nothing" to him. A few moments later, however, he hinted that he had been troubled by the tensions surrounding him.

Dr. Did you have any feelings about it at all?

Pt. I got disgusted once in a while (the patient said this with a little laugh).

Dr. What was that like?

Pt. I'd just get disgusted.

Dr. By "disgusted" you mean what?

Pt. I'd say, "What the heck, I can't do nothing about it." I'd tell the people—they'd ask me, "Ain't you doing nothing?", and I'd say, "What can I do? If you think you can do any better, go ahead." They'd burn you up that way.

Dr. You'd get a little burned up at it?

Pt. Yeah, sure. But I didn't run again for a second term. I says, "No." I didn't feel so good.

Dr. How were you feeling bad?

Pt. My wrists were starting to go with the arthritis.

Not long after this comment about the onset of his arthritis, the patient described in more detail the pressures to which he was constantly subjected. His employer, for example, failed to pay a bonus required in the contract. The employees angrily demanded of the patient that he secure the bonus from the management. The employer, when the patient approached him with labor's requirements, exploded in rage and delivered an angry harangue. Gordon was repeatedly the target of such abuse. The doctor asked him:

Dr. How would you feel then?

Pt. I'd forget about it and go back to work.

Dr. You'd forget about it?

Pt. Sure. I wouldn't forget about it all together, but, I mean, I'd go back to work.

Dr. What I was wondering was how you would feel after an argument like this and went back to work at the bench.

Pt. It didn't bother me. (Pause.) It didn't bother me. (Pause.) It didn't bother me.

Dr. Did you get pretty mad?

Pt. No, not too mad. It wouldn't do no good anyway. I'd never blow my top and get real mad and holler. I never got that way.

Dr. Why?

Pt. Well, we talked sensible. He'd holler once in a while—get mad.

Dr. But you wouldn't?

Pt. No, I'd never get mad. I figured it wasn't worth it. It never used to bother me . . . it never upset me. I just used to forget it; go back to work. I never used to let it get me. If I'd let it get me, it probably would have upset me. May have made me nervous, or something like that. . . .

Dr. When the boss would get mad or some of the workers would get mad, would it make you mad?

Pt. Not that I recall. It's so far back that I can't remember to tell you the truth. I don't think I let it get me. (Pause.) I just used to straighten it out.

Dr. It sounds like a tough situation. It sounds like a spot where you might have had a lot of feeling about it . . .

Pt. I know the boss got upset. I may have, but I doubt it. I used to try not to let it get me.

Dr. Why would you try?

Pt. Well, why let it upset me?—that's what I used to think. Heck, it's going to do me no good to worry over it. There may have been times I got mad. I don't remember; it's possible. It's so far back that I forgot.

It was not long before the patient's arthritis became so severe that he was forced to stop work and enter the hospital. That was the beginning of a chronic course of exacerbations and remissions of symptoms punctuated by short periods of work and longer periods of hospitalization.

In the hospital he was always quiet, reserved, and unemotional. He was co-operative with ward routines and stoically put up with all the procedures he was required to undergo as a subject of a research study he had agreed obligingly to take part in. In the interviews recorded with him he was notably laconic and phlegmatic; he rarely offered information spontaneously and generally waited for the doctor to indicate the direction the conversation should take. He was content to follow where others led.

From all that was learned about the patient—from his account of himself, from his family's description of him, and from observations of his behavior—it became clear that his habitual behavior was characterized by passivity and dependence, and by marked suppression, repression, and denial in the area of feelings, especially anger. His basic orientation and underlying problems were, in other words, narcissistic in nature; his surface behavior was a variation on the narcissistic theme. On the one hand he was overtly dependent without the need to revert to the defenses against this need which we have observed in patients such as Boyd C. On the other, he showed such massive defenses against anger and aggression that it was almost impossible to get a glimpse of this impulse even in situations where he was most sorely tried. Each of the two episodes of serious illness in his life was associated with environmental circumstances which in the case of his duodenal ulcer threatened the gratification of his dependent needs, and in the case of his arthritis stimulated the aggression behind his defenses. Each of these two disorders was related to a different aspect of his character structure. Let us examine the two situations in greater detail.

His *ulcer symptoms* appeared at a time when he was faced with successive losses of people on whom he was dependent. First his mother died; then by entering the service he was separated from his sister and the familiar surroundings of home and acquaintances; finally his close and only friend and roommate deserted him to ship out to sea. It was at that time that the dangerous bleeding from his ulcer first forced him to seek medical attention. Coincident with being in the shelter of the hospital and with his rapidly formed attachment to the older woman who almost at once became his wife, his ulcer symptoms completely disappeared. They remained permanently in abeyance in the ensuing years as he lived now in a dependent relationship with his wife, reunited, initially at least, with his sister.

His *rheumatoid arthritis* occurred under totally different circumstances. Here it was not the loss of persons necessary for his security that caused him difficulty, but a situation in which he was bombarded from all sides with complaints, anger, and aggression. Caught between his employer and the demands of his fellow employees who frequently lashed out at him, one would expect the patient to have reacted in kind. Instead, as we have seen, he appeared to maintain a surprising serenity, and those feelings he did admit to having were muted almost to a point of non-existence. Then his wrists "started to go."

The temporal relationship between physical illness and emotional conflict in a single case does not necessarily imply a causal connection. Our concern with Gordon C. is not to educe generalizations but to illustrate the proposition drawn from a variety of sources that emotional conflict is one of the important factors in the production of physical disorders. The many studies bearing on this proposition fall into four main categories: (1) investigations which indicate that patients who develop physical illness in relation to emotional stress have common psychological problems in the areas of dependency needs, aggressive impulses, and the defenses employed to keep these in check (58); (2) experimental correlative studies of physiological and psychological functioning under conditions of known environmental stress (55, 61); (3) statistical analyses of large groups of patients for the relationship between the appearance of illness and emotional conflict over loss, aggression, etc. (50); (4) intensive psychological investigation of the emotional conflict associated with repeated exacerbations of a physical illness in the individual patient (59), or a study of the conflict situation in a number of patients all suffering from the same disorder (47, 54).

Many questions, of course, remain unanswered—the enigma, for instance, of symptom choice: why, that is, in the face of loss does one patient develop an ulcer, another ulcerative colitis, a third a depression? Why do some patients in the course of their lives, like Gordon C., develop two, three, and even more of the disorders commonly associated with emotional stress? Are certain constellations of psychological conflict consistently related to specific illnesses? What early childhood experiences predispose the individual to such illnesses in adulthood?

It is not our purpose here either to elaborate on or to suggest ways of resolving these problems. Our task in this chapter and the last has been to recognize the fact that in considering physical illness we cannot be concerned with pathological physiological processes alone. The understanding and investigation of these of course remain an essential area of medical knowledge; but it is only a part of the task of the medical practitioner and investigator. It is necessary in addition to view the physiological processes as a part of the more inclusive process of the life of the individual person. His emotions, his relationships, and his experiences are affected by and may contribute to the production of illnesses that involve pathological changes in his body structure and functioning.

The introduction of these factors into the study of disease of course greatly complicates problems of investigation and treatment. It is natural and at times imperative to focus on only one aspect of a problem at a time. One investigator, for example, will bring his physiological knowledge to bear on a specific disorder; while another trains his knowledge of personality functioning on the same problem. The complexity of contemporary science makes such fragmentation unavoidable. The danger lies in *oversimplifying,* in losing sight of the many factors that conspire to produce illness, of singling out one aspect, whether it be psychological or physiological, as *"the* cause." Obviously in any given disorder some factors will be of more importance than others in producing illness. But the ultimate understanding of disease can result only from a synthesis of the many individual elements that contribute to its production. "Psychosomatic medicine" is not a subdivision of the field of medical practice or of medical investigation. It is a guiding concept. It provides an ideal that few can achieve within the inevitable limitations of human knowledge and skills. One dismisses, however, the importance of any of these elements, physiological or psychological, at the risk of dangerously limiting one's understanding of human illness.

XIX

The Doctor and His Patient

The complexity of the human being puts a special burden on the practitioner of medical arts. The research investigator may narrow himself to a small field of study, and though limited in his outlook, make discoveries that will ultimately become a part of a larger whole. His limited vision is detrimental only to his own scientific development and wisdom. The practitioner who limits himself, whether it be to the confines of physiology or psychology, does so to the detriment of his patient.

Our approach to the problem of illness is based on the assumption that the organism is the basic biological unit which reacts to the stimuli of its environment. The art of the practice of medicine requires on the part of the doctor an awareness that human life is a process lived in a constantly changing world which requires, for survival, a constantly adaptive response. This is a commonplace in physiology where the ideas of equilibrium and homeostasis are central concepts in its theoretical structure; it is equally true of the psychological mode of functioning. Rational treatment is based on helping the patient to return to health by combating the forces upsetting the balance—whether physiological or psychological. Although we are forced in our scientific discourse to think of man now in psychological, now in physiological terms, we must not forget that the mind and the body together form the unit of his life process. Difficulties arise when we ignore the fact that stresses arising in a man's experiences and human relationships are reflected in his physiological processes as well as in his emotions; and that stresses directly distorting his bodily functioning, especially in states of disease, are reflected in his emotions, his thinking, and his relationships. One cannot occur without the other; reasonable medical practice has to take both aspects of the process into account.

This *holistic* approach to the sick human being is a guiding concept for both research and practice. As the increasing tendency to specialization indicates, however, the complete physician, thoroughly competent in every area of medicine, does not exist. Even if he wanted to, no one man could learn all the complex therapeutic techniques peculiar to internal medicine, psychiatry, and surgery. But every physician must be familiar with a common body of fundamental knowledge about human physiological and psychological functioning to enable him to arrive at an etiological diagnosis, to carry out treatment when this is within his purview, and to refer his patient intelligently for specialized care when this is necessary.

The need for such fundamental knowledge and the ability to apply it therapeutically was evident in the case of Eleanor F. who at thirty-eight was admitted to the hospital for chronic back and leg pain resulting from a ruptured lumbar intervertebral disk. A laminectomy was successfully performed and there were no difficulties after surgery other than the expected discomfort. On the sixth postoperative day, however, the patient was found by her surgeon in a distressing state. She was crying, depressed, and acutely anxious, which was a marked change over her previous cheerful, courageous, almost stoical attitude. In addition she complained of unbearable pains, not only in the leg previously affected, but in the other leg as well, so severe that she began to demand narcotics for it. There was no evident disturbance in the operative wound nor other signs on examination pointing to a physical basis for her complaints. As this disturbance persisted during the next two or three days, her doctors turned their attention to her feelings and attitudes. A brief discussion with her revealed the following: her life had been one of service and devotion to her husband and children. Emotionally she had been the strong one in the family; although the rest habitually came to her with their problems, she kept her own troubles to herself. She gave freely of her time and energy to everyone around her; she asked nothing in return. No matter how trying a situation might be, she never lost her temper and equanimity. Her day at home was one of constant activity, maintaining her house in perfect order despite the efforts of her young, active children to keep it in chaos; she often worked late into the night to finish her many tasks to the perfection she required of herself. Despite the chronic pain in her back and leg, which had become increasingly severe during the months before surgery, she had continued her pace without abatement.

During her days in the hospital after surgery, and especially as the immediate postoperative discomfort lessened, she began to think more and more of home. She began to fear that as a result of surgery she would not be so capable and so strong as she had been accustomed to being at home. The thought came to her, and frightened her, that maybe she would be a cripple, paralyzed, in a wheelchair and completely dependent on the family she had supported for so many years. Such an idea was completely at odds with her ideal for herself as a totally independent woman who was the provider of strength for her family. As she saw herself, now sick and helpless, forced to stay in bed because of the surgery, with nothing to do but passively await the outcome, her fantasies multiplied, her fears grew, she became acutely depressed and tearful, her pains became intolerable, and she began increasingly to demand medication.

It was agreed by all observers that the patient was suffering a regressive reaction to her postoperative situation. Like the patients we have considered earlier, the dependency needs which had been restrained by her lifelong character defense of reaction formation were beginning to make their appearance through the vehicle of her physical symptoms. Lying inert and inactive in bed while her wound healed was proving too great a strain on her psychological equilibrium. It seemed important, therefore, to try therapeutically to utilize and preserve the patient's character defenses before they crumbled completely, by involving her more actively in her convalescence, by giving her the feeling that she as well as the doctors had some control over her progress toward health, and that she was not simply the passive recipient of help from others as she lay helpless in bed while nature took its course. For this reason the physiotherapist was asked to come to teach the patient a few simple exercises she could perform by herself in bed without disrupting her wound. Although there was little need for these from a physical point of view, it was hoped that they would strengthen the patient's old patterns of self-reliant activity by making her feel that she had an active part to play in her return to a healthy and useful life.

The result of this maneuver exceeded expectations. On the day after the physiotherapist's first visit the patient's behavior was strikingly different. She was cheerful, calm, and controlled and no longer complained either of the pain in her legs or of her fear of being a cripple. On the contrary, she was confident now about her ability to return home and resume the role she had lived in the past. Asked about her exercises, she replied, "The girl told me to do the exercises four times a day. I've done them seven times already since breakfast—I'm going to get out of here!"

The successful therapeutic outcome of Eleanor F.'s illness rested on a versatile medical approach. Knowledge of anatomy, physiology, and pathology was essential for making the diagnosis of a ruptured intervertebral disk. Skill in surgical techniques was needed to correct the symptom-producing disease process. Familiarity with common human conflicts combined with skill in interviewing was necessary to determine the nature of her postoperative reaction and to institute the maneuvers designed to restore her emotional equilibrium. All of these elements were required to help her get well. Attention to her emotional conflicts alone would have done nothing to correct the offending lesion responsible for her pain. A failure to take into consideration the nature of her psychological functioning would have resulted in her slipping into chronic invalidism motivated by her emotional conflicts; the beneficial effects of surgery would have been nullified.

A similar versatility was required in the management of Karl B., although the details of his treatment differed from those of Eleanor F. By the time he was fifty-three, Karl had had intermittent symptoms of a duodenal ulcer for seventeen years. These had been easily controlled by diet and medication without serious complications. Eight days before admission to the hospital he had again noted epigastric pain which had gradually increased in frequency and intensity. The night before he entered the hospital he had been on a drinking spree; the following morning while vomiting he began to feel dizzy, threw up blood, and was brought to the hospital. His was a common and simple story and it appeared evident that the irritation of the alcohol had precipitated his bleeding.

There was, however, more to his history if one inquired *what the patient had been doing* in the period before admission. In truth, for some time he had been doing very little—he had just finished serving a year's sentence in jail for nonsupport of his estranged wife and family. He had been quite contented in jail, which was a leisurely institution for the incarceration of people who, like himself, were found guilty of minor offenses. There he was well fed and comfortably housed, with no responsibilities and little work. He had had no difficulty with his ulcer during this period. His sentence expired, however, and he was released with a gift from the authorities of a new suit and a five-dollar bill. This was all he had to carry him through the period of finding a job and getting back into the pace of civilian life.

Upon leaving jail the patient felt confident of his future, for he had been promised by a friend that a job would be awaiting him on his release. Unfortunately unexpected troubles were in store for him; the promised job was not available, and he was unable to find work on his own. His five dollars rapidly dwindled, and he discovered as he made the rounds of his old friends that they could not help him either financially or to find work. He became increasingly discouraged, lonesome, and depressed, and finally at length in despair went to his estranged wife to ask her for aid. She slammed the door in his face. Tears came to his eyes as the patient recounted these events to the doctor and told how lonely, discouraged, and unhappy he felt. "I was just down and out," he said. "Nobody wanted me and I think that's what brought on these pains."

In the hospital the patient had no further bleeding, and his symptoms rapidly disappeared on a conservative regimen of diet and medication. At the end of ten days he was medically ready for discharge. He was, however, loath to leave the hospital; the circumstances of his life were unchanged; indeed, they were far worse than they had been when he was released from jail. Now he had no hope of a job, no place to go, no one to turn to, his money was gone, and his only suit was no longer new. To discharge him as medically cured without taking his situation into account was to return him to the same hopeless environment that had in the first place contributed to the symptoms that brought him to the hospital. More was needed in the management of his illness than attention to the medical aspect of his ulcer.

It was for this reason, therefore, that a social worker from the hospital's department of social service was asked to help in planning for the patient after his discharge. Her function was threefold: (1) from her knowledge of community agencies to help the patient find work and an adequate place to live; (2) to arrange for temporary funds to carry him over the initial period after hospitalization before he could support himself; and (3) through her practical help, her interest, and her availability to the patient after his discharge, to be for him a person to whom he could turn for assistance, security, and emotional support. She was "prescribed" for him, along with his diet and medication, as part of the complete program of treatment rationally devised from the doctor's knowledge of all the etiological elements responsible for his illness. His hemorrhaging ulcer was one episode in a larger process involving physical, emotional, and situational factors; effective treatment required and resulted from knowledge of all these aspects.

For both Eleanor F. and Karl B. treatment was extended beyond the specific physical measures taken to heal the local lesion, to include the necessary readjustment of environmental factors helping to produce their illness. In these general terms, the therapeutic approach was similar; in the details of the specific treatment there were major differences determined by the nature of their problems—not only that Eleanor F. was managed surgically and Karl B. medically, but there was a marked contrast between psychological maneuvers instituted for each of them. For Eleanor F. help was aimed at bolstering her flagging ego defenses, for Karl B. at supporting and partially gratifying his dependency needs. In each the therapeutic maneuver was aimed at a different part of the psychological structure; the direction was determined by the doctor's understanding of that structure and of its malfunctioning under stress. To have fostered Eleanor F.'s dependency would have increased the severity of her symptoms and regression. To have forced Karl B. into a position of self-reliance would have been to ignore the fact that his own inner resources were sadly depleted, and that the resulting despair that filled him was significantly contributing to the production of his symptoms. He needed help from others, not the opportunity to prove himself. The proper approach to each patient was determined by knowing what each required.

It is apparent that in his attempts to help the patient with the emotional component of his illness, the doctor as well as being aware of the patient's psychological functioning, turns his attention to the relationships that the patient makes with the significant people in his life. He tries to help him maintain those relationships with family and friends that are essential for his emotional well-being, and to provide new relationships when old ones are lost or ruptured. For the sick human being an especially important person in his environment is his doctor and we must turn now to a brief examination of the nature of this doctor-patient relationship.

The patient comes to a doctor with attitudes and expectations that are partly appropriate and partly inappropriate. He expects with justification that the doctor will understand illness and know how to treat it. Furthermore, particularly if the doctor is a psychiatrist, he expects him to have a knowledge of human psychology. In each case the patient reasonably anticipates that the doctor will use his specialized knowledge to help him return to health; he approaches the doctor with a healthy faith and trust in the physician's knowledge and skill.

But he brings more than this to the doctor he consults. He brings expectations and feelings that result from the tendency to regression which sickness produces, from his attitudes toward people in authority, and from his general patterns of relationships with others which have their origins in the past experiences of his life. Under the influence of these factors, his behavior and his attitude toward the doctor may be quite inappropriate to the real medical situation and the legitimate goals of treatment.

This was strikingly apparent in Marcia G., a young woman of twenty-five. She had been admitted to the psychiatric ward of a general hospital during an episode of acute anxiety. The service house staff thought she should be transferred to a state mental hospital because she manifested paranoid ideas. The patient, however, objected violently to this plan and the visiting psychiatrist was, therefore, asked for his opinion as to the necessity of further hospitalization. After hearing her history from the resident in charge, the senior psychiatrist interviewed the patient for five minutes. He decided that she might, as she wished, be discharged from the ward to carry on with the out-patient treatment which had been previously planned for her. When he told the patient of his decision, she thanked him warmly and quietly left the conference room.

Four months later the patient arrived unannounced at the senior psychiatrist's office. He was able to spend half an hour with her during which she discussed the reasons for and against her wish to move permanently west. During the brief time he spent with her, he said little, but listened sympathetically to her problems. He gave her no specific advice other than to urge her to discuss it further with the psychiatrist whom she was seeing regularly in the out-patient department.

Some weeks after this impromptu meeting a letter from her informed him that she had moved. Among other things she wrote: "You are the most sensible, just, fair and square psychiatrist I have ever come across . . . I never cease to wonder at men like you. You wear Truth, Integrity, Maturity, Ethics—and all human qualities with such honest, easy gracefulness, such extraordinary intelligence. The young, beautiful Truth and knowledge of your great mind make all lesser things burn out in your light. Men like you are so few. Your qualities are a healing power that mere knowledge cannot equal."

The patient wrote feelingly and sincerely; she believed and meant what she said; but her judgment about the doctor was utterly unjustified. He had been kind to her; he had listened to her and tried to be of help to her; he had behaved as any doctor would and should toward a patient who comes to him. There was nothing out of the ordinary about him or his actions to warrant this paean. Furthermore, in the total of a mere thirty-five minutes that the patient had on two occasions seen him, she could not possibly have learned enough about him to make anything other than the most superficial judgment about him as a physician or a person. From what took place between them she could have learned little or nothing about his intelligence, his knowledge, his integrity, or his ethics. Her feelings and attitudes were totally inappropriate to the real situation; her judgments were derived not from a rational consideration of the facts she observed during the interview. On the contrary, they arose from inner, private psychological needs and forces; they were based primarily on what she wanted the doctor to be —on her hopes and her fantasies of what an older, kindly, and helpful person should be. They were like the feelings of a small child to a parent whom he sees as omnipotent— an attitude toward people that ordinarily changes as one ripens into adulthood. Marcia G.'s reaction to the doctor was colored by her *transference* to him of feelings which might have been appropriate to other and earlier situations, but which had little bearing on the reality of the relationship between herself and the physician. Marcia G.'s was an extreme reaction. Her attitude toward the doctor appeared to be determined primarily by inner, mental factors and very little by the realities of the situation.

In most patients reality plays a larger role; in everyone, however, his relationship to the doctor is determined by a mixture in varying proportions of reality and *transference*. The latter, as we have seen, introduces a note of the irrational into the relationship, derived from earlier attitudes, relationships, and experiences, especially in childhood, which now unconscious, without his being aware of their existence, exert their influence on the patient's feelings and behavior in the therapeutic situation. It is primarily transference that leads a patient to attribute to the doctor magical, at times omnipotent, powers he does not have; to make impossible demands upon him; to rage when his, the patient's, wants are not gratified; to resent his authority, to fear him, to rebel against him.

In the regressive reaction brought about by illness, transference colored by infantile needs and impulses may, as we have noted, make the doctor's task a difficult one. A part of this difficulty results from the effect which the patient's irrational behavior and strong feelings have on the doctor himself. The physician's capacity to be helpful depends in part on his ability to distinguish the real from the unreal, and to decide rationally what needs to be done. As the hyphen in the phrase "doctor-patient relationship" implies, the doctor is as much a part of the relationship as the patient. He too has feelings and attitudes and expectations of the patient, partly in response to the reality of the situation and partly the result of his own unconscious needs and attitudes derived from earlier experiences. His *counter-transference*, especially in the face of the powerful expressions of feelings in a patient's irrational transference manifestations, may become strong and lead to feelings and behavior not appropriate to the requirements of the medical situation and possibly detrimental to his capacity to help.

A psychiatrist, for example, was listening to his patient during a therapeutic hour. The patient, who in his college years had been an unbeatable sprinter on the varsity track team, was in the process of damning and belittling both his father and his doctor. During this diatribe, the doctor slipped off into private thoughts of his own; suddenly he was aroused with the startled realization that he was completely immersed in thinking angrily to himself, "My legs are longer than this guy's—I'll bet I could beat him in any race he wanted to run." He had been so involved with his thoughts that for the moment he had forgotten the patient; his attention was completely focused on his own fantasies. As he reflected on these, he became aware that although they were partly intelligible as a response to the hostile criticism the patient was heaping on him, they were not appropriate to the therapeutic situation. The patient's hostile comments in the first place were a reflection of his transference, and as such should not have been taken personally by the doctor. In the second place, the doctor's job was not to react unthinkingly to the patient's behavior, but to maintain a position with the patient in which both of them could examine thoughtfully the patient's habitual behavior patterns which were now appearing in his relationship with the doctor. The latter's *counter-transference* had in this instance temporarily interfered with his purpose and effectiveness as a psychiatrist.

It would be unwise if not impossible for a doctor to avoid having any feelings for his patients. One cannot help at times being annoyed at a particularly hostile patient, pleased at praise that may not be entirely warranted, anxious and uneasy with some, warm and comfortable with others, charmed by the seductive behavior of an attractive woman, overcome by a feeling of helplessness in the face of hopeless situations. It is, however, of particular importance that the doctor have enough self-awareness to recognize how he is feeling. He must be able to judge whether his attitudes are really appropriate to the situation in which they arise, or whether they are a result of his counter-transference. It is even more important that he be able to refrain from acting according to the dictates of his impulses and feelings, if such actions would conflict with the rationally determined goals of treatment. It is part of the physician's job to recognize the irrational in both himself and his patients; he must be able to provide the objectivity they lack, without losing his human warmth, understanding, and empathy.

If the relationship between the doctor and his patient is full of complexity and potential danger, it is nonetheless a powerful tool in the doctor's therapeutic armamentarium. In patients whose illness is a short one and whose personality structure is reasonably mature the transference presents little or no problem; the positive elements of faith that derive both from the transference and from the patient's realistic appraisal of the doctor's knowledge and skill provide a sound basis for his trusting willingness to submit to the doctor's demands, even when these include painful and often dangerous therapeutic procedures; they carry him more comfortably through the anxieties that accompany any illness other than the most trivial. It is when the patient brings to the therapeutic situation a severe character disorder, or when he suffers from a long and serious illness that tends to evoke regressive behavior, that transference (and counter-transference) problems are liable to become of importance. The doctor must then be able to recognize these phenomena and manage his treatment so that the dangers are avoided (as, for example, in the case of Eleanor F. where the early recognition that her increasing demands on the doctor were the beginnings of a regressive dependent transference determined the post-operative phase of her treatment). In patients with chronic illness, the support and encouragement which result from the positive element of faith and trust in their doctor become essential factors not only in the courage with which they face their disorder, but often in keeping symptoms and disability at bay.

The fact that a patient with a physical disease is found to have serious psychological problems does not necessarily mean that he should be treated by a psychiatrist. The latter is valuable as a consultant in helping to define the nature of the psychological disturbance and in making suggestions as to management, but his specialized methods of treatment are often not required for the patient's emotional difficulties. The patient remains with his own physician who provides him with the requisite physical treatment and supportive psychotherapy. Supportive psychotherapy is based on knowledge of the patient's character structure and the environmental stresses distorting his psychological equilibrium. It accepts the patient as he is, and without attempting to change his basic character structure, is aimed at strengthening his existing defenses, satisfying his needs, and removing environmental stresses. It requires, therefore, that the doctor have a knowledge of the fundamentals of psychopathology.

The psychiatrist, too, is often called upon to provide supportive psychotherapy for his patients. But he must in addition be able to carry out a type of psychotherapy that his acquisition of special skills during his long training enables him alone to undertake. What is called *insight psychotherapy* does not simply accept and adapt a therapeutic program to the existing character structure which the patient brings to the doctor. He, of course, works with the existing personality structure, but his goal as well as that of his patient is to make internal changes for the better in the character structure itself, so that the patient may come himself to cope more adequately with his environmental problems. The emphasis is away from changing the environment to fit the needs of the emotionally immature patient; it is toward helping him through the process of psychotherapy to achieve autonomy through emotional maturity. In essence, the method of such treatment, which is carried out most extensively and thoroughly in the process of psychoanalysis, is to provide a therapeutic situation in which the patient can come to see the neurotic nature of his human relationships and symptoms, the initially unconscious fantasies that lie behind these, and their origin in his childhood experiences. His growing awareness of these factors, especially as he sees them emerge from his unconscious and appear in his transference to his doctor coincides with his emotional growth and development as treatment progresses. Insight psychotherapy, and in particular psychoanalysis, is a part of psychiatry as a specialty, but from it have come the basic concepts of psychopathology which form the subject of this book.

"The village doctor was a great success," wrote * the doctor-author Oliver St. John Gogarty. "His success was due to his sympathy with his patients, each of whom he treated as an individual with an idiosyncrasy of his own and worthy of special and separate consideration. It was as if, instead of giving every one mass-produced medicine, he had moulded the portrait of each on his pill. He specialized in his patients. In this way he was a real specialist, in contradistinction to the town specialists who are identified with certain diseases or disasters to such an extent that it is as much as your reputation is worth to be seen on their doorstep."

It has been our task in this book to consider psychological facts and theories about sick human beings that will help us, like Gogarty's village doctor, to "specialize in our patients." Our concern has been with basic principles of psychopathology with which every practicing physician must be familiar. A word of caution is necessary: we must be careful in thus anatomizing his psyche, as we have dissected his body and analyzed his chemistry in the laboratory, that we do not lose our intuitive understanding of man. We must not treat our intellectual concepts of his psychopathology as the thing itself, nor forget that the model we have been building to explain man's psychological disorders is only an abstract pic-

* Oliver St. John Gogarty, *Going Native*, Duell, Sloane & Pearce, New York, 1940.

ture of a living and experiencing person, that by no means encompasses the whole of him.

Intellectualization is one of the major pitfalls into which all of us as doctors are liable to tumble—whether we are thinking in psychological or physiological terms. We are prone to divorce the trouble from the man, to mistake the disease for the patient, the part for the whole, the concept of the illness for the sick human being himself, the cirrhotic liver for its jaundiced owner. In part this is useful. It gives us a distance and objectivity that help us to consider our patient's disorder dispassionately and reasonably. It protects us from the impossible pain that would follow if we were to allow ourselves in sympathy to experience to the full the whole suffering of all those we care for. It is our own defense of denial. On the other hand, there is a danger of going too far in our attempts to protect ourselves, of becoming too dispassionate, of shutting off too completely the warmth of human sympathy and understanding that every patient needs.

There are no rules or formulae to determine the proper proportions of thoughtful distance and sympathetic closeness. Each has to decide for himself what is his own most effective golden mean. Of no one should a patient have justification for saying, in the words of a stoical, uncomplaining, and courageous man dying of bronchiogenic carcinoma, "The doctors come around in droves. I like the system here; I like the teamwork, but it doesn't make allowance for any personal feelings whatsoever. It's entirely so impersonal sometimes that it hurts."

GLOSSARY

AFFECT (pronounced AF'FECT). Feeling or emotion; the subjective feeling-tone associated with drives and their discharge.

AGGRESSION. (1) The action of being aggressive, usually implying vigorous *active* striving, often with hostile and destructive intent, as opposed to passive compliant acceptance; (2) the aggressive drive; (3) the subjective feeling-tone accompanying #1 or derived from #2. (See HOSTILITY.)

AMBIVALENCE. The co-existence of ideas or affects that are antithetical; the word is most commonly used to name the subjective state of simultaneously loving and hating an object.

ANOREXIA NERVOSA. A rare psychogenic syndrome, most commonly affecting adolescent girls, characterized by a refusal to eat, marked weight loss, and (when appropriate) amenorrhea. Fatal in 10 per cent of cases, it is accompanied by marked abnormalities in character structure and interpersonal relationships.

ANXIETY. A painfully unpleasant affect characterized by physical manifestations of autonomic discharge (sweating, tachycardia, etc.) and a subjective, often not completely describable, apprehensiveness; as opposed to fear (a reaction to real external dangers that is appropriate to the stimulus), anxiety is a response to an inner affect or thought that is frightening because of the consequences, real or imagined, that would ensue if the individual acted upon the affect or thought. (See SIGNAL ANXIETY.)

ASSOCIATION OF IDEAS. The linkage of one idea, or more, with another (or others) in a relationship determined in the experience of the individual by their contiguity in space or time, by their similarity or oppositeness, by their logical connections, or by their relationship to a common factor, which may be unconscious.

AUTISTIC. Relating to private, individual affects and ideas (daydreams, hallucinations, delusions) that are derived from drives, hopes, and wishes without regard for the nature of external reality. The word most commonly refers to the private reality of the schizophrenic patient as opposed to the shared reality of the external world.

AVOIDANCE. The avoiding of objects or situations that, as a result of the phobic mechanism, provoke anxiety.

CASTRATION ANXIETY. An anxious apprehension of bodily harm or mutilation, of being made inadequate and weak, or of suffering any diminution of one's powers, capabilities, or position, deriving ultimately from an apprehension of loss or mutilation of the genitals, an anxiety that first arises during the oedipal phase (or period) of development (q.v.).

CHARACTER. This term is frequently used synonymously with PERSON-ALITY (q.v.). In a more restricted sense it refers to those aspects of the personality constituting the EGO (q.v.) which in their manifestations distinguish one person from another.

COMPULSION. A neurotic symptom that results from an irresistible impulse to carry out an act, often repetitively, despite the actor's intellectual recognition that his behavior is unnecessary, undesired, and frequently absurd.

CONVERSION. The psychological mechanism by which an unconscious psychological conflict is translated into and represented by manifestations of abnormal physiological functioning, primarily in the sensorimotor apparatus, to a lesser extent in the autonomic nervous system.

CONVERSION HYSTERIA. A symptom neurosis in which the predominating clinical manifestations result from the psychological mechanism of CONVERSION (q.v.).

COUNTER-TRANSFERENCE. The attitudes, feelings, and fantasies which the physician experiences with regard to his patient, many of them arising, seemingly irrationally, from his own unconscious needs and psychological conflicts rather than from the actual circumstances of his relationship with the patient. (See TRANSFERENCE.)

DEFENSE. A psychological mechanism, one of the functions of the ego, by means of which impulses, feelings, and fantasies are kept from conscious awareness or from action in order to avoid the anxiety associated with them.

DELIRIUM. A mental state associated with gross brain dysfunction characterized by disturbances in consciousness and the sensorium with confusion, disorientation, hallucinations, illusions, delusions, restlessness, and sometimes marked agitation.

DELIRIUM TREMENS. A clinical syndrome following the withdrawal of alcohol after a period of heavy drinking, characterized by delirium and marked tremulousness of the trunk and upper extremities.

DELUSION. The unshakable belief in an idea, or set of ideas obviously contrary to logic, to the reality of the external environment, or to the accepted communal beliefs of the individual's culture.

DENIAL. A mechanism of defense in which the facts or logical implications of external reality are refused recognition in favor of internally derived, wish-fulfilling fantasies.

DEPRESSION. (1) An affect characterized by painful dejection, sadness, loneliness, loss of interest, and loss of self-esteem. (2) A clinical syndrome characterized by depressive affect, multiple somatic complaints (insomnia, fatigue, anorexia, etc.), motor retardation or agitation, and angry self-derogation often accompanied by suicidal ideas or attempts.

DEVELOPMENT. The orderly and systematic unfolding of human potentialities in the growth of the organism, resulting from both inborn, hereditary maturational factors, and environmental influences.

DISORIENTATION. A mental state accompanying gross dysfunction of the brain in which the individual is unable to determine his location in space and time, and less commonly his own identity.

DISPLACEMENT. A mechanism of defense characterized by (1) the shifting of emotions or fantasies from the object to which they were originally attached to a substitute; (2) the shifting of the psychic energies from one form of expression to another.

DISSOCIATION. The removal from conscious awareness and voluntary control of a set of related impulses, feelings, and ideas, which may none the less indirectly affect behavior.

DRIVE. An impulse to action arising in the ID (q.v.) from biological and physiological needs of the organism and experienced in consciousness as a feeling, a fantasy, or a need to act. The libidinal and the aggressive drives are those primarily involved in psychological conflict.

DYNAMIC. The consideration of the organization of the personality at any point in time with respect to the functional equilibrium of its various parts, and without regard to the psychogenetic and hereditary developmental factors which have determined the nature of the parts under consideration.

EGO. A theoretical construct comprising that organized part of the personality structure which includes defensive, perceptual, intellectual-cognitive, and executive functions. Conscious awareness resides in the ego, although not all of the operations of the ego are conscious. (See SUPEREGO.)

EGO-ALIEN. Of conscious mental events, experienced as not belonging to oneself; as being foreign to and not a usual part of one's experience of oneself as a psychological being; as being undesired, unacceptable, and uncontrollable.

EGO BOUNDARY. The hypothetical line that divides the self as a physical and psychological unit from the objects in the environment external to it.

EGO FUNCTION. Any one of the functions of the EGO (q.v.).

EGO IDEAL. The valued image that each individual has of the sort of person he aspires to be.

FANTASY. A daydream; a more or less elaborately organized idea or set of ideas derived from an inner conscious or unconscious impulse or desire, and commonly picturing the fulfillment of that impulse or desire.

FREE ASSOCIATION. The spontaneous flow of ideas that occurs when voluntary control of thinking is abandoned and thoughts are allowed to appear without regard for their logical or ethical appropriateness. Such associations are determined more by inner conscious or unconscious drives and needs than by the dictates of logical and rational thought; as such they provide evidence for the nature of the underlying drives. For this reason, the technique of observing free associations constitutes the fundamental method of psychoanalysis for exploring human psychological function.

GENESIS (adj. GENETIC). In psychoanalytic parlance "genesis" is short for PSYCHOGENESIS (q.v.). The shortened form should be used only when there is no possibility of confusing it with "genesis" meaning "genogenesis" or "heredity."

GENETIC. See GENESIS.

HALLUCINATION. A vivid sensory perception accompanied by a conviction of its reality on the part of the person experiencing the phenomenon occurring in the absence of an external sensory stimulus—i.e. "Seeing something that isn't there."

HALLUCINOGENIC AGENT. Any substance or condition producing a HALLUCINATION (q.v.).

HYPNOSIS. A mental state induced by the suggestion of an operator. Appearing to an observer like a state of sleep, it is experienced by the subject as a condition of restricted consciousness with regard to external stimuli, but frequently of increased conscious awareness of memories and other mental phenomena that are usually unconscious in the fully waking state.

HOSTILITY. (1) The state of being angry or hostile. (2) The aggressive drive. Hostility and AGGRESSION (q.v.) (and their respective adjectives) are often used synonymously. Strictly, aggression is a more general term, in which the emphasis is on active doing that is not necessarily angry or destructive; hostility carries a stronger implication of a subjective feeling, which may or may not be expressed in action, and which is more patently angry and destructive.

HYSTERIA. A neurotic syndrome characterized by a predominance of symptoms resulting from the mechanism of CONVERSION (q.v.).

ID. A theoretical construct comprising that unorganized part of the personality structure that contains the basic drives. The Id is by definition unconscious. (See EGO, SUPEREGO.)

IDENTIFICATION. A psychological mechanism by which the individual takes on, more or less permanently, the personality characteristics contained in the image of another person internalized through a process of INCORPORATION (q.v.). (See also page 196.)

ILLUSION. The misperception of an external sensory stimulus.

IMPULSE. See DRIVE.

INCORPORATION. A psychological mechanism by means of which the individual internalizes the image of another person in such a way as to lead to IDENTIFICATION (q.v.). (See also INTROJECTION and page 196.)

INSIGHT PSYCHOTHERAPY. A form of psychological treatment in which the patient becomes aware, through the help of the doctor, of pathogenic factors in his personality structure which were previously unconscious. (See PSYCHOANALYSIS.)

INTELLECTUAL FUNCTIONS (of EGO). Those operations of the mind which comprise logical thought, judgment, orientation, attention, comprehension, and memory.

INTERNALIZATION. The taking into oneself of the image, patterns of behavior, ethical codes, etc., of another. A more non-specific term than IDENTIFICATION, INCORPORATION, or INTROJECTION (q.v.), internalization is a psychological process related to all three of these mechanisms.

INTROJECTION. A psychological mechanism of internalizing the image of another person often used synonymously with INCORPORATION (q.v.). Strictly speaking incorporation refers to a fantasied act of actually swallowing another person, part of a person or thing, thus making it a part of oneself; as such it derives from the early phases of infantile development when oral incorporative modes of functioning predominate. In introjection, the emphasis is more on the phenomenon of internalizing than on the method of internalization. (See also IDENTIFICATION and page 196.)

ISOLATION. A psychological mechanism of defense by which (1) the logical or associational connection between two ideas is made unconscious or (2) the emotional component of an idea is repressed (isolation of affect).

LIBIDINAL. Of the LIBIDO (q.v.).

LIBIDO. The sexual DRIVE (q.v.) in its broadest sense, including the mental representations of the drive.

MATURATION. That aspect of the developmental process which is contributed by inborn, hereditary factors that endow the individual with a potential personality structure which tends to come into being as he grows.

MELANCHOLIA. A depressive syndrome usually occurring in middle life and characterized by marked anxiety and agitation in addition to the usual symptoms and signs of depression.

NARCISSISM. Self-love; the investment with libido of one's own body, one's social or mental self, or one's productions.

NARCISSISTIC CHARACTER DISORDER. A psychological disorder in which the individual shows an abnormal degree of NARCISSISM (q.v.), often manifested by excessive demands for support, praise, love, and attention.

NARCOSIS. A sleep artificially induced; used primarily of sleep brought about by the administration of sedatives.

NEGATION. A mechanism of defense in which drives, feelings, or fantasies achieve mental representation accompanied by a denial of their existence.

NEUROSIS (or PSYCHONEUROSIS). A psychological disorder manifested by either symptoms or abnormalities in character structure or both, in which basic psychological functions and organizations (intellectual functions, reality testing, perception, ego boundaries) remain intact. In certain patients on the "borderline" between neurosis and PSYCHOSIS (q.v.), the disturbances in these basic functions may be partial, transitory, or fluctuating.

OBSESSION. A neurotic symptom consisting of a thought, often highly emotional, which forces itself on the individual's conscious awareness against his wish to think it or contemplate it, and despite the fact that intellectually he recognizes the logical absurdity of the idea.

OBSESSIVE-COMPULSIVE NEUROSIS. A neurotic syndrome characterized by persistent and troubling obsessions and compulsions.

OEDIPAL PERIOD. That period of development, occurring from the ages of approximately three to six, characterized by the maturation of genital libido, the love of the child for the parent of the opposite sex with rivalry with the parent of the same sex, and resulting in the development of the superego.

ORAL DEPENDENCY. A phrase signifying the psychogenetic origin of dependency in the earliest period of development in which the infant is both helplessly dependent on his parents and in the midst of the oral phase of his libidinal maturation.

PARESIS. (1) Weakness. (2) Usually called GENERAL PARESIS, a syphilitic involvement of brain cortex leading to protean psychological manifestations.

PERSONALITY. Often used synonymously with CHARACTER (q.v.), personality refers to the sum-total of the individual's drives, affects, ideas, defenses, skills and talents, social behavior, and reactions, in their over-all organization, including phenomena common to all human beings as well as those that make each person unique.

PHOBIA. Anxiety experienced when faced by an object or situation which in reality is not dangerous, nor threatening, nor conducive to fear.

PHOBIC SYNDROME. A psychoneurotic syndrome characterized by a predominance of phobias.

PRECIPITATING CAUSE. An environmental event that precipitates the onset of neurotic symptoms or behavior.

PREDISPOSING CAUSE. A factor in the individual's personality structure, the product of his development, which in conjunction with a precipitating cause leads to the appearance of neurotic symptoms or behavior.

PRIMARY PROCESS THINKING. A type of AUTISTIC (q.v.) mentation characteristic of dreams, psychoses, and the early stages of life in which logical thought processes, reality, and the restrictions of time and space are ignored. (See SECONDARY PROCESS THINKING.)

PROJECTION. A mechanism of defense in which drives and their derivatives arising within the individual are attributed to people and situations outside of himself, often with a reversal of the active mode to the passive.

PSYCHOANALYSIS. (1) A highly specialized, extensive, and intensive form of INSIGHT PSYCHOTHERAPY (q.v.) which relies on the technique of FREE ASSOCIATION (q.v.) to explore and make conscious the DYNAMIC (q.v.), PSYCHOGENETIC (q.v.), and TRANSFERENCE (q.v.) aspects of the patient's pathological behavior and personality structure. (2) The investigative method employing psychoanalytic techniques. (3) The body of observations and theories arising from psychoanalytic investigation.

PSYCHOGENESIS (adj. PSYCHOGENETIC). The derivation of adult behavior and psychic structure from infantile and childhood developmental processes.

PSYCHOGENETIC. See PSYCHOGENESIS.

PSYCHONEUROSIS. See NEUROSIS.

PSYCHOSIS. A severe derangement of psychological function (commonly called insanity) manifested by extremes of mood (mania or depression) and by marked disturbances in thought processes (loss of reality testing, delusions, hallucinations, loss of ego boundaries, disorientation, memory defects, and loss of synthetic functions). (See NEUROSIS.)

PSYCHOSOMATIC MEDICINE. A method of studying and conceptualizing illness as the response of an organism to stress by the simultaneous and related manifestations of physiological and psychological dysfunction.

RATIONALIZATION. A mechanism of defense by which occurrences arising from or motivated by irrational drives are explained as being the result of circumstances or logical thought processes. Even where the latter are relevant motivating forces, they are treated by the individual as the *only* etiological factor, and he remains unaware of the inner irrational emotional forces that contribute to the end result.

REACTION FORMATION. A mechanism of defense in which a drive, feeling, or idea is countered by a drive, feeling, or idea opposite in quality. A reaction formation may become fixed and stable to form an important component of an individual's character structure.

REALITY TESTING. A basic function of the ego by means of which the individual is able to distinguish the real, the actually existing, and the rational from the autistically imagined.

REGRESSION. The turning back from an organized pattern of behavior and mentation deriving from a later phase of development to an organized pattern of behavior and mentation deriving from an earlier phase of development—a process often serving as a mechanism of defense.

REPRESSION. The basic mechanism of defense by which drives, feelings, and ideas are involuntarily excluded from conscious awareness by a psychic force opposing their emergence into consciousness, or by which mental phenomena, once conscious, are involuntarily made unconscious and maintained in that state. (See SUPPRESSION.)

RESISTANCE. The manifestation of the operation of a mechanism of defense, most commonly observable in psychotherapy when attempts are made to uncover drives, feelings, and ideas rendered unconscious by the defense mechanism.

REVERSAL OF AFFECT. The turning of an affect of one quality into an affect of a quality opposite to it. REVERSAL is also used to describe the turning of the active mode into the passive, and vice versa.

SCHIZOPHRENIA. A psychotic syndrome characterized by major distortions of thought processes (including hallucinations and delusions), disintegration of ego boundaries, disturbances in affect (flatness or inappropriateness of affect), and serious impairment of the individual's capacity to enter into relationships with others.

SECONDARY PROCESS THINKING. Those aspects of ego function which have to do with rational judgment and the logical evaluation of the real, actually existing world, thus enabling the individual to adapt his behavior to the demands of reality. (See PRIMARY PROCESS THINKING.)

SELF-ESTEEM. The critical evaluation of oneself (physical, psychological, social, and behavioral) as measuring up satisfactorily to the standard set by one's ego ideal; the feeling of satisfaction and pleasure that accompanies that evaluation.

SENSORY DEPRIVATION. The diminution or complete blocking or removal of sensory stimuli, either through experimental techniques or as a result of disease processes.

SEPARATION ANXIETY. That anxiety that arises as the result of a threat of separation from or loss of an important person or object. The anxiety resulting from the threat of the loss of the love of an important person is a form of separation anxiety.

SIGNAL ANXIETY. That anxiety that results from the threatened emergence into consciousness of a repressed undesirable drive, feeling, or idea, and which acts as a stimulus to the ego to further defensive action to keep the drive, feeling, or idea unconscious.

SLIP OF THE TONGUE. A symptomatic act in which a person says something other than what he means consciously and rationally to say, as the result of the influence of an unconscious drive, feeling, or idea striving for expression.

SUPEREGO. A theoretical construct comprising that organized part of the personality structure, mainly unconscious, that includes the individual's EGO IDEALS (q.v.), and the psychic agency (commonly called "conscience") that criticizes and prohibits his drives, fantasies, feelings, and actions. (See EGO, ID.)

SUPEREGO ANXIETY. That anxiety that results from the threat of experiencing guilt.

SUPPORTIVE PSYCHOTHERAPY. A form of psychological treatment in which, in contradistinction to INSIGHT PSYCHOTHERAPY (q.v.), the doctor does not attempt to help the patient to an increased awareness of himself but instead, by encouragement, exhortation, suggestion, and reassurance, attempts to strengthen the patient's ego functioning; or through the emotional support of the doctor-patient relationship or by environmental manipulation tries to supply for the patient those factors necessary for the satisfaction of the patient's needs, the default of which has precipitated symptoms.

SUPPRESSION. The deliberate, voluntary attempt to control, inhibit, or keep from communicating a conscious drive, feeling, or idea. REPRESSION (q.v.) is involuntary and, unlike suppression, renders the drive, feeling, or idea unconscious.

SYMBOL. An object that stands for, represents, and acts as a substitute for another; in particular an object that metaphorically represents an unconscious drive, feeling, or idea.

SYMPTOM FORMATION. The process of creating a complex mental or behavioral phenomenon that represents a compromise between an unconscious drive, feeling, or idea striving for expression and the ego defenses countering it.

SYNTHETIC FUNCTION. That function of the ego which subserves the ability to combine percepts, ideas, and other mental phenomena into an organized, rational, and logically consistent whole.

TRANSFERENCE. The attitudes, feelings, and fantasies which a patient experiences with regard to his doctor, many of them arising, seemingly irrationally, from his own unconscious needs and psychological conflicts rather than from the actual circumstances of his relationship with the doctor. (See COUNTERTRANSFERENCE.)

UNCONSCIOUS. Not conscious; in psychiatric usage the word usually refers to what is dynamically unconscious, i.e. a drive, feeling, or idea which is forcefully held from conscious awareness by countering ego defensive mechanisms. *Unconscious* is used as an adjective, or, with the particle *the,* as a noun, referring to a theoretical construct which delineates that portion of the mind which has the quality of being dynamically unconscious.

UNDOING. An ego defense mechanism by which, with a physical or mental operation, one (often irrationally and magically) attempts to counteract the effect one assumes (often irrationally and magically) to have resulted from an unconscious drive, feeling, or idea. Undoing is frequently the mechanism underlying a COMPULSION (q.v.).

SELECTED BIBLIOGRAPHY

The list of volumes and papers suggested here makes no claim to completeness. Its aim is threefold: (1) to describe available bibliographies of the voluminous literature concerning psychoanalysis, which constitutes the primary origin of the observations and concepts relevant to psychodynamic psychiatry and psychopathology; (2) to mention a few useful volumes covering the subject of psychiatry and psychoanalysis in a general way; and (3) to indicate the source of some of the concepts and illustrative case material presented in the text. It is hoped that this will provide a useful port of embarkation.

(Note: Although the bibliography is arranged by categories, the individual items are numbered consecutively. The reference numbers in the text refer to these.)

BIBLIOGRAPHIES

1. Frosch, J., and N. Ross (eds.), *The Annual Survey of Psychoanalysis*, International Universities Press, New York, 1952-9, vols. 1-5.

   Beginning with the year 1950, all books and articles in the field of psychoanalysis are being listed and abstracted annually.

2. Grinstein, A., *The Index of Psychoanalytic Writings*, International Universities Press, New York, 1956-60.

   The five volumes of this bibliography form an incomparable reference work in the field of psychoanalysis. The first four volumes provide an author index of all writings pertaining to the subject, and the fifth consists of a complete subject index.

GENERAL ASPECTS

A. PSYCHIATRY.

3. Arieti, S. (ed.), *American Handbook of Psychiatry*, Basic Books, New York, 1959.

   Bound in two large volumes, this work covers the field of psychiatry in a series of chapters written by experts in their field. (See refs. 17, 18.)

4. Cobb, S., *Foundations of Neuropsychiatry*, 6th edition, The Williams and Wilkins Co., Baltimore, 1958.

Written, as the author states in his foreword "to start the student with a three-dimensional orientation towards neurology and psychiatry" this volume discusses the anatomical, physiological, and pathological foundations of the functioning of the brain and the mind.

5. Ewalt, J. R., E. A. Strecker, and F. G. Ebaugh, 7th edition, *Practical Clinical Psychiatry*, McGraw-Hill Book Co., New York, 1957.

A standard and comprehensive textbook of psychiatry, now in its seventh edition, which discusses and describes the psychiatric syndromes under the official classification adopted by the American Psychiatric Assocation.

6. Henderson, D. K., and R. D. Gillespie, *A Text-book of Psychiatry*, 8th edition, Oxford University Press, London, 1956.

This is a standard textbook of general psychiatry, which is particularly valuable for the copious case illustrations of the various clinical syndromes.

B. Psychoanalysis.

7. Brenner, C., *An Elementary Textbook of Psychoanalysis*, Doubleday & Co., New York, 1957.

A short, systematic, and condensed exposition of analytic theory and concepts.

8. Fenichel, O., *The Psychoanalytic Theory of Neurosis*, W. W. Norton & Co., New York, 1945.

Because of its encyclopedic nature this is not a book that most beginners find helpful as an introduction to the subject. It is, however, extremely valuable as a reference book for topics of particular interest, especially because of its extensive bibliography.

9. Freud, S., *A General Introduction to Psychoanalysis*, Garden City Publishing Co., Garden City, N. Y., 1938.

A volume of lectures presented by Freud to a non-psychiatric audience, systematically expounding his concepts as they had developed before 1920. This is an interesting and very readable exposition of concepts dealing with dreams, the unconscious, symptom formation, etc., but it is important to remember that the book was written and first published before the theoretical concepts of ego structure and function, now the main preoccupation of analytic investigators and theoreticians, had been evolved.

10. Glover, E., *Psychoanalysis: A Handbook for Medical Practitioners and Students of Comparative Psychology,* 2nd edition, Staples Press, London, 1949.

A systematic presentation of the theory and practice of psychoanalysis, with particular emphasis on its clinical applications.

11. Hart, B., *The Psychology of Insanity,* 3rd edition, Cambridge University Press, Cambridge, 1916.

First published in 1912, this little volume has run through many printings. Written to present "in as clear a light as possible" the general principles of what at the time were "recent developments in abnormal psychology" it remains a concise and excellent introductory treatise for those unfamiliar with the concepts of psychopathology.

12. Hendrick, I., *Facts and Theories of Psychoanalysis,* 3rd edition, Alfred A. Knopf, New York, 1958.

An excellent, standard work in its third edition, which provides more in the way of illustrative case material than Brenner, and discusses the application of analytic concepts to fields other than that of clinical psychiatry.

13. Munroe, R. L., *Schools of Psychoanalytic Thought,* The Dryden Press, New York, 1955.

A thoughtful and lengthy comparative discussion and critique of the various "schools" of analytic thought, dealing with Freud, Jung, Adler, Rank, Fromm, Horney, Sullivan, and others.

SPECIAL ASPECTS

A. INTERVIEWING AND OBSERVATION.

14. Bird, B., *Talking with Patients,* J. B. Lippincott Co., Philadelphia, 1955.

Written for the student and physician without specialized psychiatric training, this volume deals with a variety of problems that arise in talking with patients (both adult and child) and offers practical suggestions for handling them.

15. Deutsch, F., and W. F. Murphy, *The Clinical Interview,* International Universities Press, New York, 1955, 2 vols.

These two volumes, presenting transcripts of recorded interviews with a large number of patients with different clinical disorders, provide a demonstration of the principles and practice of interviewing.

16. Gill, M., R. Newman, and F. G. Redlich, *The Initial Interview in Psychiatric Practice*, International Universities Press, New York, 1954.

A whole book devoted to presenting the verbatim transcripts of three diagnostic interviews, accompanied by extensive comments on the content and technique of the interchange between doctor and patient. A long-playing record of the interview is available.

17. Stevenson, I., "The Psychiatric Interview," *American Handbook of Psychiatry*, S. Arieti (ed.), Basic Books, New York, 1959, chap. 9, p. 197. (See ref. 3.)

18. Stevenson, I., and W. M. Sheppe, Jr., "The Psychiatric Examination," *American Handbook of Psychiatry*, S. Arieti (ed.), Basic Books, New York, 1959, chap. 10, p. 215. (See ref. 3.)

These two articles from the *American Handbook of Psychiatry* provide a concise presentation of the principles of interviewing and observation of the patient with an emotional disorder.

19. Whitehorn, J. C., "Guide to Interviewing and Clinical Personality Study," *Arch. Neurol. and Psychiat.*, 52:197, 1944.

A detailed discussion of basic techniques of interviewing, of making observations relevant to assessing personality structure, and of organizing the psychiatric case history.

B. THE UNCONSCIOUS.

20. Bernheim, H., *Suggestive Therapeutics: A Treatise on the Nature and Uses of Hypnotism*, G. P. Putnam's Sons, New York, 1897.

Bernheim was one of the first to think of hypnosis as a psychological phenomenon. His accounts of hypnotic phenomena provide some of the observations leading to a formulation of the concept of unconscious mental processes.

21. Breuer, J., and S. Freud, "Studies on Hysteria," *The Standard Edition of the Complete Psychological Works of Sigmund Freud*, The Hogarth Press, London, 1955, vol. II.

The first paper of this volume is a clear and concise description of the role of unconscious feelings and fantasies in the production of hysterical symptoms. The remainder of the book is primarily devoted to early case studies which formed the starting point of analytic theory.

22. Prince, M., *The Unconscious,* 2nd edition, Macmillan, New York, 1924.

First published in 1914, this book presents some of the evidence on which the theory of unconscious mental processes is based.

C. PSYCHOGENESIS.

23. Freud, S., "Three Essays on the Theory of Sexuality," *The Standard Edition of the Complete Psychological Works of Sigmund Freud,* The Hogarth Press, London, 1953, vol. VII, p. 125.

In this monograph Freud presented the first systematic formulation of childhood sexuality and its relation to psychoneurosis and adult sexual deviations.

24. Hartmann, H., and E. Kris, "The Genetic Approach in Psychoanalysis," *The Psychoanalytic Study of the Child,* International Universities Press, New York, 1945, vol. 1, p. 11.

A discussion of the *dynamic* and *psychogenetic* approach to psychodynamic phenomena.

D. DREAMS.

25. Freud, S., "The Interpretation of Dreams," *The Standard Edition of the Complete Psychological Works of Sigmund Freud,* The Hogarth Press, London, 1953, vols. IV and V.

Probably Freud's most famous work, this volume gives a depth of understanding of the meaning and structure of dreams, as well as of the human psyche, that has been little deepened since its publication. It should be read by anyone interested in the essence of psychoanalytic theory or in Freud's place in the history of psychology.

E. ANXIETY.

26. Freud, S., *Inhibition, Symptoms and Anxiety,* The Hogarth Press, London, 1936.

In this volume Freud first came to grips with the problem of anxiety in a systematic fashion. He discusses the various sources of anxiety, and introduces a radically new conception of anxiety which led to the formulation of the notion of defense mechanisms.

27. May, R., *The Meaning of Anxiety,* The Ronald Press, New York, 1950.

A monograph on the problem of anxiety, discussing it from the biological, sociological, and psychological points of view. May pre-

sents a brief historical survey of the ideas concerning anxiety, as
well as a comparative discussion of its meaning in the various contemporary psychological theories, which may be read in conjunction
with Munroe (ref. 13).

F. DEPRESSION.

28. Abraham, K., "Notes on the Psycho-analytic Investigation and Treatment of Manic-depressive Insanity and Allied Conditions (1911),"
Selected Papers of Karl Abraham, The Hogarth Press, London, 1927,
chap. VI.

29. Abraham, K., "A Short Study of the Development of the Libido,
Viewed in the Light of Mental Disorders (1924)," *Selected Papers
of Karl Abraham,* The Hogarth Press, London, 1927, chap. XXVI.

The role of loss, aggression, and introjection in the production of
depression is discussed in these two classic papers.

30. Beers, C. W., *A Mind that Found Itself—An Autobiography,* 4th
edition, Longmans, Green & Co., New York, 1920.

Beers was instrumental in founding the National Committee for
Mental Hygiene, of which he was the first secretary. His book, first
published in 1907, describes his experiences in both the manic and
the depressed phases of his manic-depressive disorder.

31. Bibring, E., "The Mechanism of Depression," *Affective Disorders,*
Phyllis Greenacre (ed.), International Universities Press, Inc., New
York, 1953.

This paper, though recent, has achieved the status of a "classic" for
its presentation and discussion of depression as a phenomenon experienced by the ego and resulting from tensions occurring within
the ego-system.

32. Custance, J., *Wisdom, Madness and Folly: The Philosophy of a
Lunatic,* Pellegrini and Cudahy, New York, 1952.

Custance is the pseudonym of an Englishman who has written an
autobiographical account of his manic-depressive disorder.

33. Freud, S., "Mourning and Melancholia," *The Standard Edition of
the Complete Psychological Works of Sigmund Freud,* The Hogarth
Press, London, 1957, vol. XVI, p. 239.

A difficult, but important paper which first elucidated the dynamics
of depression. It should be read following a perusal of the earlier
paper "On Narcissism: An Introduction" (*Standard Edition,* vol.
XVI, p. 69), to which it forms a logical sequel.

34. Lewis, J., "Melancholia: A Clinical Survey of Depressive States," *J. Ment. Sc.*, 80:277, 1934.

A paper based on clinical observations which has helped to crystallize concepts about the essential ingredients of depressions. The significant extent to which thought disorders (delusions, etc.) were found in Lewis's patients should be noted as an indication of the difficulty in separating the major psychoses into sharply defined disease entities.

35. Lindemann, E., "Symptomatology and Management of Acute Grief," *Am. J. Psychiat.*, 101:141, 1944.

This study of the bereaved relatives of the victims of a catastrophic fire provides basic observations about some of the physiological and psychological aspects of acute grief.

35a. Rochlin, G., "Loss and Restitution," *The Psychoanalytic Study of the Child*, International Universities Press, New York, 1953, vol. VIII, p. 288.

35b. Rochlin, G., "The Loss Complex," *J. Am. Psychoanalyt. Assoc.*, 7:299, 1959.

In these two articles the author presents observations on children of relevance to the psychogenesis of depression and indicating the important role of loss as a precipitant of depressive affect.

G. EGO FUNCTIONS AND SYMPTOM FORMATION.

36. Æ (George William Russell), *The Candle of Vision*, Macmillan, London, 1920.

A small volume poetically describing the hallucinatory visions that resulted from the process of meditation.

37. Bexton, W. H., W. Heron, and T. H. Scott, "Effects of Decreased Variation in the Sensory Environment," *Canad. J. Psychol.*, 8:70, 1954.

The authors present experimental evidence for the role of sensory deprivation in producing psychotic manifestations in normal human subjects.

38. Coles, M. R., and J. C. Holland, "Neuropsychiatric Aspects of Acute Poliomyelitis," *Am. J. Psychiat.*, 114:54, 1957.

From their experience with patients in respirators following poliomyelitis, the authors present evidence for the role of sensory deprivation in producing psychotic symptoms in patients with physical illness.

39. Deutsch, H., *Psychoanalysis of the Neuroses,* The Hogarth Press, London, 1932.

Presented initially as a series of lectures to psychoanalysts in training, the chapters in this book constitute an excellent discussion of and introduction to the psychopathology of the common psychoneuroses.

40. Freud, A., *The Ego and the Mechanisms of Defence,* The Hogarth Press, London, 1948.

First published in English in 1937, this volume is a systematic formulation of the ideas resulting from the new interest in ego structure which had been in the forefront of investigation for the previous ten to fifteen years. It provides a basis for much of the recent concern with ego psychology.

41. Freud, S., "Psychoanalytical Notes upon an Autobiographical Account of a Case of Paranoia (Dementia Paranoides)," *Collected Papers,* The Hogarth Press, London, 1949, vol. III, p. 387.

Based on Schreber's *Memoirs* (ref. 46), this paper provided the first dynamic formulation of and insight into some of the mechanisms of paranoid delusions.

42. Hall, G. S., "A Study of Fears," *Am. J. Psychol.,* 8:147, 1897.

A long paper conceived and written in the 19th-century tradition of describing and classifying natural phenomena, it presents a panoramic view of the variety and frequency of phobias.

43. Hartmann, H., "Comments on the Psychoanalytic Theory of the Ego," *The Psychoanalytic Study of the Child,* International Universities Press, New York, 1950, vol. V, p. 74.

This paper presents a formulation of autonomous ego functions, that is, those functions of ego which are not a product of or dependent on the continued action of psychological conflict. The author (with Kris and Loewenstein) has written a series of papers appearing over the years in the *Psychoanalytic Study of the Child* which present highly theoretical expositions of many aspects of contemporary ego psychology.

44. Mitchell, S., "Remarks on the Effects of Anhelonium Lewinii (The Mescal Button)," *Brit. M. J.,* 2:1625, 1896.

An account of the author's dramatic hallucinations while under the influence of mescaline.

45. Shaw, R., "A Mixture of Madness," *Harvard Med. Alum. Bull.*, 34:38, 1958.

A striking autobiographical account of a toxic-metabolic post-operative psychosis.

46. Schreber, D. P., *Memoirs of My Nervous Illness*, trans. and ed. by Ida Macalpine, and Richard A. Hunter, Wm. Dawson & Sons, London, 1955.

Schreber wrote this book because he thought the medical profession would be interested in the unusual phenomenon of a man being changed into a woman. His family tried to buy up and confiscate all the copies of this work, but fortunately a few escaped the dragnet to provide us with a remarkable autobiographical account of a man undergoing a schizophrenic illness. It should be read in conjunction with Freud's clinical paper based on it (ref. 41).

H. PSYCHOSOMATIC MEDICINE.

47. Alexander, F., "Psychologic Factors in Gastrointestinal Disturbances: General Principles, Objectives, and Preliminary Results," *Studies in Psychosomatic Medicine*, F. Alexander, and T. M. French (eds.), The Ronald Press Co., New York, 1948, p. 103.

A pioneering attempt to understand the nature of the psychological conflict associated with a variety of gastrointestinal disorders. The emphasis is on understanding the complicated intrapsychic processes arising as a reaction to environmental stress.

48. Alexander, F., *Psychosomatic Medicine*, W. W. Norton & Co., New York, 1950.

A short but clear and concise presentation of the general principles of the psychosomatic approach to illness and their application to individual organ systems, this volume is an excellent introduction to the subject.

49. Binger, C., *The Doctor's Job*, W. W. Norton & Co., New York, 1945.

A widely known work that discusses various aspects of the doctor's encounter with his patient as a human being. It contains four chapters devoted to both general and specific problems in psychosomatic medicine.

50. Cobb, S., W. Bauer, and I. Whiting, "Environmental Factors in Rheumatoid Arthritis," *J.A.M.A.*, 113:668, 1939.

An early study of the relation of the appearance of the symptoms of rheumatoid arthritis to the presence of environmental stress.

51. Engel, G. L., "Studies of Ulcerative Colitis: II. The Nature of the Somatic Process and the Adequacy of Psychosomatic Hypotheses," *Am. J. Med.*, 16:416, 1954.

52. Engel, G. L., "Studies of Ulcerative Colitis: III. The Nature of the Psychologic Process," *Am. J. Med.*, 19:231, 1955.

These two articles, part of a series of five, systematically and carefully examine the problems involved in attempting to correlate psychological and physiological changes in the course of ulcerative colitis.

53. Lief, H. I., V. F. Lief, and N. R. Lief, *The Psychological Basis of Medical Practice*, Hoeber-Harper, New York, 1961.

Designed as a text to supply the medical student and practitioner with the available knowledge of human behavior as it is related to the psychological problems of medical practice, this volume deals with the field of psychosomatic medicine in an extensive series of chapters written by a wide variety of investigators.

54. Lindemann, E., "Modifications in the Course of Ulcerative Colitis in Relationship to Changes in Life Situations and Reaction Patterns," *Res. Pub. A. Res. Nerv. and Ment. Dis.*, 29:656, 1950.

This article presents statistical evidence of the relation between the onset of symptoms of ulcerative colitis and the presence of the loss of a significant object in the life situation of the patient, in 87 cases, and discusses in detail the nature of the precipitating crisis situation in nine patients.

55. Mirsky, A., "Physiologic, Psychologic and Social Determinants in the Etiology of Duodenal Ulcer," *Am. J. Digest. Dis.*, N.S. 3:285, 1958.

An article that presents a well-organized critical review of the facts, theories, and methodological problems arising in the investigation of the relevance of emotions to the production of peptic ulcer.

56. Nemiah, J. C., "Anorexia Nervosa; A Clinical Psychiatric Study," *Medicine*, 29:225, 1950.

57. Nemiah, J. C., "Anorexia Nervosa: Fact and Theory," *Am. J. Digest. Dis.*, N.S. 3:249, 1958.

Together these articles present a detailed clinical investigation of a group of patients with anorexia nervosa and a critical review of the English literature dealing with the subject.

58. Ruesch, J., "The Infantile Personality: The Core Problem of Psychosomatic Medicine," *Psychosom. Med.*, 10:134, 1948.

The emphasis is on those psychological features common to all patients with psychosomatic disorders regardless of which organ system is affected.

59. Weisman, A. D., "A Study of the Psychodynamics of Duodenal Ulcer Exacerbations: With Special Reference to Treatment and the Problems of 'Specificity,'" *Psychosom. Med.*, 18:2, 1956.

This article presents detailed clinical findings concerning the psychogenic aspects of peptic ulcer, derived from psychoanalytic and intensive psychotherapeutic experience with a group of patients suffering from this disorder.

60. Weiss, E., and O. S. English, *Psychosomatic Medicine*, 3rd edition, W. B. Saunders Co., Philadelphia, 1957.

This standard text, now in its third edition, contains extensive case studies of patients with a wide variety of psychosomatic disorders.

61. Wolf, S. and H. G. Wolff, *Human Gastric Function*, 2nd edition, Oxford University Press, New York, 1947.

A monograph describing a series of now famous experiments dealing with the reaction of the gastric mucosa under direct observation in a subject experiencing a variety of emotional states.

(References to patients and authors who have provided the observations used in the text are indicated by italics.)